MICHAEL HILL

Understanding Social Policy

Fourth Edition

BLACKWELL
Oxford UK & Cambridge USA

Copyright © Michael Hill 1980, 1983, 1988, 1993

First published in 1980 by Basil Blackwell Ltd and
Martin Robertson & Co. Ltd

The right of Michael Hill to be identified as author of this work has been asserted
in accordance with the Copyright, Designs and Patents Act 1988.

Second edition 1983
Reprinted 1985, 1986, 1987

Third edition 1988
Reprinted 1989, 1992

Fourth edition 1993

Blackwell Publishers
108 Cowley Road
Oxford   OX4 1JF
UK

238 Main Street, Suite 501
Cambridge, Massachusetts 02142
USA

British Library Cataloguing in Publication Data

A CIP catalogue record for this book is available from the British Library.

Library of Congress Cataloging-in-Publication Data
Hill, Michael J. (Michael James), 1937–
     Understanding social policy/Michael Hill. – 4th ed.
        p.   cm.
     Includes bibliographical references and indexes.
     Romanized record.
     ISBN 0–631–18849–5 (alk. paper)
     1. Great Britain – Social policy.   2. Welfare state.   3. Welfare economics.
     I. Title.
     HN390.H52   1993
     361.6′1′0941 – dc20   92–26626
                                                                          CIP

Typeset in 10 on 12 pt Times
by Graphicraft Typesetters Ltd, Hong Kong
Printed in Great Britain by T.J. Press (Padstow) Ltd., Padstow, Cornwall

This book is printed on acid-free paper

Contents

Preface

This book is an introduction to the study of social policy. It is based on a view that those who study this subject need to consider the way in which policy is made and implemented as well as to learn about the main policies and their limitations. It has been written for people who have had no previous training in the social sciences, with the needs of social workers, health visitors and other social policy 'practitioners' very much in mind, as well as those of undergraduates.

The preparation of the fourth edition of this book has involved a substantial revision, as did the third edition. Throughout the 1980s the Conservatives under Mrs Thatcher changed social policy dramatically, and in the process forced writers on social policy to revise the way they treated their subject. The idea that the evolution of British social policy could simply be seen as some long-run growth of publicly provided welfare had finally to be abandoned. New ways of delivering policies began to challenge the way we look at policy-making and policy implementation, particularly inasmuch as the traditional bureaucratic model for the delivery of social services was modified. This last change has been especially significant in the years since the third edition of this book, notably for health, education and the personal social services. But, above all, it is changes in the content of policies which has made revision of this book essential. This edition has been completed just as the Conservatives have won their fourth general election, in April 1992. Mrs Thatcher's successor as Conservative leader is showing signs that he will not continue to take the nation on the helter-skelter path of institutional change which characterized the Thatcher regime, so perhaps this edition will not date quite so quickly.

At this stage in the history of a textbook it becomes impossible to acknowledge satisfactorily all the people who have helped to shape the author's approach, and who have kept him up to date on developments in policy. However, a special debt should be acknowledged to two people who have been collaborators on other books, Chris Ham and Glen Bramley. Since the production of the third edition the author has been much more heavily engaged in introductory undergraduate teaching, enabling the book to be tested in use in a more robust way. Hence I have a debt to recent students, and to one in particular, Jane Wilcockson, who has helped to collect some crucial statistics and other data on new policies.

The book is dedicated to my wife Betty who, when she was a health visitor student, first helped me to identify the gap in the market, and who has taken a warm interest in the progress of the book ever since. I am happy that I have been able to share with her the fruits of its success.

CHAPTER 1

What is Social Policy?

INTRODUCTION

One way to answer the question 'What is social policy?' is to provide a
list of the areas of public policy included under that heading. Another
way is just to try to define its scope by explaining what it is that
distinguishes it from other kinds of policy. Social policy is a difficult
subject to define in this way, however. Perhaps it is best just to list the
policy areas to be discussed. However, because the process of declar-
ing different kinds of policies to be social policies, while disregarding
others having a considerable impact on the well-being of our society,
seems a particularly arbitrary exercise, it is necessary to look a little at
the rationale for doing this. It is also necessary to examine what studying social policy implies.

Readers may be familiar with textbooks that set out to define their
subject in the first chapter. These discussions are often tedious and
pedantic. They frequently appear to have been written for some private
academic argument rather than to inform prospective students. It is
hoped that this chapter will not be dismissed as an arid academic
ground-clearing exercise, since it has important things to say about the
most appropriate way to approach the subject of the book.

WHICH POLICIES?

The policy areas covered in this book are set out in the titles of
chapters 5 to 10. The first three of those chapters deal with policy areas
that everyone seems to include within their definition of social policy –
social security, the personal social services and health.

Chapter 10 looks at housing policy. Most books and courses on
social policy deal with housing, though with some uncertainty about the

extent to which they are concerned with the private sector. There are important questions about housing policy that concern the extent to which a free market can operate, in relation to the private sector, and the extent to which public housing authorities should act as if they were private business concerns. This chapter, together with the chapter on employment policy, has to give particular attention to the issues, seldom far away in any discussion of social policy, of the impact of economic policy, and of the relevance of economic and commercial considerations. These are major problems in identifying, and separating off from other policies, a specific area called 'social policy'. Whilst these are two policy areas where social and economic issues are particularly mingled they are not alone; another area where social issues arise is transport policy. This has been left out since it is less often recognized as an area in which there are social policy concerns.

The other chapter on a particular area of policy is that dealing with education policy. This is much less often included within social policy. The very fact that it is difficult to find reasons either for including it or for excluding it tells us something about the peculiarly arbitrary process involved in categorizing policies as 'social'. Clearly, the field of education is one in which there is a considerable amount of public expenditure upon services that contribute to public welfare. But is the hallmark of social policy expenditure its contribution to public welfare, and what does this really mean? If education policy is included, why not also include leisure policy or environment policy? In fact the inclusion of education, and the exclusion of the other two policy areas, is the consequence of a comparatively arbitrary decision by the author, based upon a conventional view of the limits to social policy which is clearly open to challenge.

However, even to define social policy in terms of public expenditure which contributes to public welfare raises a most misleading and widespread false assumption about the character of our subject. T. H. Marshall, in his book on social policy (Marshall, 1970), has an opening chapter with the same title as this one. In it he proclaims that 'the avowed objective of twentieth-century social policy is welfare'. Readers will find a central concern about the factors that influence social welfare a characteristic of many writings on social policy. Indeed, some of the British contributions to the study of this topic assert theirs to be a distinctive academic subject, 'social administration', which has this concern as its hallmark (see Carrier and Kendall, 1977).

However, a concern to understand social policy may be distinguished from a preoccupation with the determinants of welfare. To equate this 'avowed objective' of social policy with its real objective, as Marshall seems to do, involves an acceptance of a particular ideology about the 'welfare state' that has been challenged by various writers. Moreover, to see policies as having objectives involves confusing the character of the policies with the motives and purposes of the people who advocate, adopt and implement them.

Several recent discussions of social policy have suggested that welfare policies are promulgated not from humanitarian concerns to meet need but as responses to social unrest. Piven and Cloward, for example, argue as follows about social security policies:

> The key to an understanding of relief-giving is in the functions it serves for the larger economic and political order, for relief is a secondary and supportive institution. Historical evidence suggests that relief arrangements are initiated or expanded during the occasional outbreaks of civil disorder produced by mass unemployment, and are then abolished or contracted when political stability is restored. . . . this view clearly belies the popular supposition that government social policies, including relief policies, are becoming progressively more responsible, humane and generous. . . . (Piven and Cloward, 1972, p. xiii)

Piven and Cloward are primarily concerned to explain relief policies in the United States, but they draw on English data too, and they clearly intend their analysis to apply to other countries. Other writers have analysed British policies in similar terms. In particular, Marxists have argued that advanced capitalist societies require an infrastructure of welfare policies to help maintain order, buy off working-class protest and secure a workforce with acceptable standards of health and education (see, for example, O'Connor, 1973; Gough, 1979). Other radical analyses of social policy have seen social policy as sustaining not only class-based patterns of domination but also patriarchy and racial inequality (see Williams, 1989).

Clearly, perspectives like these give a very different meaning to 'welfare'. To the Marxist 'welfare capitalism' is a pejorative term. Policies that promote welfare are explained in terms of social control; they are measures to combat disorder and crime just like police and penal policies, measures to legitimize and prop up the capitalist system. But it is not necessary to accept totally this interpretation of public policy in order to agree that there may be circumstances under which social control motives mingle with humanitarian motives in creating what we describe as 'social policies'. Moreover, the two extreme interpretations of the origins of social policies that have been mentioned do not exhaust the range of possibilities. Joan Higgins (1978) has suggested that both rest upon rational models of political action, in which actors have motives and are able to frame policies that accurately reflect their intentions. Contemporary studies of both policy-making and policy implementation suggest that we need to give attention to some very complex relationships between the mixed goals of those able to influence policies and the varied consequences of their interventions. Outcomes may be the unintended results of policy inputs. Most policy is incremental in character, involving marginal adjustments to what has gone before and being motivated to correct what are seen as undesirable consequences of previous policies. Accordingly, social policy need not be interpreted in terms either of the continual evolution of a welfare state inspired by humanitarian ideals or of a conspiracy to manipulate a powerless proletariat. Yet the rejection of these interpretations need not imply either that individuals with altruistic motives play no part in the evolution of policy or that manipulative and social-control-motivated actions are not involved in the policy process.

This discussion implies three things for the definition of social policy: first, that the policies identified as 'social' should not be interpreted as if they were conceived and implemented with only the welfare of the public in mind; secondly, that other policies, not conventionally identified as social policies, may make a comparable, or even greater, contribution to welfare; thirdly, that public policy should be seen as a whole in which social policies are significantly interlinked with other public policies. Just because it is convenient to single out some policies for special attention, and just because there are courses on social policy that require the study of a specific and limited range of public policies, we should not therefore fall into the trap of seeing these as the main government contributions to welfare, or the 'general good'. Let us look at the implications of these arguments a little more by examining the implications, for welfare and for social policy, of policy developments in those important policy areas that no one defines as social policy: foreign and defence policy, and economic policy.

It is important to recognize that the origins of the modern nation-state lie in the achievement of a monopoly of force within a given territory. The central policy preoccupations of the government of any insecure nation are with the defence of its boundaries, the recognition of its integrity by other nations and the maintenance of order within its territories. It is only too easy for British students of public policy to lose sight of the importance of these issues. They are the daily fare of our news bulletins, but we rarely stop to think about their relevance for our own state. Incomprehension over events in Northern Ireland, and a propensity to underestimate the intensity of the feelings of some people in Scotland on the issue of devolution, stem from our tendency to take the integrity and security of the nation for granted. Yet without a secure nation-state the scope for development of what is conventionally identified as social policy is severely limited.

These facts have three implications for the study of social policy. First, social policy expenditure has to compete with other public expenditure dedicated to the defence of the realm. The case against heavy defence expenditure cannot rest simply on arguments that some of that money would be better spent on social policy; it is necessary to prove that some of that expenditure is inappropriate or irrelevant, or to face the argument that without it no social policy would be secure. Secondly, the forms of this defence expenditure have a wide range of social effects in creating employment, disrupting family life and so on. Readers may like to think about the sort of policy interactions involved by asking themselves what would be the effects upon social life and social policy of the reintroduction of a two-year period of compulsory national service. The important effects they should be able to identify will nevertheless be insignificant by comparison with the effects of mobilization for war itself. Thirdly, while social policies do not have, except in some very marginal ways, an impact on relations with other states, it is important not to lose sight of the contribution they make to integration and harmony within the nation. It is this that has led students of social policy to draw attention to the significant impact of war upon policy. Thus Titmuss has argued: 'The aims and content of social policy, both in peace and in war, are thus determined – at least to a substantial extent – by how far the co-operation of the masses is essential to the successful prosecution of war' (Titmuss, 1958, p. 86).

The development of the role of the British state in the nineteenth and twentieth centuries is often portrayed as the establishment of 'the welfare state'. To present it in this way is to emphasize social policy developments. But it is perhaps more important to give attention to the growth of the British economy over that period, and to the role played by government in relation to that economy. Two apparently conflicting political interpretations of these events lead us to ask some broadly similar questions about the relationship between social policy and economic policy.

To the followers of the 'classical economists', who argued that the industrialized state would make the greatest possible contribution to public welfare if competition were to remain unshackled, the period between the middle of the nineteenth century and the present day has been marked by extensive government interference with the economy. Some of this interference has been seen as necessary where competition has been impossible or illogical, in the public utilities and the railways for example. Some of it has been seen as justifiable because it seeks to ensure competition and prevent monopoly. But much of it has been regarded as stemming from forces eager to interfere with and undermine the free economy, shifting the locus of decision from the market place and into the political arena.

Marxists, on the other hand, interpret the same evidence the other way round. They argue that as the industrial state has grown so the 'contradictions of capitalism' have increased. Government intervention has been prompted, therefore, by a desire to save capitalism, not from a desire to undermine it. Regulation has been introduced to prevent the logic of competition from destroying the system. State interventions to protect the working class have been designed, according to this view, to stave off revolution and help the capitalist system to survive. Late capitalist society, it is argued, experiences a form of 'welfare capitalism' in which those who originally gained so much from the competitive industry are still dominant in our society.

Both these views of the relationship between government and the economy stress the extent to which social policy should be seen as dependent upon, or even a derivative of, economic policy. The key internal political issues of our age are who controls our economy, and how are the rewards that stem from our industrial achievements to be distributed. The implications for social policy are as follows: first, that the main determinants of welfare are economic; secondly, that the government's role in diverting resources into social policies must be seen to be closely interrelated with, even dependent upon, the role it plays in the management of the economy; thirdly, that social policies will be determined by views about the way the economy does, or should, operate. Specific social policies need therefore to be understood in terms of their relationships to economic policies.

The following are some examples of important questions frequently asked about social policy which are essentially about the relationship between social and economic policy. Are social security policies re-distributive? How far do the redistributive effects of social security operate beyond minimal insurance limits? How does any redistribution by this mechanism compare with redistribution that occurs through other economic mechanisms – the effects of competition, the impact of unemployment and the results of wage bargaining, for example? What are the effects of public housing upon the market of housing? How far are market forces in this area more influential than state intervention in determining who gets what housing?

It is important to take a wider view of social policy development relating it to economic policy. To what extent are there limits to the growth of public expenditure in a mixed economy, and therefore what impact may such limits (or the belief that there are such limits) have upon social policy expenditure? Similarly, what is the impact upon the economy, and also upon the whole political system, of the pattern of employment that has emerged as social policy has become 'big busi-ness'? Unlike those stressed above, these are questions about the impact of social policy upon economic policy rather than the other way round. Nevertheless, the key decisions about resources for the social policy sector will be regarded as economic policy decisions.

It has been suggested, then, that, while certain policy areas, subject to a few difficult boundary problems, are defined as social policy, any proper understanding of the forces that determine outcomes in these areas must rest upon considerations of other policies not included within the conventional social policy rubric.

STUDYING SOCIAL POLICY

Social policy may be studied in a number of ways. We may merely set out to determine the main policies in the areas in which we are interested. What is our system of social security? What benefits does our health service provide? How has the government intervened in the housing market? These and similar questions need to be answered by those who want to understand social policy. They can also be related to many other points about the way the services are organized and administered. Hence the simplest approach to the study of social policy is to describe the policies and institutions that together make up the British system of social services.

Many accounts of the system of social policy include comments on the strengths and weaknesses of specific policies. They relate what there is to what, in the authors' views, there ought to be. The study of social policy, as it has developed in Britain, has been concerned to examine the extent to which the welfare state meets people's needs. Often, indeed, students of social policy go further and explicitly analyse the extent to which it contributes to social equality. In this sense an academic discipline has been built up with an explicitly political stance. Social policy is seen as concerned with the alleviation of social ills; its objectives are accepted at face value; and it is analysed in terms of its success in achieving such goals. Many who have written about social policy have done so from the standpoint of Fabian socialism, concerned with incremental social change to create a more equal society. Few challenged this perspective until the 1980s when Conservative political thinking shifted sharply to the Right, to express much more directly suspicion of the claims of the state to regulate many aspects of our lives and to portray welfare policy as a threat to economic enterprise.

In recent years there has been among social scientists an extensive debate about the extent to which the analysis of society and of social institutions can be 'value-free'. Broadly, there is today a consensus that there are limits to the extent to which those who study and write about society can set aside their own commitments and prejudices. Some go on to argue, however, that value-freedom within the social sciences as a whole may be achieved by the interplay of arguments and evidence, each biased in different ways but contributing to the advancement of unbiased knowledge as a whole. Others are more sceptical about the extent to which a body of systematic unbiased knowledge is built up, and they argue that the value problem is ever significant. The study of social policy has been particularly conspicuous for the specific political or value commitments of those who write about it.

The strong normative bias in the study of social policy has led at times to a greater preoccupation with criticism of policies than with attempts to discover why they take the forms they do. In fact, if one believes that policies are wrong or ineffective it is important to understand why this is so, particularly if one's objective is to change them. The view that it is sufficient to point out that policies are 'wrong' is often linked with a view of policy-making in which men and women of good will are believed to be responsible and are anxious to rectify the unwitting mistakes made in the past. This approach to the understanding of the policy system was criticized above.

At this stage an author who is arguing that the study of social policy in Britain has been strong on criticism and value judgement but weak on analysis should make his own position very clear. Since he believes that students may be aided in drawing their own conclusions if writers make their own value biases explicit, it is particularly important to do this. Broadly, I am deeply concerned about the content of social policy and have contributed (particularly on social security and housing policies and on measures to help the unemployed) to the 'Fabian' critique of policy outlined above. I should not pretend that my personal motivation in studying social policy is not linked with a commitment to non-revolutionary movement towards social equality. However, I feel increasingly strongly that a concern to influence the content of social policy must be supported by an understanding of how social policy is made. This book is, therefore, concerned with what social policy is, how it was created and how it was implemented, as well as with its weaknesses and arguments about what it should be.

An understanding of the factors that influence the character of social policy must rest upon several foundations. Some attention must be given to the social and economic conditions that create the need for social policies. This is a difficult chicken-and-egg issue. One cannot simply look at the kinds of problems thrown up by particular social structures and economic situations and analyse policies as responses to those problems, since policies themselves influence the character of the societies in which they are adopted. For example, government provision of housing may be seen as a response to the inadequacies of the market as a provider of houses, but it has also transformed the character of that market. Interactions between policies and society are complex. It is important, therefore, to draw upon economics and sociology to help with the understanding of what occurs. It is also necessary to keep in mind the historical dimensions to these issues.

But social policy-making must also be seen as a political process. It has already been stressed that social policy cannot be analysed on its own, without reference to other activities of the state. Policies must be understood as products of politics, and attention must be given to the policy creation roles of politicians, civil servants, pressure groups and the electorate. Policies must also be seen as to a considerable extent products of other policies. There is a cumulative process to be analysed in which policies create needs for other policies, opportunities for other policies, and new social situations for further political responses. It will be clear that to understand social policy considerable attention must be given to the findings of political science.

An often neglected part of the study of policy is the examination of its implementation. The actual impact of any policy upon the public will depend upon how it is interpreted and put into practice by government officials. The implementation process throws light on the strengths and weaknesses of a policy, and experience at the implementation end (by junior officials and by the public) gets fed back into the policy process to influence future policy change. A particular characteristic of a state in which extensive social policies have been adopted is that it is a bureaucratic state. The organizational complexity of such a state necessarily complicates the implementation process. An understanding of these issues requires the student of social policy to give some attention to organization theory and to the study of administrative law.

The portrait of the study of social policy as presented in the last few paragraphs shows that it is a subject that draws upon a number of different academic disciplines. The problem of defining the extent to which it is necessary to delve into these disciplines is like the problem discussed earlier of ascertaining the boundaries between social policy and other kinds of public policy. There is a need to make what we can of an essentially applied subject, hoping that we can gain what is required from other disciplines without going too deeply into them. The boundaries between all the social sciences are unclear. Sometimes this is a necessary feature of subjects that put some parts of the human experience under the microscope and have to abstract this from other parts. But in other cases it is a result of historical accidents in the development of the disciplines, and if the study of society were to be initiated all over again it would surely be divided rather differently. The study of social policy particularly hives off a specific area of social activity in a way that must violate subject boundaries. If it is important to understand a number of practical policies, because of a concern about their effects upon society, it is necessary to accept studies that cannot be defined in terms of a discrete intellectual discipline.

In setting out to examine what social policy is, and how it may be studied, some answers have been suggested to the question, 'Why study it?' Many who are required to study social policy are, or expect to be, involved in its implementation. That part of a social policy course that is concerned with describing policies and the institutions responsible for them has a clear face value to the social policy 'practitioner'. But equally it is important for such a person to understand something of the way in which it works, and the internal and external forces that shape policies.

It may also help to understand other agencies to which a 'practitioner' has to relate, particularly as a great deal of policy depends, or is intended to depend, upon successful co-operation between organizations. It has been stressed that no policy area is discrete, that policies in one area affect those in others. This is particularly true of social policies, where their impact upon the public depends upon the way they interrelate. Successful treatment of the sick requires attention to their housing and income maintenance problems; the care of the neglected child depends upon co-operation between health service workers, personal social services staff and schoolteachers; the homeless often face income-maintenance problems as well as housing problems; and so on – the examples are legion.

Hence the most obvious case for studying social policy is a need for the staff of the various social services to understand the system in which they operate. But that is not all. A characteristic of many of the people who are drawn to work in the social services is a strong commitment to those services. In this sense it is not surprising that the study of social policy has been deeply concerned with the improvement of policies. Many social services staff care considerably about the inadequacies of the policies they administer. But achieving policy change is never an easy process, particularly if one is a comparatively junior participant in a large organization. To make a contribution towards this end requires not only knowledge of alternatives and commitment to putting them into practice, but also an understanding of how social policy is made and implemented.

These arguments for studying social policy have been addressed to people likely to be involved in the social services. In the earlier versions of this book the word 'employed' was used in this context. Recent changes to social policy have, however, increased the extent to which private and voluntary organizations are involved in the delivery of social policy. They have also made it very clear that many social welfare services are not delivered by state agencies but are left to the slender resources of families, neighbourhoods and communities. Hence this is a book for all concerned citizens who want to influence social policy. Its underlying justification is that participation in policy-making, for a group of services of considerable importance to us all, must rest upon understanding: understanding of what the policies are, of how they are made and implemented, and of the implications of the many prevailing suggestions on how to change those policies.

SUGGESTIONS FOR FURTHER READING

This has been an introductory chapter in which it has been suggested that students do not need to delve deeply into the debate about the definition of the field of study of social policy. The essay by Carrier and Kendall (1977) explores that debate, and arrives at a more positive stance on the distinctive character of the subject as an academic discipline than that suggested here.

Richard Titmuss was the outstanding exponent of the liberal socialist standpoint on the study of social policy; indeed, he can be said to be virtually the founder of the systematic study of social policy. His main essays on social policy have recently been put together in a single volume (Titmuss, 1987). Marshall (1970) has produced the other major elementary discussion on this subject in the same tradition.

A more radical perspective, from the Left, is provided in Fiona Williams's *Social Policy: A Critical Introduction* (1989). Exponents of the Marxist viewpoint include O'Connor (1973) and Gough (1979). Perhaps the strongest assertion of the Radical Right's perspective come from an American source, Charles Murray (1984). Green (1986) provided a British account of this point of view.

Good overviews of the competing perspectives on social policy can be found in two books by Mishra (1977 and 1984). A reader edited by Loney (1987) provides good examples of some of the key views.

CHAPTER 2

The History of Social Policy

INTRODUCTION

This chapter deals with some of the key events in the development of British social policy, relating them to social, economic and political trends in our society. It is not intended as a comprehensive potted history of the subject; it is, however, important to have a historical perspective, particularly on the relationship between social and political change, in order to understand the character of British social policy today.

At one level the story is simple. The growth of state involvement with the social welfare of its citizens can be related to the development of an industrial society, and its subsequent maturation, or perhaps decline, into what some writers have described as 'post-industrialism' (Bell, 1973). Alongside this industrial development are political developments, associated with the extension of the suffrage, involving citizens more thoroughly with the activities of the state. Accompanying these are changes to social life, and particularly family life; and changing views of the respective responsibilities of the individual, the family and the state for remedies to social problems. The result is a package of developments – of the state's role, the character of the economy, the nature of political processes and of ideologies – which those without a very dogmatic belief about the motive forces in political development find difficult to disentangle in cause–effect terms.

This version of the story of the development of the state's role in social welfare can be applied to a number of industrialized nations – to the United States, to most of the other countries of western and northern Europe and to Australasia – as much as to Britain (this theme has been widely analysed, see, in particular, Wilensky and Lebeaux, 1965; Ashford, 1986; Esping-Andersen, 1990). But while these 'broad brush' features of the story must not be forgotten it is important also to try to single out characteristics of Britain's development that help to explain the particular shape of its own social policies. A proper understanding of this subject requires consideration of the general factors, which may apply to a distinct group of nations; of the special factors, which are perhaps unique to one nation; and, furthermore, of a number of factors that do not fall neatly into either of these categories. Included in this last group is, for example, the 'insurance principle' in social security, adopted in a variety of ways by various governments who clearly attempted to learn from each other's experiences (see Heclo, 1974; Baldwin, 1990).

DEVELOPMENTS BEFORE THE TWENTIETH CENTURY

It is always very difficult, in dealing with the relationship between past events and contemporary policies, to know how far to go back in time. To understand British social policies some consideration of the history of the poor law, with its roots in Elizabethan legislation, is necessary. The Tudor age saw considerable population movements, with changes in agriculture, the growth of towns and some rudimentary developments in manufacturing. The government found it necessary to try to impose a centrally determined framework on what had hitherto been entirely local, and often monastic, charitable initiatives. It placed responsibility for the poor upon each parish, with the requirement, under the Acts of Settlement, that the itinerant poor should be returned, if necessary, to their parishes of origin. The parishes were required to levy rates to provide for the relief of the poor.

The history of the poor law between the sixteenth and twentieth centuries was one of attempts to make this formula work – for local initiative with broad guidelines laid down centrally – despite social changes. As Britain became industrialized and urbanized a strictly local system of administration came under strain. Population movements gradually rendered the Acts of Settlement obsolete. The tasks of the poor law became more complex as parishes had to cope with, for example, trade recessions and outbreaks of infectious diseases, each affecting large numbers of people in the new towns and cities. By the middle of the nineteenth century developments in medicine offered a new challenge to the parish 'guardians' who had previously provided only the most rudimentary care to the sick.

The most significant nineteenth-century attempt to modernize the poor law was the Poor Law Amendment Act of 1834. This set up a national Poor Law Commission to superintend the system, and formed the parishes into groups known as poor law unions. This important step towards the development of a national system was only a limited success. However, its main contributions to the development of policy were the 'workhouse test' and the doctrine of 'less eligibility'. The aims of these were to curb indiscriminate outdoor relief; if the poor were not sufficiently desperate to enter the workhouse they could not be really in need. The system was intended to ensure that those who received help were worse off ('less eligible') than the poorest people in work. In practice many poor law unions did not strictly enforce the workhouse test, and as the years passed the elderly and the sick were increasingly given outdoor relief. Nevertheless, the elimination of the workhouse, and the abolition of the means test adopted to confine relief-giving, became an important preoccupation of twentieth-century critics of the poor law. The principle of less eligibility has continued to influence decisions about relief up to the present day.

While the basic nineteenth-century response to poverty was to try to strengthen older institutions, some of the consequences of urbanization and industrialization posed problems for which entirely new responses were necessary. Measures were taken to curb the hours worked by women and children in factories, and to improve safety and working conditions. This significant development in state intervention in the economy seems to have come about as a result of a mixture of growing humanitarian concern and embryonic working-class pressure. The enforcement of this legislation was put into the hands of a central government inspectorate, the first of a number of such inspectorates to be set up in the nineteenth century and to operate, according to Roberts (1960), as an important source of pressure for further social reform.

The rapid spread of infection in areas where people were crowded together was, like the exploitation of child labour, not a new phenomenon. But in an increasingly urbanized society it took new forms more apparent to political opinion, and more threatening to life and industry; and there were very many more large, populous areas devoid of the most elementary arrangements for disposing of waste or supplying pure water. Furthermore, it was only during this period that scientific advance identified the main links between insanitary conditions and disease. In a few areas local government agencies took some steps to tackle this problem, but real progress did not come until central government gave local authorities powers to act effectively, and also required them to take such action.

Here, then, was an important area of government intervention, pushing local authorities to tackle some of the problems of their own areas. The local government system of the time had been given some shape by the Municipal Corporations Act of 1835, but it was not until the end of the century that it acquired a structure that would enable it to take on the range of functions it carries out today. In the nineteenth century, therefore, some reforms required local authorities to take action and to employ professional staff, such as the medical officers of health required by an Act of 1871. Others, however, set up *ad hoc* authorities to take on functions delegated by central government.

The evolution of state education during the nineteenth century provides a good example of a series of *ad hoc* responses. Religious societies had begun to become involved in the provision of cheap basic education for the children of the poor early in the century. By 1833 they had persuaded the government to provide a small grant towards this work. In 1839 the government set up an inspectorate to further central supervision of the way the growing state aid was being spent. It was not until 1870, however, that the government moved really forcefully into the provision of primary education. Motivated, it is widely believed, by a concern about the illiteracy of the growing electorate (the franchise had been considerably widened in 1867), but also undoubtedly by a recognition of a need for a better-educated workforce, Parliament provided that school boards, to set up state-financed schools, could be established where there was a clear educational need and where the voluntary schools were insufficient in number. In 1880 a further Education Act made schooling compulsory for children between five and ten, and in the 1890s it was established that most elementary education should be free. During the last years of the century some of the school boards even became involved in secondary education, producing a confused pattern of educational growth that was to prompt government action at the beginning of the twentieth century.

Reference has already been made to the way in which developments in medicine began, in the late nineteenth century, to render inadequate the traditional poor law approach to the care of the sick. Alongside the development of poor law hospitals many voluntary hospitals, assisted by charitable funds that enabled them to provide cheap or free services to the poor, were founded or grew in strength from their earlier origins. The local authorities were also given powers to establish hospitals to fulfil their duties to contain infectious diseases and to care for the mentally ill. Medical care outside the hospitals grew in importance in the second half of the century, becoming more than the prerogative of the rich. This was partly a poor law development, partly the extension of the services of the voluntary hospitals, and partly an aspect of the growth of insurance against misfortune widely practised by the more prosperous of the working classes. In all, a very mixed package of health care measures was evolving. This complex mixture, dominated by a powerful medical profession firmly established during the nineteenth century, posed problems for subsequent attempts to rationalize the health services, and therefore influenced the shape the national health service eventually achieved.

At the end of the nineteenth century the verdict of the legal philosopher Dicey (1905) was that *laissez-faire* had given way to collectivism; that government had begun to assume a role in society that had taken Britain well on the way to becoming a socialist state. The factory legislation, and the government intervention in the cause of health and safety, implied important changes in the role of the state. The educational system at the primary (or, as it was known then, the elementary) level had received a crucial injection of public enterprise. The poor law, on the other hand, had been changed but little. A need for new policies in that area was just beginning to become apparent at the end of the century, as scientific surveys (Booth, 1889; Rowntree, 1901) and journalistic investigations charted the existence of severe problems of poverty caused by factors, in particular sickness and old age, largely outside individual control.

It was suggested earlier that the agencies set up during the nineteenth century to implement social policies were often *ad hoc* bodies. While local government was responsible for public health, and for the rudimentary planning, housing and hospital functions required to help achieve more sanitary urban areas, education was made the responsibility of separately elected school boards. The poor law, of course, came under yet another kind of authority, the boards of guardians, descendants of the former parish officials. However, legislation late in the century provided a new local government structure much better able to take on a wide range of functions. Local government Acts in 1888 and 1894 set up a system of local authorities that was to remain almost unchanged until the 1970s. They gave a shape to local government, with a split between the highly urbanized areas and the rest of the country, that dominates local politics to this day. The less-urbanized areas acquired a two-tier system of county government accompanied by lower-tier urban and rural districts. In many urban areas county boroughs were set up as single all-purpose authorities. London acquired a special two-tier system of its own.

It is very convenient, for the presentation of historical accounts, when a specific date can be identified as a watershed. It further adds neatness when that date is the beginning of a century. While there is always an arbitrary aspect to the choice of such dates, particularly in social history, the dividing point between the nineteenth and twentieth centuries seem a particularly significant one. At this time the large working-class male element added to the electorate in 1885 was just beginning to influence political thinking. The Labour Representation Committee was set up in 1899 to try to get more working men elected to Parliament. This body was to turn itself into the Labour Party in

1906. The major political parties, the Conservatives and the Liberals, were increasingly aware of the need to compete for working-class support. For the Conservatives the formula was an interesting blend of imperialism and social reform (Semmel, 1961). The Liberals had a radical wing, temporarily disadvantaged by the jingoism of the Boer War, but ready to push the party towards acceptance of a package of new social measures.

Late in the nineteenth century Britain had begun to discover that an advanced industrial nation is vulnerable to alarming economic fluctuations, owing to the unco-ordinated nature of much business decision-making and the international complications of the trade cycle. New competitors had also emerged as other nations – Germany, France, the United States – industrialized rapidly. The Empire still looked secure, but the competition for new trading outlets was increasing dramatically. At the same time as doubts were beginning to be felt about Britain's economic vulnerability, the working people were increasingly organizing in trade unions to try to secure, or guarantee, their share of the progress. The political price of economic failure was being raised. New initiatives to preserve the unity of the nation were required.

1900 TO 1914

The period immediately before the First World War was dominated by a series of reforms adopted by the Liberal Government after 1906. However, before those reforms are considered two earlier events require comment. In 1902 the Conservatives enacted an important Education Act. This passed the responsibility for state education from the school boards to the county and county borough councils, and devised a formula for the comprehensive financial support of the church schools that preserved a measure of voluntary control. The other important feature of this Act was that it legitimized expenditure on secondary and technical schools, and thereby stimulated the growth of this element of state education.

The other significant event was the Boer War. This rather inglorious episode in British imperial history had a considerable significance for social policy. In general it led to a concern to examine what was wrong with Great Britain that she should have been unable to fight effectively against apparently fragile opposition. In particular, politicians, in this age when Britain's imperial success was believed to have been based upon racial superiority, sought to examine why so many volunteers to fight had been found to be unfit to do so. Hence, as Fraser argues:

> In that bizarre way which again and again seemed to link imperialism and social reform (sometimes as allies, sometimes as competitors), it seemed to some that Britain would only be able to sustain its Empire if she ensured that the new generation of children, tomorrow's Imperial Army, was properly nourished.   (Fraser, 1973)

An Interdepartmental Committee on Physical Deterioration was set up. It reported in 1904, urging the establishment of a school medical service and the provision of school meals within the public education system. Both these measures were adopted by the Liberals and implemented soon after they came to power.

Before they lost office the Conservatives also responded to the growing evidence on the extent of poverty and the inadequacies of existing measures by setting up a Royal Commission on the Poor Laws in 1905. The report of this body, which did not appear until 1909, contains a most thorough discussion of British social policy at that time. There was both a majority and a minority report, and the latter provided a well-argued critique of the system. However, without waiting for the Royal Commission, the Liberal Government decided to promote two pieces of legislation that significantly modified the role of the poor law in the provision of social security: the Old Age Pensions Act of 1908 and the National Insurance Act of 1911.

These two pieces of legislation provide interesting contrasts in approaches to the provision of social security. The old-age pension was non-contributory and based upon a simple test of means. It was an extension of the outdoor relief given by some boards of guardians, but its means test was a personal and not a family one. The national insurance scheme, on the other hand, was contributory but not means-tested. It provided cover against sickness and unemployment for some, initially limited, categories of workers. The contribution was to come jointly from the employee, the employer and the state. The sickness scheme provided not just cash benefits but also medical treatment, from a 'panel' doctor who was remunerated on a 'capitation basis' in terms of the number of patients he accepted on his panel. The friendly societies and insurance companies, who were already involved in the provision of sickness cover for many working people, were allowed to participate as agents for the scheme and providers of additional benefits. The scheme protected only employees themselves but no members of their families.

The National Insurance Act is most important for introducing the 'insurance principle' into British social security legislation. A number of European countries had adopted state or municipal insurance schemes during the last years of the nineteenth century. The British policy-makers were particularly aware of the German scheme. Heclo provides, in the following passage, an interesting account of the role played by Beveridge, one of the architects of the new scheme, in introducing insurance ideas:

> In his first column for the *Morning Post*, February 16, 1906, he had dismissed contributory social insurance on the German pattern, as had all British investigating committees, with the standard view that it would require an 'un-British' amount of regulation of the individual. Beveridge, however, studied the German experiment more closely during the next year and concluded that the contributory insurance principle could not only reduce costs; it could also eliminate reliance on means tests. (Heclo, 1974, p. 81; see also Harris, 1977, on Beveridge's role)

The idea of social insurance had been adopted in the conservative society of Bismarck's Germany because it offered a low cost mechanism to meet some social needs whilst committing workers, as contributors to their own benefits, to the social and economic status quo.

This adoption of the insurance principle had important consequences for the development of social policy. In various measures after 1911 governments extended benefits in ways that undermined the *true* insurance basis of the scheme; but the contributory principle remained an important political symbol, and from time to time attempts were made to return the scheme closer to its roots. It is always difficult to combine the hard-headed actuarial principles of insurance with a concern for effective and comprehensive social security; yet, as Beveridge recognized, when the only viable political alternative is means-testing, the contributory principle has a great appeal. Beveridge was to play an important part in the 1940s in maintaining the insurance approach to social security.

The 1911 National Insurance Act had implications for more than social security policy, in two ways. The provision of medical services under the sickness benefit scheme used a model for the state payment of general practitioners that has continued in the National Health Service to the present day. Abel-Smith (1976, ch. 2) has pointed out that before 1911 the doctors were in conflict with the friendly societies about the conditions under which they were hired to care for members. Hence they were predisposed to secure contracts under the state scheme which preserved their freedom. This right to operate as independent contractors rather than as salaried servants of the state has been zealously preserved by general practitioners.

It is also important to perceive the National Insurance Act as the sort of response to the problem of unemployment that has remained dominant in Britain. The earlier years of the twentieth century saw a number of small experiments in combating unemployment by providing publicly subsidized work. Yet these did not achieve any scale, perhaps because of suspicions of their implications for state involvement in the economy. There was however one measure, adopted in 1908, the Labour Exchange Act, that came to assume importance. The insurance Act gave the newly set up exchanges the role of administering the system of unemployment benefit. This was the activity with which they came to be most closely identified in the first 50 years of their existence. The hallmark of the British response to defects in the working of the labour market became the provision of relief to the unemployed, and neither the creation of special work programmes nor measures to facilitate movements of workers between jobs (see Harris, 1972). Not until the 1970s was this emphasis really challenged.

The Liberal government could, of course, have developed their social security measures as direct measures to redistribute incomes without either means tests or contributions. Neither their measures nor any of the social security measures that have succeeded them have involved the wholesale redistribution of resources. However, both the early measures required quite large subventions from taxation. It is important, therefore, to bear in mind the significance of the budget that Lloyd George introduced in 1909 to finance both social welfare reforms and increased government expenditure on other matters such as defence, by increasing taxation and making it more redistributive. This seems to have been the first occasion on which a British government's annual budget was presented, or perceived, as an instrument for the redistribution of income. This in itself is of note. Lloyd George, whose penchant for the rhetoric of class warfare gives a misleading impression of his readiness for the reality of such conflict, described the budget as follows: 'This is a war budget. It is for raising money to wage implacable warfare against poverty and squalidness.' Its most controversial part was a group of measures to tax land. Lloyd George defended them by an aggressive verbal attack on the privileges of landowners:

> The ownership of land is not merely an enjoyment, it is a stewardship. It has been reckoned as such in the past, and if the landowners cease to discharge these functions, the time will come to reconsider the conditions under which land is held in this country. No country, however rich, can permanently afford to have quartered upon its revenue a class which declined to do the duty which it was called upon to perform.   (Speech at Limehouse, 1909)

Such was the populist rhetoric of the time. It did not usher in a revolution, but it helped to change the tenor of British politics. Inside Parliament the working-class interest was advanced by a comparatively cautious radical Liberal group, supported by an equally cautious small caucus of Labour MPs. Outside, Marxist socialism was beginning to be given attention by orators, and syndicalist trade unionists were beginning to flex their industrial muscles. Against all this the landowning interests – not, it must be noted, the industrialists – fought a rearguard action. The House of Lords threw out Lloyd George's budget. The consequence was a Parliament Act, with which the Lords eventually acquiesced after two general elections and the threat of mass creation of peers, which curbed the power of the Lords to block Commons legislation.

The events of 1909–11 have been given comparatively lengthy attention. The political balance in Britain tipped quite markedly at that time, with important implications for social policy. Such was the ferment of the times throughout Europe, and such was the rising volume of political controversy within Britain (bear in mind also the Suffragette agitation and the conflict over the future of Ireland), that a more dramatic tipping of the balance than actually occurred in the next few years might have been expected. Certainly, many new social policies were shortly to come, but these did little to disrupt the status quo; indeed, many must be seen as designed to preserve it.

1914 TO 1939

It is important that we do not regard the development of social policy in Britain as simply involving two dramatic jumps forward in the periods 1906–11 and 1944–9. Between these a great deal happened to influence policies and to give them a character they often retain.

In the First World War Britain experienced conscription for the first time, and the mobilization not only of the whole work-force but also of many women, hitherto not in employment, to assist the war effort. The war economy produced many domestic shortages. Initially the government was reluctant to impose controls and rationing, but its desire to curb wage rises and industrial unrest forced it to intervene. In general, then, the 'collectivist state' advanced considerably during this period. Civil servants learnt to carry out, and members of the public came to expect, government policies in areas of life never before influenced by state action. This was the general impact of war upon public policy. Its specific impact upon social policy was more limited. The imposition of controls upon private rents was a rare, but significant, example of social policy innovation in this period.

However, during and at the end of the war the government made many promises for a better future. Even before the war ended an Education Act was passed which recognized the case for state support for free education up to the age of 14. At the end of the war Lloyd

George promised 'homes fit for heroes', and one of the first pieces of postwar legislation was a Housing Act that provided government subsidies to local authorities to build houses for the working classes. This Act, known as the Addison Act after its sponsor, the Minister of Health, while not the first legislation to allow local authority house-building, was the first to subsidize it. It effectively initiated a pro-gramme of council house-building that has continued, albeit subject to regular modification as governments have changed the subsidy arrangements, until the present day. After the Addison Act both of the minority Labour governments, in power in 1924 and in 1929–31, extended the local authority house-building programme by means of further subsidies. In the 1930s there was a shift in housing policy, with the government encouraging local authorities to put their emphasis in house provision upon clearing the slums. The strict rent control, intro-duced in the war to protect private tenants, was partly lifted during the interwar period. But with this, as with council-house building, no real attempt was made to turn back the clock on processes that were ulti-mately totally to transform the character of Britain's housing market.

The evolution of relief policies for the unemployed in the interwar years is an interesting story. Unemployment was a recurrent problem throughout this period. Immediately after the war the government mismanaged the discharge of servicemen back into civilian life, and unemployment rose rapidly. Then the economy picked up and the problem abated. But this proved to be a temporary respite, and by 1921 registered unemployment was over two million. It remained over a million throughout the period, falling back a bit in the middle 1920s but then rising steeply in 1930. By 1931 it was over two million, and it did not fall below two million until 1936.

The 1911 National Insurance Act provided unemployment benefit only for workers in a limited number of trades which at that time were not liable to extensive and prolonged unemployment. It also contained strict rules to protect the insurance fund. Benefits were dependent upon past contributions, and the duration of weekly payments to individuals was limited. The scheme was not designed to provide widespread relief in a period of mass unemployment. Gilbert, in his detailed study of social policy in this period, has shown that politicians were alarmed by the reports they received of unrest and agitation among the ranks of the unemployed (Gilbert, 1970). They were particularly conscious of the expectation of ex-soldiers that they would receive generous treat-ment from the government. Hence the government faced a dilemma. They resolved it by breaching the strict insurance principles and ex-tending the scope of the unemployment benefit scheme.

It would be inappropriate here to set out all the convolutions in public policy on relief for the unemployed. What a whole succession of ministers and official committees had to try to resolve was the conflict between the demand for economy in government expenditure and the rising cost of an insurance benefit scheme no longer entirely restrained by insurance rules. Broadly, the compromise reached was to have extended but not unlimited insurance benefits, the operation of strict and quite unrealistic tests to ensure that people were 'genuinely seeking work' (a measure particularly aimed at unemployed females: Deacon, 1976), the use of additional means-tested benefits known then as 'doles', and acceptance that the poor law authorities would give extensive 'outdoor' relief to the unemployed. Eventually rationalization came in 1934 when a unified national means test scheme for benefits additional to insurance benefits was devised, to be administered by the Unemployment Assistance Board (UAB). This new organization was the forerunner of the National Assistance Board set up in 1948, and therefore of the Supplementary Benefits Commission that operated until 1980. The UAB provided a model that enabled central government to take over the functions of the poor law agencies. It transferred responsibility for means-tested benefits for the unemployed to this national organization in 1934, added similar benefits for the elderly to its responsibilities in 1940, and added most other cash aid in 1941. By 1948, when it was finally killed, the poor law was all but dead already.

The demise of the poor law was also assisted by another piece of legislation in this period, the Local Government Act of 1929. This handed over responsibility for the poor law from the boards of guardians to the local authorities. As far as the administration of relief was concerned this made little difference; the public assistance committees of the local authorities could be regarded as broadly the guardians under another name. However, the handover of powers brought the institutions that had evolved from the old workhouses into the hands of authorities that could more effectively bring them up to date. This was particularly important for the hospitals, since now a unified public service could be provided. It constituted an important step towards a national health service, though in practice few authorities did much to modernize their facilities. Instead, the transformation of the hospital service awaited the special arrangements that were made to co-ordinate their activities with those of the voluntary hospitals during the Second World War.

While little attempt was made to alter the character of the patchwork of health services available in the interwar period, all the parties that were to be involved in their transformation in the 1940s were beginning to examine the weaknesses of the existing provision and to formulate alternatives. In view of the importance of medical acquiescence in the system eventually adopted, it was probably necessary for many doctors to become aware of the need for change.

Education services similarly went through a phase of detailed examination of their weaknesses and future potential during the interwar period. Here, however, the roles given to the local authorities by the Acts of 1902 and 1918 left scope for innovation where money allowed. The teaching profession grew in strength at this time, developing a formal system of training to replace the nineteenth-century pupil-teacher system. Education beyond the primary stage grew in various ways, and this part of the system was ready for rationalization by the end of the 1930s.

This section has described the interwar period as a period of consolidation in social policy. But at least one really significant innovation occurred: the development of a public housing sector; and the inroads made into poor law were of considerable significance for the future. One other element of this that deserves a brief outline was the adoption in 1925 of a contributory pension scheme to run alongside the non-contributory one. This period is often thought of as one of failure in British politics: of failure to cope with the rise of Hitler and Mussolini abroad, and failure to deal with unemployment at home. It was, however, also a period when complete adult suffrage was achieved, and in which a political consensus was built up that enabled the Labour Party to establish itself alongside the older parties, so that an element of working-class power developed without turning into a revolutionary force. The key Conservative politicians of that age, Baldwin and Chamberlain, were very much men of the 'consensus', eager to promote cautious innovation in social policy. The key Labour politician, Ramsay MacDonald, was equally eager to occupy the middle ground. Some readers will no doubt regard this consensus politics as another of the failures of this age, urging that the compromises by the Left prevented radical change from occurring. Its significance, however, for social policies was that it created a platform for changes to occur in the 1940s, changes that secured very widespread social and political acceptance.

THE 1940s

The government was very much more ready to mobilize all the nation's resources in the Second World War than it had been in the First. Regulation and rationing were not adopted reluctantly but as measures essential to the war effort. Politically, at least after Churchill replaced Chamberlain as prime minister in 1940, the nation was more totally united. The Labour Party regained its self-confidence; it had been deserted by its leaders, who formed a National Government in 1931 that then heavily defeated Labour in the ensuing general election. It regarded attention to social policies as one of the conditions of its involvement in a coalition government. Although Churchill sometimes appeared to be unhappy about it, planning for the peace was widely accepted as a legitimate political task during the war. But before looking at the two most important examples of planning for peace, the Beveridge Report and the Butler Education Act of 1944, it is important to note a number of ways in which peacetime policy changes were foreshadowed by *ad hoc* wartime measures. In the last section reference was made to the way in which the Unemployment Assistance Board, which was renamed the Assistance Board in 1940, took over various functions from the public assistance committees in the early part of the war. Mention was also made of the integration of the hospital services during the war, under the Emergency Hospital Scheme. The evacuation of children called for the development of special services, foreshadowing developments in child-care practice after the war. Rents were again strictly controlled, and empty houses were requisitioned. The wartime state had many of the characteristics of the 'welfare state', which is popularly regarded as having been created after the war.

The Beveridge Report was the report of a committee on *Social Insurance and Allied Services*, published in 1942. This recommended the adoption of a contributory social security system that improved on the existing system by protecting all citizens against sickness, unemployment and old age. The new system should, it was argued, include family allowances, maternity benefits and provision for widows. The contribution principles should be insurance ones, involving the employee, the employer and the state, as before, but the coverage of the scheme should be universal and therefore involve a national pooling of risks. There was, in the arrangements for dependants and widows, inevitably built into the scheme certain assumptions about the male breadwinner and his relationship to the family unit, which have left a difficult legacy for attempts in our own age to balance the interests of men and women. Otherwise it is still possible to evaluate the British system of social security in terms of the extent to which it matches up to the model outlined by Beveridge in 1942.

Beveridge argued that other social policies were necessary to underpin his insurance scheme. Support for children would be necessary through a universal 'family allowance' scheme. A system of means-tested assistance would be necessary as a 'safety -net' for the minority whose needs were not adequately covered by the scheme. The maintenance of full employment would be essential to enable social insurance to work properly. A national health service should take over the provision for medical care in the old insurance scheme and effectively underpin the new one.

Beveridge's insurance scheme was broadly put into legislation. Family allowances were provided by one of the last measures of the coalition government. The rest was enacted by the postwar Labour government, though there was one crucial departure from the insurance principle in that the qualifying period for a full pension was very short. This deviation from Beveridge's plan made the scheme expensive to general taxation, and probably tended to prevent the adoption of benefit levels sufficient to provide subsistence incomes to those with no other resources and to inhibit subsequent increases to keep up with the cost of living.

The Education Act passed in 1944 and often identified by the name of the minister responsible, R. A. Butler, provided the framework for the education system we have today. The Butler Act provided for universal free state secondary education, but did not specify the form it should take or rule on whether or not there should be selective schools.

At the end of the war the coalition broke up. In the ensuing general election both parties promised substantial social policy reforms, but the electorate swung strongly towards the Labour Party, rejecting the old war leader Churchill in favour of Labour's clearer commitment to a vision of the 'welfare state'. The social security reforms embodied by the Labour Party in the National Insurance Act of 1946 and the National Assistance Act of 1948 have already been mentioned. With the adoption of these measures came the abolition of the poor law, its income maintenance responsibilities going to the National Assistance Board and its responsibilities for residential care and other welfare services going to local authority welfare departments.

In 1946 the creation of the National Health Service provided another crucial innovation in social policy. General practitioner and hospital services were provided free for everyone, in a complex structure designed to unify the hospital sector while leaving general practitioners as independent contractors and other community services in the control of the local authorities. This structure was achieved after hard bargaining between the minister, Aneurin Bevan, and the doctors, who were deeply suspicious of state medicine (see Eckstein, 1960; Pater, 1981). The scheme was funded out of general taxation, though an element of payment for the health service remained in the national insurance contribution, creating a confusing illusion that this was what paid for the service. The notion of a totally free service did not last for long. Very soon Chancellors of the Exchequer, exploiting concern that demand for services was much greater than expected, secured, first, small payments for spectacles and dental treatment, and then prescription charges, as ways of raising revenue.

Among these widely publicized social policy reforms came another measure, that had much less impact upon the general public but nevertheless had important implications: the Children Act of 1948. The origins of this reform of the services for deprived children seem to have been in a child care scandal, the O'Neill case, which led to the setting up of the Curtis Committee to investigate contemporary practice (Packman, 1975, ch. 1). The Children Act consolidated the existing child-care legislation and created departments in which professional social work practice would develop in child-care and, in due course, in work with families.

The Labour Government of 1945–51 did not alter the system of subsidizing local authority housing that had developed in the interwar period, but, by the Housing Act of 1949, it did substantially extend the subsidies available. The Act formally removed the limitation confining local authority provision to housing for the 'working classes'. The government's concern throughout the late 1940s was to stimulate building to make up the deficiencies in housing stock arising from bomb damage and the wartime standstill in house-building. However, postwar shortages of materials made it difficult to accelerate new building. The Labour Government laid its emphasis upon local authority housing rather than on private building for sale. It also involved itself, as no government ever had before, in an attempt to secure effective land-use planning and to curb land speculation. The Town and Country Planning Act of 1947 provided a grand design for this purpose, though one of limited success, but was subsequently dismantled by the Conservatives. Another crucial planning innovation, with major implications for the provision of public housing, was the New Towns Act of 1946. This provided jobs and houses in new communities for people from overcrowded cities and run-down industrial areas.

Government involvement in planning the use of national resources, which had been one of the necessities of wartime, was continued by the Labour Government as a matter of principle. This in itself was important in enlarging the involvement of government with many aspects of life in Britain. There was a commitment to the maintenance of full employment, with the Keynesian doctrine (Keynes, 1936) that budgetary management could achieve this now a matter of economic orthodoxy. In the 1940s such economic management was slightly inflationary, but this was broadly seen as a reasonable price to pay for full employment and economic growth. In retrospect it is hard to judge the extent to which the success of this policy (and, for all the worries it caused at the time, it was a success by comparison with the economy management disasters of the 1960s and 1970s) was due to good management, and the extent to which it was due to external and internal economic factors outside government control, in particular to the postwar recovery and the stimulus provided by the continuing military activity of the 'cold war'.

The 1940s were, in both war and peace, crucial years for building the system of social policy Britain has today. But it has been shown that few of the innovations of this period were without precedent in the policies of earlier years, and that much of the crucial thinking about the form these new institutions should take had been done in the interwar period. Continuity is also evident in the behaviour of the two major political parties. The Butler Education Act and the Family Allowances Act were both measures of the Conservative-dominated wartime coalition. Preliminary work had also been done during the war on the ideas for the social security scheme, and a start had been made on drafting plans for a national health service.

The political continuity is also apparent in the fact that the Conservatives did comparatively little, on returning to power in 1951, to dismantle the 'welfare state'. The Labour Party policies that they did contest, and partly reverse, were its nationalization policies, not its social welfare ones. Otherwise, they shifted the house-building emphasis from public to private building but by no means eliminated a substantial public element from their enlarged building programme; they were marginally more ready to increase health service charges; and they were, perhaps, rather slow to raise social security benefits. In the later 1950s they encouraged education services to flourish; and some local authorities began to innovate in this policy area in ways that in due course came to be regarded as radical and politically contentious.

SINCE THE 1940s

The presentation of policies in this section will be sketchy because they are generally covered more fully in the appropriate detailed chapter later in the book. The aim here is to give the flavour of the key developments in this period as part of the history of social policy.

Broadly the period 1951–92 can be divided into four parts: 1951–64, a period of comparatively little social policy innovation that may be regarded as a time of consolidation or stagnation, according to one's political viewpoint; 1964–74, a period of fairly intense policy change stimulated by both political parties, in which considerable difficulties were experienced in translating aspirations into practice; and 1974–79, a period in which rapid inflation and government by the Labour Party without a parliamentary majority administered a severe shock to the political and social system, and to all who believed that there was still a need for developments in social policy; and 1979–92, when much more explicitly anti-welfare state Conservative administrations reinforced that shock by deliberately treating inflation as more deserving of its attention than unemployment, attacking public services which were seen as inhibiting economic recovery, and seeking ways to 'privatize' public services. Bearing these points in mind, let us look at developments in each of the main policy areas over the whole period.

The period 1951–64 was a boom period for house-building, both private and public. It was during this time that two kinds of tenure began to dominate in Britain: owner-occupation and local authority tenancy. The decline in the size of the privately rented sector was rapid, and towards the later part of this period it was accelerated by slum clearance. In 1957 the government, believing that the private renting market could be revived if rent controls were removed, passed a Rent Act that allowed some decontrol. The main impact of this measure was that many landlords used the freedom to evict allowed under decontrol to sell previously let properties for owner-occupation. In the 1960s the Labour government legislated to restore security of tenure and to allow rent levels to rise only to levels that fell short of market prices.

When Labour returned to power they were committed to reversing the emphasis upon building for owner-occupation within the building boom, but at the same time they wanted to produce even more houses per annum. The use of restraints upon building investment as an economic regulator to prevent excess domestic demand made it difficult for them to achieve their targets. By the end of the 1970s the additions to the housing stock had been so considerable that arguments were increasingly heard that Britain had enough houses. What complicated this debate was the question of whether there were enough houses of the right kind in the right places. Certainly some of the earlier building activity may have been misplaced effort. In particular, many local authorities produced poor quality, system-built high-rise flats which were hard to let (Dunleavy, 1981).

Another of Labour's policy commitments was to try again, like their predecessors in 1946, to do something to rationalize planning and curb the activities of the land speculators. While the central problem here was the unrestrained inner-city office and commercial development, the concern about this issue also had implications for owner-occupied housing. Politicians of both parties have, since 1960, become increasingly concerned about the problems of house-buyers, in the face of spiralling land and building costs and high rates of mortgage interest.

When they came to power in 1970 the Conservatives decided that public expenditure on local authority housing needed to be curbed. Their Housing Finance Act of 1972 set out to adapt the 'fair-rent' principle, which Labour had applied to private rents in the 1960s, to the local authority sector. They linked this with a national rent rebate scheme, rationalizing the variety of local schemes that had been set up over the previous decade, to offset the costs to the poorer tenants. This Act was designed to reduce the general subsidy to council tenants; it was linked to changes in the system of national subsidies to local authorities designed to phase out indiscriminate help of this kind in due course. Labour opposed this measure and limited its impact, but on returning to power in 1979 the Conservatives, by reducing new expenditure on public housing, modifying the subsidy formula and encouraging rents to rise, set out to eliminate most subsidies to public housing other than means-tested benefits to individual occupiers. Measures at the end of the 1980s prevented local government subsidy of council housing and accelerated the rate at which central subsidies were withdrawn.

In addition, legislation enacted in 1980 to give local authority tenants a 'right to buy' has also made extensive inroads into the system of public housing. An Act passed in 1988 sought further to dismantle the system of local-authority-owned public housing. It aimed to replace it by a mixture of housing associations, tenant co-ownership schemes and further individual ownership. In practice such changes have been slow to occur.

The Conservatives did little to change the social security system in the period 1951–64. Towards the end of the period the two parties began to produce competing plans to superimpose an earning-related pensions scheme on top of the inadequate flat-rate system. In 1959 the Conservatives introduced a very limited graduated pension scheme. In 1964 the Labour Party came to power committed to a much more comprehensive scheme. However, they failed to complete its preparation before they lost office in 1970. The Conservatives then took up the idea in a slightly more limited way, but Labour returned to power and put their own scheme on the statute book in 1975. This provided for a mixed scheme of public and private pensions, with many of the better-paid and more secure groups of workers able to 'contract out' into private schemes so long as these were at least as good as the State Earnings Related Pensions Scheme (SERPS). Conservative legislation in 1986 has extended the scope for contracting out, allowing investment in schemes which do not necessarily compete favourably with the state scheme and also reducing the benefits available under SERPS.

In the early 1960s a number of academic studies were published showing that the 'welfare state' had by no means abolished poverty (Cole and Utting, 1962; Lynes, 1962; Abel-Smith and Townsend, 1965). This 'rediscovery of poverty' would seem to be a function of an academic and political interest that had emerged, the aim of which was to look at the adequacy of social policies. Indeed, it can be said to be a consequence, but also a cause, of the growth of the academic subject with which this book is concerned. It was not, at that time at least, a consequence of any particular social or economic change between the late 1940s and the early 1960s, except inasmuch as increased affluence for many highlighted the 'relative' poverty of those left behind (Townsend, 1954; see also Townsend (ed.), 1970; Townsend, 1979; Holman, 1978). The emphasis upon the weaknesses of existing social security policies for the relief of poverty led to a reappraisal of those policies. The Labour Government of 1964–70 made a number of changes, therefore. Some of them raised some people's incomes, and there were a number of increases in benefit rates. Inflation was, however, increasing, and public resources were, as ever, limited and in great demand for a wide range of policy objectives.

The main social security policy changes in this period were the introduction in 1965 of earnings-related supplements to sickness and unemployment benefits and of a redundancy payments scheme. Also, in 1966 'national assistance' was replaced by 'supplementary benefits'. This reform was designed to remove the stigma of assistance by making rights to these means-tested benefits much clearer, particularly for pensioners.

One particular focus of attention in the debate about poverty was family poverty, and particularly the problems faced by the low-wage earner. The principle, adopted in 1834, that wages should not be subsidized had been carried forward in social security legislation, but the margin between the income of those in work and those out of work sometimes made the principle of 'less eligibility' appear under threat. The Child Poverty Action Group, a pressure group set up in the 1960s, urged governments to deal with this problem by increasing family allowances. These had fallen in value, in real terms, since little effort had been made to update them properly. However, the conventional political view was that family allowances were an unpopular and indiscriminate handout. The 'poverty lobby' sought to persuade the government that family allowances could be increased at the expense of child tax allowances. This approach was gradually accepted, though not before inflation had reduced the tax threshold so low that most poor wage-earners were also benefiting from the tax allowances. In the 1970s the Conservatives floated an alternative approach, a form of negative income tax called 'tax credits'(HMSO, 1972) and implemented a means-tested benefit for poor wage-earners, 'family income supplement'. Labour, on return to power, decided to press on with the development of a new family allowance scheme, called 'child benefit', designed to replace the older allowance. They extended it to the first child in each family, and offset it against the abolition of tax allowances (see McCarthy, 1986, for a discussion of these developments). But it did not abolish family income supplement.

On first returning to power in 1979 the Conservatives set out to make piecemeal adjustments to the social security system. They reduced the value of contributory benefits by altering the procedure for inflation-related increases and by extending the taxation of benefits. They shifted responsibility for the provision of sickness absence for the first 28 weeks from the national insurance scheme to a statutory sick pay scheme to be run by employers. They attempted also to rationalize the burgeoning supplementary benefit scheme by developing a stronger rule-based structure, and they introduced a housing benefit scheme.

However, in 1983 they decided that more radical reform of social security was necessary. It was an element in public expenditure which they were finding very hard to control; not surprisingly in the face of an ageing population, rapidly rising unemployment, and government measures designed to shift the subsidy of housing on to the social security scheme. Proclaiming themselves to be engaged in the most radical review of social security since Beveridge they set up a number of ministerially dominated committees to explore options for reform. The eventual outcome was the 1986 Social Security Act. This legislation modified SERPS (in the way outlined above), replaced supplementary benefits by 'income support' and family income supplement by 'family credit'. The rule structures for these two new schemes are much more simple than those for supplementary benefits. Housing benefit was altered to bring it in line with these other two benefits. Some anomalies which had been arising as a result of the previous piecemeal evolution of means-tested benefit were eliminated. The maternity grant and the death grant, two benefits initiated in the Beveridge era but not properly updated in line with inflation, were abolished, to be replaced by means-test-related benefits for the very poor. The system of single payments available to help people on supplementary benefits with specific needs was replaced by a much more limited system, known as the 'social fund', under which all that most people could get were loans.

Alongside these major structural changes the Conservatives substantially weakened the benefits designed to protect the unemployed, making support for under-18s conditional upon undergoing training and sharply reducing the help available to other young unemployed people. Penalties for refusing to undergo training and for leaving jobs were made very severe.

In many respects the Beveridge design for social security had been undermined before 1979 by failures to uprate insurance benefits adequately, by rising unemployment and by the need to provide means-tested benefits for the increasing number of single-parent families. The policy changes of the 1980s continued that process, ensuring that means-tested benefits were increasingly of key importance for the relief of poverty. In particular, the 1986 Act extended and rationalized means tests but it did not take social security in the radical new direction that 'negative income tax' or 'social dividend' advocates were suggesting (for a further discussion, see Hill, 1990, ch. 9).

In the period 1951–64, of all the policy areas with which this book is concerned it was probably education that saw the most innovation. It was, however, very much localized and piecemeal within the general structure laid down by the Butler Act. That had, as was stressed, laid the foundation for the creation of a sound secondary education system. Initially the orthodox view was that such a system should be selective and tripartite, with children routed at eleven-plus into grammar, technical or secondary modern schools according to their aptitudes and abilities. The concept of a separate form of technical education did not become established (Sanderson, 1991). Then, as time passed, even the notion of a bipartite system was increasingly questioned and an alternative, non-selective, comprehensive model was championed. Various local authorities began to introduce comprehensive schools in the 1950s, motivated sometimes by political and educational ideology but sometimes, particularly in rural areas, by a recognition that such schools were a more realistic response to local needs. It was not until the 1960s that battle-lines began to be drawn up, with Labour in favour of comprehensivisation and the Conservatives against; and even then the Conservatives in central government were not hard-line opponents of this policy in the way that, by the end of the decade, Labour had become hard-line advocates. Nevertheless, Labour legislation requiring local authorities to introduce comprehensivisation schemes, enacted in 1976, was repealed by the Conservatives in 1980.

In a variety of other ways the Conservative governments of the period 1951–64 rapidly increased the resources available to state education. In many respects this was a necessary response to the child population 'bulge' created by the 'baby boom' of the immediate postwar years. This in itself created a need for new schools and teachers, and therefore provided a platform for educational innovation. But clearly governments were ready to encourage innovatory thinking. Advisory groups were created to look at various educational issues. These produced a memorable series of reports: on early leaving (Central Advisory Council for Education, 1954); on education between 15 and 18 (ibid., 1959); on the education of less-academic children (ibid., 1963); on higher education (HMSO, 1963); and on primary education (Central Advisory Council for Education, 1967). The crucial policy changes influenced by all this committee activity were the rapid expansion of higher education in the 1960s, the raising of the school-leaving age to 16 in 1973 (after delays in implementing a change first announced in 1964), and a distinct shift away from streaming and selectivity at all stages before the teenage years. But it was the change in amounts of public money spent on education that was most important. By the mid-1970s the 'bulge' had nearly worked its way through the system, and this, together with disillusion with innovation in education, brought to an end the role of the education service as an expenditure growth-leader among the public services.

This reversal was extended in the 1980s to some extent, particularly in the case of higher education, in advance of the fall in the size of the relevant generation. At the same time education-based expenditure on meals, milk and transport came under attack.

The late 1970s also saw the initiation of the questioning of the value of educational growth. Controversy grew about some of the bolder experiments in egalitarian education, and it was increasingly alleged that basic education, the 'three Rs', was being neglected. Some people put some of the responsibility for the growing youth unemployment on educational inadequacies, giving sustenance to the Department of Employment's bid to control low-level post-school education. Once the Conservatives came to power in 1979 the unrest began to be translated into policy form. The completion of the comprehensivation programme was arrested, and new opportunities were created for state-financed places at private schools. The 1980 Education Act, which extended parental choice of schools, was seen as creating pressures for the raising of academic standards and had the effect of increasing the tendency towards social segregation.

The 1988 Education Act was much more fundamental, largely replacing the 1944 Act as the framework law for state education in England and Wales. This Act laid down a requirement that there should be a 'national curriculum' of 'core' subjects (English, maths and science) and 'foundation subjects'. It requires children to be tested regularly, starting at the age of seven, to assess the extent to which attainment targets have been achieved, and the government is determined that collective information about test outcomes shall be published. Local government control over education is weakened by this legislation, which strengthen the autonomy of individual school managements and enables schools to apply to become directly funded by central government. This legislation, supplemented by further legislation, also extended central control over higher education and removed the last vestiges of local authority responsibility for this sector.

In the 1950s the principal government concern about the health service was with difficulties in controlling costs. No substantial changes resulted from this preoccupation. The relationship of the doctors with the government was, and remains, a sensitive area. A great deal of attention was given to their terms of service and remuneration.

The only major item of legislation in the health field between 1951 and 1970 was the Mental Health Act of 1959 which altered the procedures for the compulsory admission and retention of the mentally ill in hospital, abolishing the old 'certification' procedure. The treatment of mental illness was advancing considerably at that time, and it probably contributed more than the legislative change to reducing both the use of compulsory procedures and the incidence of long stays in hospital. A further Mental Health Act in 1983 continued the liberalization of the treatment of the mentally ill.

In the 1960s, as part of the wholesale review of the institutions of central and local government, proposals were introduced for the reorganization of the National Health Service. Two green papers were produced, suggesting different ways of doing this (HMSO, 1967 and 1968b). Eventually the change was effected by the Conservatives in 1974. This change created a new structure with the former local authority health services integrated with the rest of the service. Lay participation in the running of the service was reduced; in its place community health councils were created to represent the public. The new structure was criticized as over-elaborate – with its three tiers of regions, areas and districts – almost as soon as it was created. Discontent over the operation of the new service was one of the factors that led the Labour Government to set up a Royal Commission on the National Health Service in 1976. This reported in 1979 (HMSO, 1979) recommending the removal of a tier; the government responded in 1982 by eliminating areas but enlarging some districts.

Two important stimuli to the search for the right structure for the NHS throughout this period were a concern about effective policy control in the face of professional domination, and anxiety about the extent of inequalities in health between social classes and between regions. These two concerns were brought together during the 1970s with the development of a system for the allocation of resources between regions and districts based upon health indices (RAWP, see chapter 7). They, and particularly the former, also fuelled a concern to strengthen management. In the Griffiths report (Department of Health and Social Security, 1983), a hierarchy of general managers was advocated for the NHS, weakening the influence of the nominated regional and district 'authorities'. This proposal was enacted.

Despite these changes, the rising costs of the NHS, an effect deriving more than anything else from the ageing of the population, led the Conservatives to explore further structural changes. Their right wing urged them to privatize the system. Whilst being unprepared to go this far, the government, in legislation enacted in 1990, encouraged hospitals to become quasi-independent 'national health service trusts', and general medical practices to become 'budget holders'. Both of these measures are designed to bring about increases in efficiency, accompanied by general arrangements for a managerial split between 'purchasers' and 'providers'. The overall aim is to create an 'internal market' system within the NHS in which hospitals are in competition with each other. There has been an eager scramble by hospitals to achieve trust status. General practitioners have been slower to seek budget-holder status.

The development of the personal social services between the 1940s and the 1970s is a story of steady consolidation and one important structural change. At the end of the 1940s local authorities organized these services within two or three departments. Children's services were the responsibility of one department, required by statute. Children's departments built up a body of social work expertise, and gradually extended their activities from work to deal with acute child-care problems into work designed to prevent child-neglect and abuse and work with delinquent children. Two Children and Young Persons Acts, in 1963 and 1969, legitimized and encouraged these changes in emphasis.

The other local authority welfare services, or personal social services, were organized by welfare departments and by health departments (or by departments that combined these two functions). A social work career was developed in connection with this work, but not so effectively as was the case in the children's departments. A government report in 1959 made recommendations that influenced developments in the training of social work staff of this kind. But the activities of these departments were growing in other ways, too. Their legacy from the poor law was a stock of homes, for the elderly and disabled, that were ex-workhouses. A central task, therefore, was to phase out these institutions, replacing them by smaller, more welcoming and civilized homes, and also to seek to develop ways of caring for people within the community. Developments in day care, the home help and other domiciliary services were the currency of growth in these departments. In 1970 the Chronically Sick and Disabled Persons Act placed obligations upon the local authorities to identify and help disabled people. But progress in this area of policy should not necessarily be measured by statutes. Earlier, permissive legislation had already enabled some authorities to innovate in services for disabled people.

The important structural change for all these local authority services was an Act passed in 1970, on the recommendations of the Seebohm Committee (HMSO, 1968a), which created integrated 'social services' departments in local authorities in England and Wales. In Scotland the Social Work (Scotland) Act of 1968 had already created integrated 'social work departments', including the probation officers, who in England and Wales remained in a separate service independent of local government.

The structural change in England and Wales was accompanied by a change in central government organization, whereby the Home Office's responsibility for children's services was passed over to the Department of Health and Social Security, which was already responsible for other welfare services. These changes represent another example of the statutory creation of a 'platform for growth'. This duly occurred, but by the 1980s had been checked.

With that check came renewed questioning about the balance between services provided by the social services departments and the many forms of family, neighbourhood and commercially purchased care that they supplemented. Within social work the quest continued for the best way to organize a service that could be responsive to community need (Barclay, 1982). From outside social work doubts were increasingly raised about the adequacies of that profession, particularly in the face of a growing number of child abuse 'scandals'.

A related problem, exacerbated by the ageing of the population, has concerned the balance between community and residential care. This is a complex issue, because it is not merely an issue about forms of care but also about who should bear the costs of care. The community care debate is about *both* care *in* the community and care *by* the community. In the 1980s a strange piece of government carelessness brought the whole issue to a head. The social security minister relaxed the rules under which means-tested benefits could be used to subsidize private residential care. The result was an explosive growth of this sector, making demands upon the social security budget that were hard to control. A whole range of anomalies developed about the relationship between residential and community care (Audit Commission, 1986). The Conservative government's eventual response to this problem was to try to develop a version of the health service's purchaser/provider split in which local authorities would be purchasers and the various forms of community care would be provided by a range of organizations in which private and voluntary enterprises would be dominant. The 1990 Act, which developed similar ideas for the NHS, authorized this, but at the time of writing the government's difficulties about local government finance (see below) have delayed part of its implementation. April 1993 is the expected starting date for the full scheme.

During the period 1964–91 the local government structure, within which many of the social services are based, came under review. In 1972 the Local Government Act made the first major change in the local government system of England and Wales, apart from the 1963 restructuring in London, since the nineteenth century. This reform created a new two-tier system of local government. In the metropolitan areas the model, like the earlier one adopted in London, was of most-purpose, lower-tier authorities and of top-tier counties responsible primarily for structural planning. Outside the metropolitan areas the division of the social policy functions was more even: the counties acquired responsibility for education and social services while the districts were made responsible for housing. Similar changes followed in Scotland soon afterwards. Then, in 1986 the Thatcher government abolished the metropolitan counties. Their functions were either devolved to the districts or given to *ad hoc* joint boards.

An accompanying central government preoccupation about local government in this period was the fact that it was becoming an increasing spender (not surprisingly in the light of central government's expectations of it in areas like education, personal social services and housing). In the period up to the middle 1970s central government steadily increased its grant contributions to local expenditure. It also struggled, rather fruitlessly, to find ways to wholly or partly replace the system of local taxation, the rates assessed on property. In the last year of the 1964–9 Labour government the first cuts in the central contribution to local expenditure were made. The Thatcher government continued this process, much more zealously, developing a formula which deliberately penalized those authorities they deemed to be overspenders. Then, in addition, they decided they must limit local authorities' powers to go on increasing local rates. They developed a power which enabled them to 'rate cap' a group of authorities whom they deemed to be high spenders. Finally, they decided to abolish rates and replace them by a poll tax known as the 'community charge'. This measure proved to be enormously unpopular and contributed to Margaret Thatcher's political downfall. Her successor as Prime Minister, John Major, rushed legislation through Parliament to try to get rid of the stigma of the poll tax. He sharply increased the central subsidy to local finance and enacted a modified version of the old domestic rating system to be known as the 'council tax'.

What is clear from this flurry of activity concerning local government and its finance is that central control over the resources available at the local level has become very strong, and is likely to remain so. Any measure which extends local taxation powers is likely to be unpopular and difficult to enact. There is an increasing search, in the face of all these changes, for a new system of local government, which may be simpler and may involve regional authorities.

This section has described policy developments in a period in which the Conservatives and Labour alternated in power. Thirteen years of Conservative rule was followed by nearly seven years of Labour rule. Then there was an episode of nearly four years of Conservative government. After that Labour 'enjoyed' a period of four years in government in which their continuance in office depended upon the support of the Liberals. Then, in 1979, the Conservatives won a clear majority. They won a second term of office in 1983, and a third term in 1987. In April

1992, as this edition of this book was completed, the Conservatives were elected to power for the fourth time in succession, but with a marked fall in their majority.

In the first edition of this book it was argued that levels of controversy over social policies since 1951 had not been particularly high. Conservative ideologists had had much to say about the case for bringing market conditions more effectively to bear upon the distribution of social services, but it was only in the housing field that Conservative governments had taken steps that represented major responses to this viewpoint. Labour had disappointed many of its supporters, who closely identified the party with the advancement of the welfare state. A succession of economic crises had limited the money available for new social policies. Yet both parties had considerably advanced public expenditure, particularly on social policies, to the point where some economists had argued that this kind of expenditure had become an inflationary force, limiting the scope for new wealth-creating private investment. This is a view both parties had taken very seriously. The most staggering growth had been in public employment and in social security transfer payments, two forms of growth politicians find very hard to limit.

However, political dominance since 1979 by a Conservative government much more openly hostile to the welfare state has changed the political atmosphere. Hence the title of this chapter was changed for the 1987 edition from the positive word 'growth' used in the two earlier editions of the book to the more neutral word 'history'. In fact, however, as is shown in some detail in chapter 11, while the Conservatives have been very committed to public expenditure restraint and have stopped the growth of public employment, they too have found social policy expenditure hard to curb.

Public sector housing expenditure has experienced severe cuts. Education expenditure has risen a little in real terms. Health and personal social services expenditure trends are harder to interpret. The figures suggest growth, but needs and costs have grown faster and some decline has been experienced. Nevertheless, social policy expenditure as a whole has grown, driven upwards by the considerable growth in its major component, the social security budget (see Hills, 1990, for a detailed analysis of these trends).

Undoubtedly, the political and economic climate for social policy growth has chilled. In the 1950s Keynesian economic management techniques were employed to try to retain full employment without inflation. Critics of policies of that period, such as Samuel Brittan (1971), have suggested that chancellors found it difficult to time their uses of the economic 'brake' or 'accelerator' properly, and that the 'stop–go' pattern that emerged provided a poor economic environment

for investment decisions, and thus inhibited British growth. The particular motivation for some fairly panicky use of the 'brake' was a
concern with Britain's tendency to run into balance of payments
problems, importing more than it was exporting. However, during this
period a rate of growth was achieved that was good by later standards,
full employment was maintained, and inflation, while ever-present, was
never so high as to cause alarm.

In the 1960s, despite an increasing commitment to economic planning, the cyclical pattern got worse. Inflation increased, balance of
payments crises forced strong restraints to be applied to public expenditure and private incomes on a number of occasions, and, at the
depressed point of the cycle, quite marked increases in unemployment
occurred. In the mid-1970s Britain faced a more severe crisis, in which
very high inflation, a balance of payments problem and continuing high
unemployment occurred all at the same time. Measures to cope with
the first two by traditional means worsened the third. At a time when
governments seemed to have learnt a great deal about economic management they found it increasingly difficult to practise it. In fact, the
rise in economic management problems can be correlated with the
dramatic increase in the number of economists in the civil service!

Different schools of economists have preached different solutions
to these problems. On the Right the 'monetarist' school of thought
became increasingly influential, arguing that governments must control
the money supply and let economic forces bring the system under
control (Friedman, 1962, 1977; for an overview of this theory, see
Bosanquet, 1983). This viewpoint was put partly into practice in the
1970s, but politicians were reluctant to let bankruptcies and redund-
ancies occur on a sufficient scale to really test the monetarist hypothesis. More influential, and more in conformity with Keynesian
orthodoxy, were those economists who argued that income restraint
was necessary to bring unemployment and inflation into balance, and
to prevent Britain's balance of payments getting out of hand as rising
wages led us to import goods we could ill afford while making it more
difficult to sell things. As far as they were concerned, what happened
was that wage bargaining was no longer restrained by the social and
political forces that had hitherto limited rises to figures that would not
disrupt the economy. Incomes policies were seen as crucial to help
solve our problems, yet over and over again governments found that
political pressures made these very difficult to sustain for any length of
time. The whole picture was, however, complicated by changes in the
pattern of trade in the world, and particularly by rises in prices of
primary commodities.

After 1979 the 'monetarist' theory was more boldly put into practice.
The government treated the money supply and particularly the public

sector borrowing requirement as the key phenomena to keep under control. It was prepared to let unemployment rise rapidly in the cause of the war against inflation. It abandoned incomes policy in the private sector, seeking only to keep pay increases to public employees tightly under control. Initially it found the removal of pay controls and its own taxation adjustments produced severely inflationary effects. But then it was successful in bringing inflation under control, but achieved that at the expense of a rapid increase in unemployment. Numbers registered as out of work rose from just over a million in 1979 to over three million in 1983.

Later in the 1980s the government abandoned any rigorous attempt to keep the money supply under control, but continued its tight control of public borrowing. By the 1990s, with the economy depressed and an election time approaching, even the latter monetarist nostrum was abandoned by the Conservatives.

Changes to the official method of counting makes comparison of data difficult after the end of 1982. Significant numbers of the unemployed, in particular people registering for work but not receiving benefit, were excluded from the count. There was a real fall in unemployment in the second half of the eighties, but it was not as large as the official figures suggested. Moreover many of the jobs created at this time were part-time or temporary.

Then, at the end of the decade a new recession developed. In February 1992 the official count made United Kingdom unemployment about 2,600,000 (9.2 per cent of the workforce), a figure that the Unemployment Unit estimates represents a real figure of about 3,700,000 (Unemployment Unit, March 1992, p. 18).

In chapter 9, one of the issues which will be examined is whether social policy measures can help to cope with unemployment or whether it is primarily an economic problem. Doubts are increasingly raised about whether specific national policy interventions can counter a developing trend towards lower job opportunities. There is evidence that the character of demand for labour is changing, and that new investment is essentially capital-intensive and therefore unable to absorb much labour. Analysis of the issue is complicated by questions about the changing composition of the labour force, which large numbers of married women have joined since the war, and about the extent to which the unemployed lack the skills and capacity now required by industry (Gilbert, 1989).

Early in this chapter it was pointed out that at the beginning of the century British governments adopted an approach to the relief of unemployment that largely ruled out the creation of specific employment opportunities. In the early 1970s interest was awakened in Britain in the case for the development of 'active labour market policies' of the kind adopted in Sweden (Mukherjee, 1972). These involved such things as assisting labour mobility, expanding training when unemployment rises, and creating special work projects for the unemployed. Their appeal was that they were conceived in Keynesian terms as helping to alleviate unemployment, in a largely fully employed economy, without creating inflation.

Their adoption in Britain occurred at a time of high unemployment. Accordingly, instead of serving the economic function for which they were originally advocated, they have been modified to serve the political function of reducing the number of unemployed whilst minimizing intervention in the economy as a whole. There has been a particular concentration on measures for young people to the extent that many who leave school at 16 can expect up to two years in government schemes which combine work experience with training. Indeed, at the end of the 1980s the government adopted a strategy for employment policy which largely abandoned other job creation measures but strongly emphasized training (Department of Employment, 1988 a, b).

These reflections upon some of the problematic relationships today between economic and social policies conclude this chapter on the development of social policy in Britain. It has been hard to decide what should be given attention, and how much detail should be included. It was important to sketch in some of the history of developments in social policy. In our complex society so many of the peculiarities of our institutions and policies can be explained only by what has gone before. It is also necessary not to view policies in a static way; they have been built up slowly over a long period and they are still changing. The factors that helped to build them will be examined further in the next two chapters by looking at the forces that influence the making and implementation of social policy. After that we shall be ready to look at specific policies in more detail.

SUGGESTIONS FOR FURTHER READING

Such is the wealth of historical literature that it has been difficult to decide what to reference in this chapter. References have been confined to some of the more significant primary sources and to secondary sources that readers may find particularly interesting or readable. Some of the major historical works upon which the author has depended have not been cited.

Derek Fraser's *The Evolution of the British Welfare State* (1973) is a good general historical textbook but is stronger on the nineteenth than the twentieth century. Pat Thane's *The Foundation of the Welfare State*

(1982) deals with the period from 1870 onward. The interwar period is well covered by Gilbert (1970). A number of recent books deal with the 1945–51 Labour government. Amongst these, K. O. Morgan's *Labour in Power* (1984) is recommended. Morgan has also written an account of the whole period 1945–89 (1990), but of course it gives comparatively little attention to social policy. However, Nicholas Deakin's *The Politics of Welfare* (1987) provides the rudiments of an account of social policy over this period. There is also a forthcoming study of social policy since 1945 by an economic historian, Rodney Lowe.

The impact of Thatcher's governments upon social policy has provoked various accounts, each rapidly dated by further developments. The most up to date are contained in books edited by McCarthy (1989) and by Savage and Robins (1990).

CHAPTER 3

The Making of Social Policy

INTRODUCTION

This chapter deals with the social policy-making system, introducing the key institutions involved in the process in Britain. The next chapter looks at the implementation of social policy. The two chapters must be considered together; dividing the policy processes between 'making' and 'implementation' is, in various respects, difficult. It is hard to identify a dividing line at which making can be said to be completed and implementation to start. There is also a considerable amount of feedback from implementation which influences further policy-making, and many policies are so skeletal that their real impact depends upon the way they are interpreted at the implementation stage.

The starting point in the chapter is the ideal to which the British system of government is presumed to correspond, in which policy-making is seen as the responsibility of our representatives in Parliament, who answer to the people at the general election for their stewardship of the public interest. The chapter will first look at the features of the system that correspond to this model, and at the institutions that are reputedly responsible for the policy-making process. It will also look at the implications of the presence of lower-tier organs of government, at local levels, and at the way in which representative government seems to be expected to work within them.

Having done this, the discussion will then turn to consider the various ways in which the model of representative government is modified, or perhaps even undermined, in practice. It will consider how the people's will is translated into political action. It will look at the part played by pressure groups in the system, and it will examine the case that has been made for regarding democracy as significantly undermined by 'political elites'. The relationship between government and Parliament will be scrutinized, together with its parallels in local government. Attention will be given to the role played by the machinery of government, by the civil service and by local government officers in the policy-making process, and some general points will be made about what we mean by that 'process'. These later issues will lead naturally into the examination of the implementation process in the next chapter.

THE REPRESENTATIVE GOVERNMENT MODEL

When the systems of government in Britain, the United States, most of Western Europe and much of the Commonwealth are claimed to be democratic, that opinion rests upon a view that a form of representation of the people prevails in their governmental systems. Clearly, these systems do not involve direct democracy since in complex societies large numbers of decisions are taken by small numbers of representatives. Some countries seek to involve the people more directly, from time to time, by the use of plebiscites.

There is a further sense in which representative government is indirect. A distinction is often made between representatives and delegates. Delegates are regarded as mandated by those who elect them to support specific policies and to return to explain their subsequent decisions. British politicians have persistently rejected the view that they should be regarded as delegates, arguing instead that their duty is to make judgements for themselves in terms of their understanding of their constituents' best interests, while recognizing that they may, of course, be rejected at the next election if they become seriously out of touch with the people they represent. In this sense they claim to be concerned with the interests of all their constituents, and not just of those who voted for them. This doctrine was first expounded by Edmund Burke in the late eighteenth century. Today, of course, the importance of political parties makes it difficult for Members of Parliament to claim to represent all their constituents; but equally it makes it difficult for them to assume delegate roles. The presence in Parliament, and in the local councils, of party groups exerts an influence in favour of party programmes and away from a direct relationship between member and constituency. The modern modification of representative democracy is therefore to see the public as being allowed to choose from time to time between two or more broad political programmes, and being able to reject a party that has failed to carry out its promises (Schumpeter, 1950).

If this model of democracy prevails, it may be expected that social policies will be determined by the commitments of the political parties, and proposals for policy changes will be set out in election manifestos. The growth of the welfare state will be clearly relatable to the growth of democracy, with the people *choosing* to see their society change in this way. The limitations of this view of the policy-making process will be explored, but first there is a need to identify more explicitly the institutions of government to which such an analysis must relate. Those who have previously done courses on the British constitution may wish to skip the next two sections.

THE CENTRAL GOVERNMENT SYSTEM

The curious feature of the British constitution is that Britain has democratized institutions that were created in an undemocratic age. Most countries have systems of government that are relatively modern creations, either designed after cataclysmic political events which required the setting up of entirely new institutions, or set up to meet the needs of newly created or newly independent states. The governments of France and Germany, for example, fall into the first of these categories, and those of the United States and the Commonwealth countries into the second. The British pride themselves on having developed a system of government that has been a model for the rest of the world. The truth is that, while certainly many constitutional ideas *have* been borrowed from Britain, the British system contains features that no one designing a system of government today would conceivably want to adopt.

The monarchy and the House of Lords are the two most significant British 'anomalies'. Formally, neither has much influence on the policy-making process. Monarchs have relinquished their rights to interfere; the House of Lords has been largely stripped of its rights by successive parliamentary Acts since 1911. This discussion need not go into the residual rights and responsibilities of these two.

The House of Commons is elected from over 600 constituencies (an exact number has not been quoted as regular constituency boundary changes alter it), each of which returns the person who wins a simple majority of votes at each election. After a general election the monarch has the formal responsibility to ask the leader of the majority party to form a government. On most occasions the monarch's duty is clear, but situations in which there is no party with a clear majority may complicate the task. Broadly, the expectation is that the monarch will not have to take a decision that will then prove to be a violation of the democratic process, because it will be up to whoever agrees to form a government in these circumstances to prove that he or she has adequate parliamentary support. In other words, the position of a minority government can be made untenable if all the other parties combine against it. There are, however, ambiguities in such a situation, as the lives of minority governments may be prolonged more by a reluctance to force them to resign than by any positive commitment to their support.

The newly appointed Prime Minister will then form a government, giving a hundred or more governmental offices to his or her supporters. Again, the normal assumption is that these will be members of his or her own party, but exceptionally a coalition may be formed in which government offices go to other parties. All those given office will normally be, or will be expected to become, members of either the Commons or the Lords. Most will be members of the Commons (known as 'Members of Parliament'). The choice of members of the government rests significantly upon the preferences of the Prime Minister. However, he or she cannot disregard interests and factions within his or her own party, and will obviously give some attention to the competence of those appointed.

The most important prime ministerial appointments will be those of the members of Cabinet. The normal practice is to appoint a Cabinet of 15 to 25 members. It will include the main departments of government, together with some members without departmental responsibilities who may be given political or co-ordinating roles. The cabinet, chaired by the Prime Minister, is the key decision-making body within the government. New policy departures of any significance and new legislation will need Cabinet approval, and conflicts of interests between departments will have to fought out in the Cabinet or its committees. Each Cabinet sets up a number of committees to do more detailed work. Some of these will draw on the help of non-Cabinet ministers.

The government departments to which attention must be given in the discussion of social policy in England (the different situation in the other component countries of the United Kingdom is outlined later) are the Treasury, the Department of Health, the Department of Social Security, the Department of the Environment, the Department for Education and the Department of Employment. Two other departments, the Cabinet Office and the Home Office, also play a small part. Readers must be warned that it has been the practice of governments in recent years to alter the departmental structure from time to time, ostensibly in an effort to find the best possible framework for policy co-ordination, but – it may be suggested – with less elevated political motives in mind too. Accordingly, it may be the case that by the time this book is in your hands departments may have new names and policy responsibilities may have been moved from one department to another. For example, since the previous edition of this book the formerly combined Department of Health and Social Security has been split into two.

The Prime Minister is technically the First Lord of the Treasury. This archaic title serves to remind us that, while today we regard the Chancellor of the Exchequer as the senior Treasury minister, the Prime Minister is, above all, bound to be involved in major decisions on expenditure, taxation and the management of the economy. The importance of this aspect of policy is so great that there are often other Treasury ministers in the Cabinet, such as the Chief Secretary to the Treasury and the Paymaster General. These may be expected to play important roles in relation to decisions on public expenditure.

Each of the departments listed above has its senior minister, the secretary of state, in the Cabinet. Again, the Prime Minister may choose to have other ministers from specific departments as Cabinet members. Each department head has the support of several junior ministers, known as ministers of state or under-secretaries, who may take on particular responsibilities for specific policy areas. The recent trend towards 'super ministries' taking on several different but related areas of policy has made this political division of labour particularly important.

The role of the minister who is also a Cabinet member involves a quite considerable conflict between a position as a member of the central policy co-ordinating team within the government and responsibility for the protection and advancement of the interests of a department. In his *Diaries of a Cabinet Minister* (1975–7) the late Richard Crossman gave considerable attention to this problem. It is personally difficult for any individual to give wholehearted attention both to departmental issues and to the main political strategy problems arising outside his or her own responsibilities. There is likewise a crucial problem for a rational approach to government in which strategic questions may not be best resolved by bargaining between a group of individuals all of whom have conflicting, 'tunnel vision' images dictated by departmental needs and priorities. Clearly, the members of the Cabinet without departmental responsibilities are expected to help to resolve this problem, but they often suffer from a sense of being outsiders without the detailed departmental briefs possessed by their colleagues (see ibid., vol. 2). The creation of a group of special civil servants, including individuals recruited from outside the public service for their expertise or political connections, has been seen as a further device to strengthen strategic thinking in government. There would seem, however, to be a continuing and inevitable conflict here.

As far as his or her departmental duties are concerned, a minister's work will fall into roughly four categories. First, he or she may be responsible for putting forward new legislation. Clearly this is something the ambitious politician will want to do. He or she will hope to secure a job that involves the initiation of policies from the party's programme. Secondly, he or she will have a large amount of day-to-day administration to oversee. Much of this will involve the formulation of new policies that do not require legislation, or the determination of responses to new crises within the department. It is in this kind of work that the distinction between policy-making and implementation becomes so unclear. In many respects any issue that a department regards as requiring a ministerial decision is likely to be describable as a 'policy issue'. Thirdly, the minister will have to deal with questions from Members of Parliament about the policies and activities of the department. While this may be seen primarily as a defensive kind of action, involving much routine work by civil servants who are required to produce the information required for parliamentary answers, it may also provide opportunities for publicizing new policy initiatives. Indeed, many questions are planted by friendly MPs, from the back benches on the minister's own side, to enable activities to be advertised. Fourthly, the minister has a wide public relations role beyond Parliament. This will involve a programme of speeches, meetings and visits relating the department's activities to the world outside.

Several references have already been made to the support of ministers by civil servants. It is self-evident that civil servants have an important role to play in implementing policy. What also needs to be emphasized is that civil servants are also heavily involved in making policy. Until recent changes in the structure of the civil service, designed to reduce barriers between the various grades and to stress the importance of many of the managerial roles played in connection with policy implementation, it was possible to draw a fairly clear distinction between the 'administrative class', containing the 'higher' civil servants responsible for policy, and the rest of the civil service. Now, the policy-making group is a little more difficult to define. Each major department has at its headquarters a group of a hundred or so civil servants, up to the top position of 'permanent secretary', who are concerned with decisions of a 'policy' kind, many of which require ministerial approval. The theory of representative government clearly requires that they be called the *servants* of the minister, providing information and evidence on policy alternatives but not taking policy decisions.

The British system of government involves more than a network of departments headed by ministers. Responsibility for various specific public services is hived off to a range of special agencies, though in each case ultimate responsibility for policy lies with one of the central departments. Again, these subordinate bodies could be described as being concerned with implementation and not with policy-making. But, while this is broadly true, many do this within only general guidelines and have therefore an important, if subordinate, policy-making role. Students of social policy will come across a number of important examples of bodies of this kind; some with a nationwide remit, others with local or regional responsibilities. They have grown in numbers and importance in recent years, as a result of what has come to be called the 'next steps initiative', which aims to delegate most routine governmental tasks to separate agencies. In social policy the most significant of these agencies are those concerned with the social security system, particularly the Benefits Agency, and the Employment Services Agency.

The discussion in this section has moved from the consideration of the composition of Parliament and the nature of the relationship of government to Parliament to a more detailed account of the agencies concerned with policy-making. There is a need, however, to look a little more at the role of Parliament. It has been shown that about 100 of the 600 Members elected to Parliament become involved in specific government jobs. What role do the rest play in policy-making?

Primary policy-making involves the promulgation of Acts of Parliament. The overwhelming majority of these are promoted by government, and thus the initial 'Bills' are prepared by civil servants within the departments. Bills then go through four stages in each House: a 'first reading', which simply involves the formal presentation of the Bill; a 'second reading', at which there is likely to be a large-scale debate on the basic principles of the Bill; a 'committee stage', when the legislation is examined in detail (normally by a small 'standing committee' and not by the whole House); and a 'report stage' and 'third reading', at which the Bill that emerges from the committee is approved, but may be re-amended to undo some of the actions of the committee. Clearly, Members without ministerial office may participate in all these stages, and Opposition Members will take particular care to scrutinize and attack government action. The leading Opposition party organizes a 'shadow cabinet' to provide for a considered and specialized response to the activities of the government.

Back-bench MPs may be able to promote new policies through 'private Members' bills'. These cannot have direct financial implications for the government, and they have little chance of becoming law without government support. Occasionally governments assist private Members with their Bills, particularly by allowing extra parliamentary time. Some significant social policy measures have become law in this way. The Abortion Act of 1967, for example, was promoted by a Liberal MP, David Steel, and became law because many key ministers were sympathetic. In this case the Bill concerned an issue of conscience on which many felt it would be inappropriate for Parliament to divide on party lines. The abolition of capital punishment and reform of the law on homosexuality came about in a similar way. In the 1970s the Labour government supported a private Members' Bill which took over an item which would have been included in its own programme if there had been sufficient parliamentary time. This curious reversal of roles may have owed something to the agreement of the Liberals to support a government without a clear majority; the legislation was the Housing (Homeless Persons) Act of 1977 promoted by a Liberal, Stephen Ross.

In addition to Acts of Parliament, both Houses have to deal with a great deal of what is known as 'subordinate' or 'delegated' legislation. Many Acts allow governments to promote subsequent changes and new regulations. It is important to recognize that many policy changes pass through Parliament in this way. It would be an extravagant use of parliamentary time to require new legislation for all detailed changes of this kind. Controversy arises, however, over the extent of the use of delegated legislation, since some Acts convey very wide scope for this kind of ministerial action. To promote subordinate legislation the government has to publish a 'statutory instrument' which is open to scrutiny by MPs. Some of these require parliamentary approval; others may be annulled if a negative resolution is passed by either House within 40 days of their initial publication. Hence back-benchers may intervene to prevent subordinate legislation. A joint committee of the Commons and the Lords has been set up to scrutinize statutory instruments, and therefore to facilitate parliamentary review of subordinate legislation. They have, however, a mammoth task and only give detailed attention to a limited number of the statutory instruments that are put before Parliament.

Readers will find a good example of legislation for which statutory instruments are important in the 1986 Social Security Act. They will look in vain for detailed information on, for example, the housing benefit scheme or the 'social fund' in the Act: this is contained in subsequent regulations. In particular, actual benefit rates are not included in such legislation, but set out in regulations which are regularly updated and amended.

Reference has already been made to parliamentary questions as providing an opportunity for back-bench scrutiny of government actions. Members put down initial questions in advance. Many questions are answered in writing, but those that receive oral answers may be followed up by supplementary questions. In addition to the powers to ask questions, various parliamentary procedures provide scope for MPs to promote short debates on topics that concern them. More specific facilities of this kind are extended to the main Opposition party, so there are days allocated for debates on topics of its own choice.

One peculiar characteristic of the British Parliament that distinguishes it from many legislatures in other countries, and particularly from the United States Congress, is the slight use made of specialized committees. This is also a difference between the central government system and the local government system in Britain. The committees that consider Bills are in no way specialized; they consider new legislation in rotation, regardless of subject, and do not do any separate investigatory work.

There is also, however, a system of select committees. Perhaps the most important of these is the Public Accounts Committee, concerned to look at the way in which public money has been spent. Then there are select committees on the work of the Parliamentary Commissioner for Administration (the 'Ombudsman'), on statutory instruments and on European legislation. In 1979 a system of 14 committees was set up to be concerned with the work of specific (or in some cases two specific) government departments. In the field of social policy the social services committee has conducted a number of influential investigations of issues. *Ad hoc* committees may also be set up to investigate specific subjects. However, such is the power of the executive in our system that it is doubtful whether these new committees can do other than play a rather superior pressure-group role. They investigate specific topics, with the aid of specialist advisers, and have issued some influential reports. But, as stressed above, they have no role with regard to legislation.

This account of the institutions of British central government has shown that elected representatives have a wide range of parliamentary duties. If they belong to the party that wins power they may well take on a government office of some kind. If they do not achieve office they are still in a special relationship to government in which, while some advantages may accrue from being a member of the ruling party and having many colleagues and friends in office, there may also be disadvantages, in that party allegiance implies a duty to support the government. Some of the scope for the criticism of policy that comes to Opposition members is denied to government supporters. On the other hand Opposition, in a Parliament organized strictly on party lines, implies a situation in which it is very hard to secure majority support for your own ideas.

REGIONAL AND LOCAL GOVERNMENT

The term 'regional government' is used here to cover two phenomena: the government of Scotland, Wales and Northern Ireland, and the organization of the government of specific services on a regional basis.

Northern Ireland had a devolved system of government between 1922 and 1972. The Government of Ireland Act of 1920 conferred a considerable measure of self-government upon Northern Ireland. All social policy legislation was the responsibility of the Northern Ireland government, and revenue was raised partly by local taxes and partly by the United Kingdom taxation system. In practice, legislation at Stormont, the Northern Ireland Parliament, tended to follow legislation at Westminster quite closely but often a few years behind. The people of the province were represented both at Stormont and at Westminster. The British government possessed reserve powers, so that it could interfere in the government if it so wished. Until the 'troubles' of the late 1960s it studiously refused to do so. However, in 1972 the Northern Ireland (Temporary Provisions) Act suspended Stormont and imposed direct rule from Westminster. In 1974 an attempt to begin to restore self-government through a new Northern Ireland Executive, elected by proportional representation to try to provide for the involvement in government of the Catholic minority, was brought to an end after a strike by Protestant workers. Government of Northern Ireland is through a secretary of state for Northern Ireland at Westminster who heads a Northern Ireland Office. Within Northern Ireland itself the former separate departments operate but all are technically under the jurisdiction of the Northern Ireland Office. The various junior ministers in the Northern Ireland Office share the 'ministerial' responsibilities for these departments. Naturally, the Northern Ireland departments operate on the basis of legislation passed before the demise of Stormont. This is supplemented by special legislation from Westminster where appropriate.

Scotland's affairs are conducted from Westminster by way of a secretary of state for Scotland and a separate Scottish Office, which is split into several departments. Much Scottish legislation is already separate. Those social services that come under local government – housing, personal social services and education – have their control devolved to the Scottish Office and are regulated by separate legislation. The health service in Scotland has a slightly different structure and some separate legislation, but here the centralizing tendency for control from London has been very strong. The social security system, on the other hand, operates throughout Great Britain. Within Parliament there is a convention that only Scottish MPs participate in debates on Scottish matters. Since the 1987 general election the ranks of Scottish Conservative MPs have been reduced to a very small number. This has brought the arrangements for Scottish legislation under strain, and increased the pressure for political devolution.

Devolution to Wales is not so extensive. Whilst there is a separate Welsh Office, most legislation deals jointly with England and Wales.

In many respects the Welsh Office is little more than an integrated 'regional office' bringing together, in a way not present in the English regions, concerns about health, personal social services, education and housing.

Acts were passed in 1978 allowing for devolution of most of these administrative powers to elected assemblies in Scotland and Wales. These were subject to acceptance by the people of those countries, who were consulted by referenda early in 1979. The people of Wales conclusively rejected the proposals. In Scotland there was a majority in favour of devolution but it fell short of the 40 per cent of the total percentage of the electorate required by the statute.

The Channel Islands and the Isle of Man have substantially more-independent systems of government, and do not send MPs to Westminster. In view of their small size, however, it does not seem appropriate to say anything more about them.

In the context both of the discussion of devolution to Scotland and Wales and of the consideration of the reorganization of local government, some attention has been given to the case for regional government in England. While it is hard to predict whether or not a real system of regional government will be developed, it is important to note that most government departments with responsibilities for local services have systems of regional offices. These regional structures appear to have comparatively little significance for policy-making, with perhaps one exception of some importance for social policy. This is that the National Health Service is administered through regional health authorities, consisting of a small body of people appointed by the secretary of state. This is an important tier, within the complicated government structure set up for the health service, with responsibilities for the allocation of resources and for strategic planning.

Local government in England and Wales is organized into two distinctive systems. In the metropolitan areas of London, West Midlands, South Yorkshire, Greater Manchester, Merseyside and Tyne & Wear there has been, since the abolition of the Metropolitan Counties (see p. 38), a one-tier system of metropolitan districts responsible for personal social services, education and housing. There are *ad hoc* bodies dealing with some of the functions of the former counties, but these need not detain us as their tasks do not fall within the main concerns of this book.

In the rest of England and Wales there are county authorities which are responsible for education and personal social services, but also a lower tier of districts which include housing amongst their responsibilities. Planning responsibilities are shared between the two tiers. At the time of writing, this arrangement is again under review and some of the larger districts are likely to be promoted to unitary authority status and to take over responsibilities from the counties within which they are situated.

There is also a third tier comprising parish councils, with minimal powers. Whilst many of these are old parishes, others are towns that previously had significant powers of their own, some retaining mayors and calling themselves town councils. In Wales these third-tier authorities are known as community councils. None of these third-tier authorities have significant social policy responsibilities, so they will not be examined further here.

In Scotland there is a two-tier system very similar to that operating in the non-metropolitan areas of England and Wales. The top-tier authorities there are known as regions, a more appropriate title perhaps, as one of them, Strathclyde, contains half the population of Scotland. There are great variations in population size between the regions, a probably inevitable consequence of the uneven way population is distributed in Scotland. In those parts of Scotland that are most isolated (Orkney and Shetland and the Western Isles), there are single unitary authorities which deal with all local government functions.

Local government in Northern Ireland has been stripped of almost all its significant powers. It had previously been notorious in some areas for the manipulation of electoral boundaries and for the practice of religious discrimination. Health services and personal social services come under four appointed boards. Education is the responsibility of three separate education and libraries boards. Public housing is the concern of the Northern Ireland Housing Executive.

The health service, outside Northern Ireland, has its own separate system of regions and districts, designed with some regard to local government boundaries.

National legislation defines the powers of local authorities, and may set limits to those powers. It also imposes upon local government a range of duties. The relationship between central and local government in Britain is a complex one. Local government is not autonomous, but neither is it merely local administration. Some statutes impose fairly clear tasks for local authorities. But many give powers, and indicate ways in which those powers should be used, without undermining the scope for local initiative. Other Acts of Parliament merely grant powers to local authorities, which they may choose whether or not to use. Exceptionally, a local authority may itself promote a 'private' Act to secure powers to undertake new ventures. Local authorities are therefore able to make or elaborate policies and are not merely implementing agencies.

However, the relationship between central and local government involves both partnership and conflict. Central government seeks to impose its will not merely through legislation but also through the communication of large amounts of guidance. This may be embodied in circulars, regularly sent from central departments to local authorities, or through less-formal communications from ministers, administrators and professional advisers. Central intervention will be justified in terms of national political commitments, to ensure that central policies have an impact upon all localities. There is an inherent conflict between the demands of local autonomy and the principle of 'territorial justice', requiring that citizens in different geographical areas secure comparable treatment.

Central government also justifies its interventions in local government in terms of its concern with national economic management. It is its financial control over local government that tends to weaken its claim that the central-local relationship is a partnership. The problem is compounded by the lack of a satisfactory way for local government to raise its own revenue.

Local authorities have three major sources of income: local taxes, payments for the provision of services and government grants. The first of these was, until the mid-eighties, a system of rates upon property, both domestic and commercial. Then the government replaced domestic rates by a tax on individuals, the community charge or 'poll tax', and centralized control over commercial rates. The poll tax was met by a popular reaction which contributed to the end of Mrs Thatcher's career as Prime Minister. After her fall her successor sharply increased the central government grant to soften the impact of the poll tax, financing this out of an increase in value added tax. He also promised to replace the poll tax by a new tax which would largely reinstate a system of domestic property taxation. It involves a simplified version of the former rates, to be known as the 'council tax', with the number of adult occupants of the property being partly taken into account. At the time of writing, legislation to introduce the council tax has been passed through Parliament. Its implementation will occur in April 1993.

This turmoil has involved a sharp reduction in the independence of local government. Even before the poll tax the Conservative government had given itself powers to prevent local authorities raising local taxation over centrally prescribed limits. It continued this 'capping' practice after the introduction of poll tax. At the same time the centralization of the commercial rating system had the effect of bringing three-quarters of local revenue under direct central control; and the panic reaction to reduce the impact of the poll tax, after Mrs Thatcher's fall in November 1990, had the effect of pushing the centrally controlled proportion up to around seven-eighths of local government revenue. Given the inflexibility of property-based taxation systems, by contrast with income tax or value added tax, it is unlikely that any future government will dare to reverse this situation.

Central government also maintains control over local authority borrowing. The trend in recent years has been away from a system of strict, item-by-item controls to broad limitations upon total borrowing. The system is currently a complex combination of these two approaches to control.

Policy-making in local government is the responsibility of elected members. These represent districts, or wards, within each authority in much the same way as MPs represent constituencies. Today a great deal of local politics is arranged along party lines, and most councillors represent the political parties that are also found at Westminster.

Local authority members each belong to a number of committees. Most business in transacted in these committees, so that the meetings of the full councils are largely rubber-stamping affairs, affording opportunities for making political points. The committee structures are primarily related to the various functional responsibilities of the authority. Many local authorities operate 'policy committees' which aim to co-ordinate the activities of the authority as a whole. In most authorities the parties are represented on the committees in proportion to their distribution on the whole council. Generally the majority party will assume the chairmanship of each of the committees. The politicization of local government has intensified the conflict between central and local government. This was particularly sharp in the early 1980s between radical Labour authorities and the central Conservative administration.

THE VOICE OF THE PEOPLE?

It has already been noted that in the British system of government MPs and councillors are elected in individual constituencies on the basis of a procedure in which the candidate with a simple majority is the winner. It is generally the case that the voter has to choose between two to four candidates, each of whom is the representative of a specific political party. In this way electoral choice is peculiarly structured. Voters have to make their decision on the basis of assessments of particular people with their own special policy commitments, in relation to the more general political biases and policy commitments of their parties. The parties' intentions are perhaps of more importance than individuals' commitments. However, what the parties offer are broad packages of policies, within which voters may like some items while disliking others.

Hence, the individual voters' starting point in trying to influence policy through the electoral process is a situation of very limited choice in which it is general policy biases, or even more general considerations, often described as 'party images', that must govern his or her selection of an MP. Moreover, his or her vote will be taken together with large numbers of other votes perhaps motivated by very different policy preferences. Hence, one person's voting choice may be influenced by a party's commitment to raise pensions, which leads him or her to support it despite its commitment to other policies – say, increasing educational expenditure – with which he or she disagrees. But others who vote for the same party may be motivated by directly opposite considerations – a strong commitment to education, say, but no concern about pensions. Furthermore, the candidate for this party in one constituency may stress a commitment to education, while colleagues in other constituencies may make the pensions increase the central plank in their programme.

The above example was chosen to illustrate the basic underlying problem about the use of choices between representatives as a means of settling policy priorities. The reality is that party platforms are considerably more complex, with choices between desirable ends deliberately obscured. No party presents the electorate with explicit choices between widely desired ends; they generally seek to convince it that they can bring a little more of everything that is wanted. Voters are forced to discriminate between the parties in terms of their general ideologies, value biases and images.

Furthermore, most voters do not really make electoral *choices*. Many vote for the same party every time they vote, and probably give little attention to the personalities or policies of specific candidates. Voters behave in ways that, as far as the collective pattern of choices is concerned, political scientists are to a large extent able to predict from their occupations, social origins and personalities. Only a minority of the electorate changes sides between elections. Indeed, many of the changes that alter the balance in power in Parliament are no more than changes between voting and non-voting or vice-versa. Research findings suggest, moreover, that the people most likely to change their votes – the floating voters – are generally the least informed within the electorate, and are thus not people who can be said to be making careful choices between policies. It is suggested, instead, that political *images* are particularly significant – the personalities of the leaders, their projections of competence and of their capacities to deal with the nation's problems. An important consideration at a general election is the success or failure of the government in power in coping with the economic situation. In this sense a verdict may be given on its policies, but only in a very general way.

Clearly, therefore, electors are not normally provided with the opportunities to make clear choices about social policies or between social policy options. There are certainly general characteristics of the parties' approaches to social policies that may help people to decide between them; and at particular elections (such as for example the general election of 1945) one's social policy commitments may be particularly clear. But at other times it may be very difficult to single out policy issues that divide the parties. In 1970 the Child Poverty Action Group attacked the Labour Government's failure to deal effectively with family poverty and secured a pledge from the Conservatives that family allowances would be increased. The Conservatives did not increase these allowances, but it is doubtful whether many voters were influenced to change their allegiances on this issue. Those who studied the parties' platforms carefully would have had to relate the Labour Party's generally stronger commitment to universal social security policies to the Conservative's specific pledge. It may be suggested that what the Child Poverty Action Group expected, and wanted, was a new Labour government returned to power, chastened by criticism of their family policies, and not a Conservative government (see McCarthy, 1986).

Another characteristic of social policies is that, while some involve broad responses to popular needs and wishes, many are specific measures to assist quite small disadvantaged groups in the population. Policies to assist disabled drivers, for example, may be viewed as generally desirable, and in that sense may have electoral appeal; but the number of people they benefit directly or indirectly is a very small minority in the population. Disabled drivers may be a relatively 'popular' minority group; but what about policies to help the long-term unemployed, rehabilitate criminals or provide facilities for vagrant alcoholics, for example? If there were a direct relationship between the pursuit of electoral popularity and the determination of social policies, surely minority causes would receive much less attention than they do now, and unpopular minority causes would receive no attention at all (or even more punitive responses). Opinion polls suggest that a variety of social reforms carried out in Britain since the 1940s – the abolition of capital punishment and the liberalization of the law relating to homosexuality, for example – were enacted in the face of popular opposition.

Other survey evidence suggests, moreover, that, whilst there are strong public commitments to pensions and the health service, other social policies which favour those most in need of help from the welfare state, such as the unemployed and single parents, have little popular support (Taylor-Gooby, 1985; Edgell and Duke, 1991).

It is additionally important to add to this examination of the impact of 'the voice of the people' upon social policy determination the observation that our 'first past the post' electoral system can convey a very ambiguous message. In 1987 the British elected a Conservative government for the third time on the basis of a minority of the votes cast.

After that election Mrs Thatcher had a large majority in Parliament and thus claimed to have a very clear mandate. But her opponents were able to point to the majority vote against her. This was, of course, split, largely speaking, between the Labour Party and the Liberal/SDP Alliance. Moreover, over a quarter of the electorate did not vote, and the disadvantaged will have been disproportionately represented amongst the non-voters. It can also be shown, as has already been suggested with reference to Scotland, that in our very centralized political system government support was nevertheless very low in some regions. The 1992 election continued this pattern, albeit with a much lower Parliamentary majority for the Conservatives. However, of course, the introduction of some kind of proportional representation system would not necessarily solve this 'political arithmetic' problem; policy priorities would then be influenced by the way negotiations between potential coalition parties developed.

PRESSURE GROUPS AND POLITICAL ELITES

Much of the detailed analysis of the role of pressure groups in the policy-making process has been carried out in the United States. There the political system has several characteristics that particularly facilitate the mobilization of small groups of people to influence decisions. First, power within the system is very fragmented – between President and the two houses of Congress, between the federal government and the states, and between the state government and local government. Secondly, in that vast and diverse country political choices are much more dictated by local interests than they are in Britain. Hence the relationship between a congress member and his or her local electorate is much less affected by national party considerations. Thirdly, at federal level the parties are accordingly much less unified by political ideologies. Political actors are therefore readily influenced by small groups which can effectively threaten to have an electoral impact.

In Britain pressure groups are probably just as much in evidence as they are in the United States. A number of studies (Finer, 1958; Wootton, 1970; Roberts, 1970; Jordan and Richardson, 1987) have dispelled the notion that they are of no importance in the British system. But there is a need to beware of the assumption that they have as direct an impact upon the political system as they have in the United States. Their importance in the politics of that country has led political scientists to propound a modification of the theory of representative government in which the weakness of the individual voter, discussed on pages 57–9, is seen as compensated by his or her membership of interest groups (Dahl, 1961). Democracy is thus seen as 'pluralist' in character with politicians engaged in continuing processes of compromise with multiple groups. Such a theory is then seen as explaining the deference of politicians to the interests of minorities; and a new and perhaps superior version of democratic theory is presented which has as its hallmark the achievement of a political consensus in which minority interests are protected.

This theory has, however, come under fire in the United States. It has been pointed out that there are biases in the system that make it much easier for some interests to be heard than others, and much easier for modifications to the status quo to be vetoed than to be supported (Schattschneider, 1960; Bachrach, 1969).

These general points about the plurality of pressure groups are worthy of our attention since they suggest important questions about the way the British system operates. The contrasts made above between the political systems on the two sides of the Atlantic suggest that it may be much more difficult for British pressure groups to identify points at which the political system is particularly open to influence. In individual constituencies grievances with the established political parties have to be very deeply felt, and very widely shared, to upset the normal national electoral swings. Direct interventions in elections motivated by local issues are rare, except in the areas where nationalist parties can have an impact. Outside Scotland and Wales politicians have often been able to be singularly insensitive to local issues. And the current three or more party system further distorts the picture.

There are similar problems for a national pressure group in persuading political parties that disregard of its case carries electoral dangers. Furthermore, any interest group able to threaten in this way probably has a special relationship with a major political party, and is acknowledged as important in that sense. Many of the most powerful of the British pressure groups tend to have an established relationship with one or other political party. The trade unions are, of course, the clearest example of this phenomenon. They played a key role in the original establishment of the Labour Party, and provide a large proportion of the party's funds today. Correspondingly the other side of industry is an important paymaster for the Conservative Party. It is unlikely that the major elements in either of these groups will actually change sides, but it may be threatening to the parties if they are lukewarm in their support. However, there are ambiguities even in these power relationships. While it is arguable that the Labour Party dances to the trade union's tune, it is also the case that the special relationship facilitates bargaining. By contrast, the danger of union opposition to the Conservatives is that the strike weapon may be used to resist policies. Similarly, the Labour Party has to face, when in power, a commercial and financial establishment that can de-stabilize the economy through speculation and the movement of currency.

These reflections lead us to an alternative view of pressure group power in Britain: that the strongest weapons are forms of direct action and not the manipulation of electoral choice. If this is correct, it gives a very different emphasis to political pluralism, one that makes democracy through the ballot box of much less importance. Attention must be given to ways in which pressure groups secure or resist policies through their power to take actions that directly affect either the success of policies or the stability of the political system. This suggests the need to examine the power of groups whose co-operation is needed to implement new policies, and the influence of agencies that are expected to play a crucial part in the policy process. What, for example, is the basis for the influential role doctors have been able to play in health service policies? Why does government give attention to the views of the associations that represent the various groups of local authorities? What is the significance of organized resistance to rent or rate increases? The threat of direct action seems to put a very different complexion upon political bargaining processes, transforming the view of the significance of pressure groups. Yet in the 1980s the capacity of a determined government to 'sit out' forms of direct action – most obviously in the case of the 1984–5 miners' strike – raises doubts even about this form of pressure group action.

It is important to look more closely at the ways in which, regardless of the possession of a direct capacity to disrupt the political system, particular groups enjoy an institutionalized relationship to the political system. In particular, it is necessary to go beyond the examples of close relationships to political parties to consider whether the positions some groups enjoy in relation to the political system owe nothing to particular party allegiances. Indeed, there are groups whose very power in Britain might be jeopardized if they were seen as identified with specific political parties.

The power of some pressure groups can only be explained in terms of what may be called an 'insider' status within the policy-making system. This implies a further deviation from democratic theory, a system within which some individuals and groups have special statuses. A number of political scientists and sociologists have suggested that societies possess a political 'elite' (see Bottomore, 1966; and specifically on Britain, Urry and Wakeford, 1973; and Stanworth and Giddens, 1974), that decision makers are drawn from a narrow spectrum within a society. Traditional Marxist analyses of the social structure suggest that the political system is dominated by representatives of the bourgeoisie, the capitalist class. Modern updates of this theory have pointed out the relevance of patterns of domination based upon race and gender as well (Williams, 1989). But other political theories, notably those of Pareto and Mosca, suggest that there is a ruling elite that is not necessarily characterized by the possession of economic resources.

Modern interpretation of elite theories seek to show either that key policy offices are held by people from a narrow spectrum of social origins, or that a limited number of people, characterized by close links with one another, dominate decision-making roles. For Britain it has been shown that Cabinet ministers, senior civil servants, members of key advisory bodies and the heads of prestigious organizations tend to be drawn from a relatively narrow social class group, characterized by education at public schools and Oxbridge and by having had parents in a similarly narrow range of upper-middle-class occupations. The picture is, however, not simple, and there is some evidence that the backgrounds of top decision-makers have changed to embrace a slightly wider range of social origins in recent years. While certainly it seems plausible to suggest that, if there are people from similar social or educational backgrounds in a number of key roles, the relationships between those people will facilitate the sharing of ideas and opinions, the processes involved cannot necessarily be explained as simply as this.

What is more important to explain the relationship of some of the pressure groups in Britain to the structure of power is to examine the sense in which the policy-making process is perceived as involving assumptions that some interests should be consulted. Such assumptions rest upon several foundations. One of them is that expertise conveys the ability to help with public decision-making. This is the technocratic view: that experts' opinions carry a greater weight than other people's. It is the basis upon which academics sometimes secure a measure of influence in government. Similarly, some pressure groups secure attention because of their expert knowledge. In the educational and medical fields such 'heavyweight' pressure groups abound.

Another foundation upon which pressure groups may secure influence is by way of their association with traditional elite groups. Voluntary organizations benefit by royal sponsorship and by the acquisition of prestigious figures as vice-presidents and supporters. Such sponsorship is not always easily earned. It is clearly helpful to have a cause that readily attracts the sympathy of influential people. It may also be important to behave in ways that are deemed respectable. This is a curious feature of this kind of pressure group activity; to some extent the power of groups depends upon their ability to forswear the more direct weapons in the pressure group armoury, to avoid mounting vociferous opinion-forming campaigns or threatening forms of direct action. This supposition is based upon a belief that there is an underlying elitist approach to government in Britain. A fairly narrow range of people are responsible for key decisions; some of them attain such positions through democratic representational procedures, but they co-opt others to their ranks. These other people may be individuals of shared social backgrounds, but the process of co-optation may be more haphazard. Individuals from pressure groups, or at least representing specific interests, secure entry into the ranks of those who exercise power by virtue not only of expertise but also of personal qualities, such as persistence and charm, which enable them to persuade that they have something to contribute to public decision-making. They also generally have to establish that they understand some of the unspoken rules relating to public participation: that they don't embarrass their sponsors by the use of direct tactics or indiscreet communications with the press or unseemly behaviour in committee situations. In so doing they join that list of people who have been called upon over and over again to sit on public committees and advisory bodies.

This argument, then, is that political influence may be secured in Britain without the aid of independent power. The system co-opts others to join its ranks, and pays attention to some citizens very much more readily than to others. In this day and age people are rightly cynical about propositions concerning the power of ideas. They look around for other explanations and ulterior motives. But in the study of social policy, the importance of individuals should not be wholly under-estimated. There are examples of people who, through the strength of their commitments and the power of their attention to detail, have secured a place in the policy-making process. In the first half of this century William Beveridge (Harris, 1977) was such an individual. More recently Richard Titmuss (Gowing, 1975) seems to have played an important role. In the 1980s experienced businessmen were turned to as advisers, and one (Sir Roy Griffiths) had an important influence on the organization of the health service and on community care policy. There are many lesser examples around, of people whose influence upon policy-making owes nothing either to any notion of representative government or to the cruder theories about pressure group activity.

A great deal of pressure group activity is, of course, concerned with 'good causes'. Again, a theory of the policy-making process needs to find room for 'good causes' as well as for 'good people'. There are important questions that should not be brushed aside about the place of altruism in policy-making. It is not naive to argue that politicians, or, if you prefer, some politicians, have commitments to ideals. It is certainly important to recognize that many politicians want to be seen as supporters of 'good causes'. Hence, pressure groups for the disabled, the old, neglected children and so on will exert influence out of proportion to their naked power. For them the skilful use of mass media may be important, and key contacts in positions of power will be a great help.

No account of social policy-making should disregard the potential influence of these 'good causes', however much there may be scope for controversy about their real power in situations where interests are in conflict. Indeed one of the frustrating phenomena many pressure groups of this kind experience is continuing assertions by politicians that they do matter that are accompanied by minimal concrete action. It is very hard to predict the political circumstances that will favour interests of this kind, but manifestly many have secured benefits without the use of any perceptible political 'muscle'. It is perhaps useful here to bear in mind the distinction often made in the study of pressure groups between 'interest' groups and 'cause' groups, though in the tactical struggle for influence each may seek to co-opt the support of the other. Interests seek to be recognized as 'good causes', and causes try to enlist the backing of more powerful 'interests'.

It has been suggested in this section that pressure groups provide a crucial qualification to the notion of a simple relationship between electors and elected. Some writers have suggested that they solve the problem of the powerlessness of the individual in relation to the political machine (Dahl, 1961; Beer, 1969). While there are many circumstances in which that is true, it seems important to acknowledge that the political system contains biases that make it much easier for some groups to secure influence than others. In addition, in Britain there is the peculiar phenomenon of the exercise of influence by groups that, according to the crude calculations of political arithmetic, do not seem to have a power base at all. This must lead us to look at the shortcomings of the 'how many divisions has the Pope' approach to the estimation of political influence. It implies, however, a recognition that the minority who occupy powerful positions in British society are able to make choices, based neither upon notions of democracy nor upon calculations about who has power, about whom they will listen to or consult.

MINISTERIAL POWER: THE ROLE OF OFFICIALS AND THE INFLUENCE OF OUTSIDE GROUPS

In *The Sociology of Public Administration* (Hill, 1972) the author developed a typology of local government styles to try to elucidate different characteristics of politician/official relationships in different political situations. The emphasis was upon local government because it was felt that it was easier to develop a comparative analysis drawing upon the considerable number of studies of local decision-making in Britain and the United States. However, the typology was intended to have a more general relevance and provides a useful starting point for this discussion. Three types of political system were identified: 'ideological politics', 'administrative politics' and 'bargaining politics'.

A system of 'ideological politics' relates most clearly to the model of 'representative government'. It is one in which the traditional distinction between politics and administration is most easily made. Political parties compete to win elections by submitting distinct programmes between which the electorate can choose. Politicians instruct administrators to frame policies compatible with their mandates and commitments. The Thatcher governments have stood out as examples of this phenomenon.

'Administrative politics' describes a contrasting system in which full-time officials are much more clearly dominant. The 'politics' are organizational rather than public, and many of the key conflicts are between departments. Ministers in central government, while formally possessing the key decision-making powers, in fact find themselves involved primarily in expounding views and defending policies generated within their departments. Politicians of the majority party without ministerial office find themselves frustratingly shut out from a decision-making process into which they are given few insights. In British local government the committee system provides scope for the wider use of elected representatives in an administrator-dominated context, though here such involvement may further undermine representative government since it will depend primarily upon personal characteristics. J. M. Lee has described such a situation admirably:

> It is misleading to think of the County Council primarily as a body of elected representatives who make decisions of policy and then order officials to execute them. Although such a view constitutes the theory, the reality is vastly different. It is better to regard the system of county government as a body of professional people placed together in a large office at County Hall, who can call upon the representatives from all places throughout the area which they administer. Some of these representatives by sheer ability and drive make themselves indispensable to the successful working of the machine; others merely represent points of view which come into conflict with it.   (Lee, 1963, p. 214)

The concept of 'bargaining politics' was derived from examination of accounts of local politics in the United States. In recent years, partly as a result of exposure to the American literature and partly because of a desire to adopt a tough-minded approach towards power, British social and political scientists have increasingly been on the look out for signs of a similar system in Britain. In such a system political outcomes are seen to depend upon inputs of resources of power. Those who hold elected positions are not 'representatives' so much as 'brokers' bringing together coalitions of interests. Their desire for re-election forces them to adopt strategies in which they are highly sensitive to pressure groups. Some reservations about this view have already been suggested, but it was acknowledged that elements of bargaining are by no means absent from the British scene. Bargaining politics implies a clear role for politicians which may suggest that officials will occupy subordinate positions. While this is true inasmuch as political futures are at stake, it has been suggested that in Britain deals with quite explicit electoral implications are rare. Bargaining may therefore be more concerned with the maintenance of specific policies or particular organizational arrangements. If this is the case, it may be that officials have more to lose, or have more explicit commitments, than the politicians. Key conflicts concern relationships between departments and the outside world; ministers are expected to help defend departmental interests.

It is not suggested that the individual types fit any specific political system. British central government must be noted as a context where conflicts often appear to be of an ideological nature and where the representative model is treated as of some importance. Yet a key theme in discussions of relationships between ministers and their departments has been the extent to which politicians enter with apparent policy commitments but become socialized into roles determined by the permanent administrators and particularly by the need for 'policy maintenance' within their department (this has been cleverly satirized in the television series *Yes Minister*). Furthermore, a related theme to the ministerial discovery that cherished policy innovations are not administratively feasible is the recognition that vested interests and pressure groups carry a political 'clout' that had not been realized when policies were planned outside government. Policy-making outcomes may be determined by the interaction of three forces: political input (ideological politics), organizational considerations within departments (administrative politics), and external pressures (bargaining politics).

Beyond these generalizations, the more detailed study of the factors that influence the way policy is made needs to take various considerations into account. First, what are the kinds of policies involved? This raises the question so far evaded in this chapter: What is policy? Writers on policy analysis are agreed that a policy is something more than a decision. Friend and his colleagues suggest that 'policy is essentially a *stance* which, once articulated, contributes to the context within which a succession of future decisions will be made' (Friend, Power and Yewlett, 1974, p. 40). Jenkins (1978) similarly stresses the notion of interrelated decisions concerned with the selection of goals and the adoption of a course of action. Smith suggests that 'the concept of policy denotes . . . deliberate choice of action or inaction, rather than the effects of interrelating forces': he emphasizes 'inaction' and reminds us that 'attention should not focus exclusively on decisions which produce change, but must also be sensitive to those which resist change and are difficult to observe because they are not represented in the policy-making process by legislative enactment' (Smith, 1976, p. 13).

Policies are thus not easy to define. It is doubtful whether much can be gained by trying to achieve any greater precision than that suggested in the definitions above. It is more fruitful to look in a concrete way at the relevance of policies to the activity of a minister and his department. On appointment to office a new minister will take over responsibility for many departmental policies. The overwhelming majority of these will be just existing ways of doing things. A good many will be enshrined in Acts of Parliament. But these will be accompanied by organizational arrangements, systems of administration and working conventions which will also help to define policy. There is a distinction to be made between policy and arrangements made for its implementation. This will be explored further in the next chapter; here it must be stressed that these arrangements will in many cases have a quite fundamental impact upon the character of the policy and may thus be deemed to be part of it.

It is this existence of policies determining most everyday practice in a department that provides the most crucial group of constraints for a new minister. Existing policies keep most people occupied most of the time. Innovations depend upon finding opportunities for staff to work on developing new policies. They may also depend upon getting people from within the department to work to change old policies which have hitherto been regarded as quite satisfactory. Clearly, an innovating minister has to find ways to get a vast operational organization to change its ways.

What is perhaps more significant is that a new minister will also find that his or her department is developing new policies. These are not necessarily merely the left-over business from a previous administration. Many of them will derive from weaknesses in existing policies that have been recognized within the department and that administrators are striving to correct. Some, moreover, will have their roots in changes in the world upon which existing policies operate, changes that are making those policies unsuccessful or irrelevant. This group of policies or 'would-be policies' is important. The new minister may find that his or her own, or the party's, policy aspirations mesh with the policy issues upon which the department is working. In such circumstances he or she may find it comparatively easy to become, or to be seen as, an innovator. But the minister may have to face the fact that his or her own view of the department's policy needs are regarded as irrelevant to the main problem being tackled within it, or even that his or her own commitments lead in quite opposite directions to those being taken by the people concerned with policy innovation in the department. Popular discussions of the success or failure of ministers are often carried out in terms of their personalities and their experience. Of course, it is often possible to distinguish 'strong' and 'weak' ministers; but it must not be forgotten that the comparatively temporary incumbent of the top position of a large organization may be just lucky or unlucky: in arriving when key advisers are likely to agree that exciting innovations are necessary or, conversely, in finding that the consolidation of existing policies or the confronting of unpleasant realities is more important than the policy changes the minister cherishes.

There are various kinds of policy initiatives. Some policies may be enacted by the passing of a law. Reform of criminal law, for example, may have no administrative implications. A second category of policies with only indirect consequences for the minister's own department are those whose enactment and implementation depend upon another agency. Legislation giving powers, and even sometimes duties, to local government comes into this category. The Chronically Sick and Disabled Persons Act of 1970 is a classic example. While it seems to involve the development of a national policy for the disabled, in practice its dependence upon local government makes it a gesture in which central government involvement is comparatively slight. This measure arose as the result of an initiative by a private Member, Alf Morris. A later piece of legislation on this issue, the Disabled Persons Act 1986, seems to have similar characteristics. Individuals and voluntary organizations are likely to have to work hard to make local government implement it. Clearly, it is easier for a minister to accept this sort of legislation than to develop a policy that effectively changes the direction of a great deal of work going on *within* the department. In the above case the policy-making may be more 'symbolic' than real; ministers may hope to derive kudos without really introducing innovations.

Once a minister seeks to enact policies that require the expenditure of 'new money' he or she becomes engaged in what is inevitably a more difficult political exercise. Formally the approval of the Treasury is required and probably also the support of the Cabinet in one of its priority-setting exercises, where the minister is involved in competition with colleagues who have alternative expenditure aspirations. What this implies for the minister's relationship with civil servants is altogether more complex. The specific expenditure commitment will be by no means the only one the department might undertake. Hence there will be an intra-organizational battle about the case for that particular innovation. What the outside world sees as a minister promoting a particular project is probably the end of a long process in which different groups of civil servants within the department have argued about the case for that venture as opposed to other ventures. A minister who says

'I want to do X' will have to face civil servants who argue 'but we need money for X, Y' and so on. The political negotiations between a minister and the Treasury ministers will be matched by much more elaborate negotiations between civil servants. A case that is comparatively weak when argued within the department will come up against further problems in this tough forum, and a minister who successfully overrides objections within his or her own department may well lose in this wider battle. Students of government have, moreover, raised questions about the extent to which civil servants will fight effectively for their minister against the Treasury, in view of the prestige and power of the latter within the civil service as a whole (see Heclo and Wildavsky, 1981).

In differentiating different kinds of policies, and in interpreting their implications for ministerial power, it must be recognized that some policies have implications for more than one department. A new approach to assistance with housing costs, for example, may have to be considered both by the Department of Social Security, with concern for social security policy, and the Department of Environment, with its responsibility for housing policy. In addition, local government is likely to be involved. This adds a form of complexity that greatly enhances the significance of negotiations between civil servants, and the related tendency for the maintenance of the status quo. Such policies place strains upon the unity of the political group involved. Two key aspects of government emphasized in the Crossman diaries are the difficulties facing a minister with departmental responsibilities who tries to take an overall view of government policies, and the related tendency for ministers to take narrowly departmental views which sabotage inter-departmental co-operation.

This discussion has distinguished between policies that ministers can enact with relatively slight implications for their own departments and those that require elaborate departmental involvement. It has implied that where ideological commitments are involved a distinction may be made between relatively easy gestures and hard administrative battles. Yet it may also be the case that some difficult aspects of 'bargaining politics' are involved where policy success depends upon the response of other organizations.

It is, of course, outside the field of social policy, in industrial relations, that the best examples are found of the undermining of policy innovations by groups outside government. The 1964–70 Labour Government found that their alliance with the trade unions limited their scope for action in this field. The Thatcher Governments found some of their ideas for tax and social security reform affected by the reservations of small business about new tasks for government. Within social policy, however, the power of the doctors provides related examples. In this case the problem comes, if not exactly within the secretary of state's own department, at least from within a public agency. More important, however, for the analysis of social policy is the interplay between central government and those other organs of government, particularly local government, which have a crucial role to play in the implementation of policy, but are also themselves in certain respects policy-makers.

A new minister with an overall responsibility for the health and personal social services within the Department of Health, or for education, or for housing policy (together with local government in general) within the Department of the Environment will find an 'established' relationship between the department and local government or the health service with certain key characteristics. There will be a body of enacted legislation, a pattern of grants from central government, a range of procedures relating to the sanctioning of new initiatives including the taking up of loans for new capital expenditure, perhaps a pattern of inspection or policy review, and a variety of policy expectations enshrined in circulars and related messages from the centre. In a few cases the obligations of the local authorities will be quite clear. In a rather larger number of situations the authorities will have quite explicit duties but will not have been given detailed guidance on how to carry them out. In yet other important cases the local authorities will regard themselves as the key policy-makers; the central requirements will have been specified in such general terms that the decisions that really dictate the quality of the service given to the public are made locally. Then there will be some situations in which central government has made it very clear that the policy initiative rests with the local agency, by *permitting* activities if they so wish. Finally, there will be a few situations in which local authorities have been almost entirely the innovators, in which they have sought to promote local acts through Parliament or in which they have interpreted general powers given to them in quite novel ways.

The new minister who wants to introduce changes into this pattern has a variety of options open, but each may involve complications wherever there is resistance to new ideas. New policies are expressed as much in ministerial statements, White Papers and circulars to the local authorities as in new statutes. In each case the minister may be able to back up a recommendation with indirect weapons: by control over loans and other powers to permit or limit activities, by co-operation or its refusal in situations in which joint central–local action is necessary. In the National Health Service the control over funding also facilitates policy change from the centre.

The local authorities often fight hard to try to protect their independence. They may be unresponsive to ministerial suggestions, and they may make this opposition very clear through the local authority associations.

The threat of non-co-operation from the local authorities may make the minister think again. The most publicized cases of such non-cooperation have occurred where some authorities have stood out against the minister on a highly political issue. It may be suspected that issues on which there would be widespread local resistance, but where a party political split is not clearly in evidence, rarely hit the news headlines because they are quietly negotiated in private discussions between the minister, or civil servants, and the local authority associations. The public conflicts of recent years have involved confrontations between different political ideologies: the resistance from the Clay Cross Urban District Council to the Conservative Housing Finance Act; the rejection by Merthyr County Borough of the Conservatives' withdrawal of free milk for schoolchildren; the resistance of a number of Conservative education authorities to the Labour commitment to the introduction of comprehensive secondary education; the resistance of Labour local authorities to the Conservative Government's legislation on the sale of council houses; and the forms of creative accounting developed in the mid-1980s by some local authorities to evade expenditure restraints. The evidence suggests that a determined central government, generally backed by the courts, has, at least since 1979, been able to impose its will in most central–local battles. The new financial controls, described above (p. 56), have surely strengthened this domination.

Although the local authorities are themselves, as has been suggested, policy-makers, the force of influence for policy change is, however, not just one-way. Just as the new minister encounters groups of civil servants within his department with policy concerns that conflict with his own, so too does he encounter local authorities keen to take new initiatives. They will be eager to protect their own autonomy, but may also seek to convince the minister that their local initiatives should be enshrined in national policy.

Hence, as sources of local initiatives local government may be as important as central government. The example of comprehensive education is again interesting. Before the 1964–70 Labour Government made it Department of Education and Science policy, a number of local authorities had already set up comprehensive schools. It is significant that, while in some areas, such as London, this development was motivated by a political commitment, in other places, for example rural Devon, it was educational administrators who had convinced councils, of a broadly Conservative persuasion, that the development of such schools was the most appropriate policy. It is equally interesting to note that the trend towards comprehensivization continued after the Thatcher Government repealed the legislation which had been forcing the pace in the late seventies.

In this section the discussion has ranged over many of the influences upon policy. Using the notion that is particularly associated with representative government, of a new minister with explicit policy commitments, attention has been given to the pressures that frustrate such commitments, or replace them by commitments derived from other sources. It has been stressed that there are strong forces in favour of the maintenance of existing policy, and that many new initiatives are in fact derived from concerns not so much to innovate as to correct the imperfections of existing policies.

Hence, it is interesting that, while the historical account of social policy tended to stress a variety of significant contributions to policy, building constructively on the past – the 1911 National Insurance Act, the 1944 Education Act, the 1946 National Health Service Act – perhaps a key theme in modern writings on the policy process is the absence of rational forward planning but in its place a phenomenon that has been called 'disjointed incrementalism' (Braybrooke and Lindblom, 1963). Is there a conflict of approaches here?

Braybrooke and Lindblom, the theorists who drew attention to the significance of 'incrementalism', were particularly concerned to attack that portrayal of the policy process which perceived it as, or able to become, a rational appraisal of all the alternative consequences of alternative policies followed by the choice of the best available. If incrementalism is perceived in these terms there is little difficulty in understanding its applicability to social policy. As the historical chapter showed, the development of social policy has been very much a process of piling new initiatives on top of older policies, without ever clearing the ground to facilitate a fresh start. Then, as this piling-up process has proceeded, it has created new interests which future developments have to take into account. Since political values have often been at stake in conflicts over social policy, the very character of the ideological issue has precluded a cool appraisal of all the policy options.

If the choices are between understanding policy-making as a pure exercise in rational decision-making, as the putting into practice of ideologies, or as a quite incoherent process of bargaining and muddling-through, it is sensible to reject each alternative. It is a compromise between all three, with perhaps the first least apparent and the third most in evidence.

SUGGESTIONS FOR FURTHER READING

Like the previous chapter, this one has drawn upon a vast literature, this time largely from the discipline of political science. Reference notes have largely been chosen to include some of the classic works that expounded particular theoretical viewpoints together with text-books that most clearly interpret theories and issues for British audiences. The following suggestions for further reading will be primarily in the latter category.

For those who require a basic textbook on British government Hanson and Walles's *Governing Britain* (1970) is recommended. An alternative with a strong constitutional law bias is Hartley and Griffith's *Government and Law* (1975). Jowell and Oliver's *The Changing Constitution* (1985) reviews some emergent issues of importance. For more advanced accounts, written from a strong political science perspectives, books by Dearlove and Saunders (second edition 1991) and Jordan and Richardson (1987) are worth consulting, the former offering a comparatively radical account of events, the latter a more conservative one.

An account of the local government system is provided by Tony Byrne (fifth edition, 1990), whilst Stoker's *The Politics of Local Government* (1989) offers an account of some of the recent developments. This is a rapidly changing scene on which there is no totally up-to-date account. Travers's *The Politics of Local Government Finance* (1986) and Loughlin's *Local Government in the Modern State* (1986) explain the development of the central/local government conflict discussed in this chapter, and will hopefully be updated soon.

Valuable discussions of the policy-making process in social policy are found in Hall et al.'s *Change, Choice and Conflict in Social Policy* (1978), and in Banting's Poverty, *Politics and Policy* (1979). Chris Ham and the present author's *The Policy Process in the Modern Capitalist State* (1985, new edition due 1993) explores many of the theoretical issues about the study of policy-making.

CHAPTER 4

Implementation

INTRODUCTION

Why devote a chapter in a book on social policy to the study of policy implementation? What is the significance of this issue for our subject? There are several reasons why it is important. First, the discussion of policy-making in the later part of the last chapter suggested that many new initiatives stem from the recognition that older policies are failing to meet desired goals. This may be because these goals have changed, but it may equally be because the social world for which the original policies were designed has changed. This is an implementation problem. It may also be because there were weaknesses in the older policies, many of which became apparent once policies were implemented. In this sense it is important to scrutinize the implementation process with some care.

Secondly, this concern with the ineffectiveness of policies is now recognized as requiring that we ask not only questions about the character of policy but also about what is wrong with the implementation process and the organizations responsible for implementation. It may be that the policies are at fault, or it may be that corrective action is most appropriately applied to the implementing agencies. This is the central concern for what we may call the 'top down' approach to the study of implementation: Why don't those who are expected to carry out policies do what is required of them?

Thirdly, and finally, while it is true that the impact of all policies must be subjected to careful scrutiny, it is clearly particularly important to give attention to what it feels like to be on the receiving end of social policy. This may be described as a concern with 'impact' rather than with 'implementation'. However, it is this concern that has led students of social policy to give increasing attention in recent years to the activities of that group of public servants who may be called 'street-level bureaucrats', to ask questions about what actually happens in the exchanges between these people and the public.

Before, therefore, exploring any further the phenomenon of policy implementation, a brief account of the main groups of people responsible for social policy implementation in Britain is appropriate. An examination of the wide range of people involved, of the many different roles they play and of their varying involvement in or distance from the policy-making process will help to stress the importance of giving attention to implementation and to introduce the more theoretical discussion that is to follow.

Social security benefits are calculated and paid to the public by a very large number of civil servants based in regional and local offices throughout the country. These people now come under one of five public 'agencies' carrying out functions delegated to them by the Department of Social Security to whom they are ultimately answerable. The most important of these is the Benefits Agency responsible for payments but there is also an agency to deal with contributions and one to enforce child-support obligations on parents.

The Benefits Agency deals with payments of both contributory and means-tested benefits. The former are determined by a largely computerized central system. The calculation of means-tested benefits is also increasingly concentrated in a small number of offices, leaving the local offices in touch with the public to take in applications and to deal with queries. A minority of Benefits Agency staff, social fund officers, are concerned with the highly discretionary 'social fund', where the determinations are still made at the local level.

There is only one other large group of people defined in Britain as civil servants that is concerned with the implementation of the social policies discussed in this book: those involved in the employment services. They come under the Department of Employment, and are again organized into an agency (the Employment Services Agency). This also services local Training and Enterprise Councils whose membership is drawn from employers.

Otherwise field-level social policy implementation is the responsibility of National Health Service and local authority officials, who, since they are not employees of the central government departments, are not regarded as 'civil servants'.

However, to relate to local implementation systems a number of central government departments have regional offices. Examples relevant to social policy implementation are the Department of the Environment's system of regional offices which handle many aspects of relationships with the local authorities, and the Department of Health's regional social work inspectors who help the Department to relate to the local social services departments.

The implementation of health policy is devolved by the Department of Health to regional (RHAs) and district health authorities (DHAs). The latter are concerned with field-level policy. The important feature of this system for policy implementation is that the districts have both policy-making and implementation responsibilities. However, the Conservative government, in its health policy changes enacted in 1990, endeavoured to create a system in which DHAs purchase services from 'providers'. These may be hospitals and community units under their direct control but may also be independent National Health Service Trusts or units under the control of other DHAs. They describe this as creating an 'internal market' system within the health service, and expect that it will enhance efficiency.

While, since the changes recommended by Griffiths, there is a key managerial cadre in district health authorities, health remains an area of social policy in which professionals – particularly doctors and nurses – have extensive degrees of autonomy. It is often difficult to make the policy implementation distinction with reference to a service operated by professionals. Day-to-day service provision decisions may actually determine, or pre-empt, priorities. In this sense they can be described as policy decisions. The purchaser/provider split is seen as limiting the scope for this to happen.

The peculiar feature of the health service organization is that the regional links in the chain, the regional health authorities, are semi-autonomous organizations, standing between the Department of Health and the district health authorities. There is speculation that with the emergence of the purchaser/provider split at district level one or other tier will come to be regarded as irrelevant. Purchasing could shift to the RHAs, or the DHAs could come to stand alone relating to a system in which all health delivery units became semi-independent like the NHS Trusts.

Primary responsibility for the implementation of education policy lies with local authorities in England and Wales. As suggested in the previous chapter, there has been a considerable amount of conflict in recent years about the autonomy of these authorities as 'policy-makers'. To some extent the implementation issues in this service concern the relationship between the authorities and the schools. While the chain image is not entirely appropriate, since varying responsibilities and degrees of autonomy are involved, and individuals in the chain may be bypassed, it is important to acknowledge that implementation may depend upon the following series of links: education committee, chief education officer and his or her administrative staff, local authority inspectors and advisers, school governing bodies, head teachers, departmental heads within the schools, and class teachers. The examination of policy implementation in the education service raises a number of interesting questions about local authority autonomy, the role of school management and the place of professional discretion.

The 1986 Education Act has strengthened the powers of school governing bodies, laying down rules to determine their budgets and giving them autonomous responsibilities. It also enables them to apply to the Secretary of State to become directly accountable to him or her, rather than remain under local authority control. Comparatively few have achieved this status so far, but the possibility further weakens local government influence. Whilst the government has seen this as a form of decentralization, increasing the feasibility of parent power, the weakening of local political control through the provision of a centralized administrative framework can equally be seen as increasing centralization (see Glennerster et al., 1991). The latter impression is further reinforced by the development of the national curriculum.

Higher education in Britain has required special forms of organization designed to take into account the fact that many colleges serve more than the local authority area in which they are based, and to acknowledge the special claims to autonomy of the universities. For the university sector a special intermediary body has long existed. However, the 1986 Education Act replaced the comparatively independent University Grants Committee by a more directly government-controlled University Funding Council. At the same time it took the polytechnics out of local authority control, setting up a special funding council for them. Subsequently the Further and Higher Education Act 1992 brought the polytechnics under the same Funding Council as the universities and brought the remaining local authority colleges of higher education under direct ministerial control.

The personal social services are the responsibility, inasmuch as they are under public rather than voluntary control, of social services departments within local authorities. While professional discretion and autonomy is also to some extent an issue in this service, implementation is not complicated by either a multi-tiered structure like that of the health service, or by powerful institutions like the schools and colleges. While many directors and senior staff in social services departments are professionally qualified social workers, a relatively small proportion of the staff is engaged in social work. Other key workers include home helps, residential care staff and occupational therapists. Policy implementation is often influenced by the character of co-operation between these different occupational groups. It may also be heavily dependent upon voluntary effort, much of which is only loosely co-ordinated and partly subsidized by the public departments. However, after 1993 local authorities will be expected to operate community care policies using a purchaser/provider framework, rather like that in the health service, with a wide range a private and voluntary organizations able to operate as providers.

While for education there is a major department of state, the Department for Education which is responsible for national policy and the relationship between the centre and the local authorities, the personal social services are very much a small proportion of the policy concerns of the Department of Health. One implementation problem here is that the main central department responsible for local government is the Department of the Environment. This department, together with the Treasury, deals with the main financial and legal links with local government, but has no responsibility for education or social services. This exacerbates a tension, at the local level, between the demands of an integrated and corporate approach to local government and the separable service interests of these two large, heavy-spending departments of education and social services. For social services the link with the Department of Health encourages the giving of attention to relationships with the health service. The Department of Health has been engaged on seeking to co-ordinate the planning of health and social services. This is a development of some importance for the evolution of integrated caring services in the community. A special device that cuts across the link between social services and the rest of local government but strengthens that with health, has been the 'joint financing' of social services ventures with health service money. The new community care policies continue this development by establishing the direct funding of all work by local authorities in the mental health field.

Local authority housing is the responsibility of the lower-tier local authorities. In Northern Ireland protests about discrimination by local authorities led to the creation of a province-wide Housing Executive; and in Scotland there is an important nation-wide public housing authority to supplement the work of the local authorities. There is also in England and Wales a Housing Corporation, responsible for the provision of funds for housing associations. A feature of recent government policy has been a quest for new ways of managing and financing housing. This is increasing the importance of bodies like the housing associations, financed by public money or by a combination of public and private money.

The implementation of housing policy is fragmented not only because of the mixture of kinds of housing authorities. This is an area of social policy in which many significant decisions are made by private agencies. Since there are four main types of housing tenure – renting from a local authority, owner-occupation, renting from a private landlord, and renting from a housing association – and the government intervenes, or has intervened, to try to influence the quality and cost of each type, policy implementation is often a very complex matter. In studying it, attention has to be given not only to the relationship between government and the local authorities, but also to government attempts to influence the behaviour of building societies and landlords. There are also some other public–private interactions of some significance for housing policy. For example, there have been government efforts to influence the price of land and to curb land speculation, government intervention in the money market, and government manipulation of the costs and benefits of various statuses in the housing market by means of taxation and social security policy.

Finally, it is misleading to suggest that these relationships between government and the various private sectors are of no concern to the local housing authorities. The latter increasingly seek to influence housing opportunities of all kinds in their areas, and to give advice to those they do not house themselves. Moreover the housing authorities, of course, have a significant interest in land prices, and have planning responsibilities to relate housing activities to other kinds of developments in their areas. Housing policy implementation has many dimensions.

THE RELATIONSHIP BETWEEN POLICY AND ITS IMPLEMENTATION

In the previous chapter it was suggested that policies are complex phenomena which are hard to define with any precision. This obviously makes for difficulties in distinguishing policy-making and implementation, and for identifying implementation issues and problems. The distinction between policy-making and implementation seems to need to rest upon the identification of decision points at which a policy is deemed to be made and ready for implementation, like a commodity that is manufactured and ready for selling. This is not, however, to imply two separable processes. The difficulty, however, with this analogy is that policy-making and implementation merge. The policy-making process is like the design of a building for a specific occupant by an architect; the implementation process affects policy design quite early on and will continue to influence some details of it even after implementation has begun, just as modifications are made to buildings after occupancy.

Policies have characteristics that must affect the nature of the implementation process. Many policies will be complex, setting out to achieve objectives x, x1, x2 ... under conditions y, y1, y2. ... These complexities may very well influence the implementation process.

Some policies will involve vague and ambiguous specifications of objectives and conditions. These will tend to become more specific during the implementation process.

Constraints are not merely contained within new policies themselves. While it is possible, in the abstract, to treat policies in isolation from other policies, in practice any new policy will be adopted in a context in which there are already many other policies. Some of these other policies will supply precedents for the new policy, others will supply conditions, and some may be in conflict with it. The process of inaugurating new policies will continue after the adoption of the policy and will then further affect implementation.

A further general constraint that must not be overlooked is, of course, the fact that the scarcity and control of public finance frequently sets limits to policy development. In some cases these limits are quite explicitly set by central government. Perhaps they arise because the government does not recognize the true costs of their new policies, or perhaps because of a resistance to making a particular policy effective which comes from within the central government machine. In other cases the split between central government as a policy initiator and local government in the role of implementer produces a situation in which central intentions appear to be thwarted by local scarcities. Hence the Chronically Sick Disabled Persons Act of 1970 expects local authorities to provide a range and scale of services that in practice they rarely can. However, since central government in Britain is the dominant influence upon the availability of local finance, there is a certain political duplicity here in legislation which requires local agencies to provide benefits that the centre knows they are unlikely to be able to afford.

Policy goals are often specified, as has been pointed out, in general, or unclear terms. We may identify a number of different reasons for this lack of clarity. First, it may be simply that policy-makers are far from clear what they really want. The lack of clarity may be so total that it is comparatively meaningless to seek to identify a policy or to study its implementation. Some of the 'policies' of this kind derive from political aspirations to demonstrate a popularly desirable commitment. It was suggested in the last chapter that some so-called 'policies' may be merely symbolic.

Secondly, it is important to take account of the extent to which a lack of clarity about policy stems from a lack of potential consensus. Policies emerge that are not merely compromises, but also remain obscure on key points of implementation. Where this occurs it is likely that there will be a lack of consensus among the implementors, too. Hence wide variations in practice may emerge, together with a range of conflicts surrounding the implementation process. The 1977 Housing (Homeless

Persons) Act provides examples of implementation problems – concerning the definition of priority groups, the extent of the duty to provide help and advice and the identification of the responsible authority – that would seem to have emerged from the conflict during the legislation process. In the same way, the author has elsewhere suggested that some of the difficult 'value' problems faced by the former National Assistance Board (NAB) staff stemmed from the ambivalence of legislation:

> The traditional attitude to the poor had been to regard them, in the absence of unambiguous evidence to the contrary, as undeserving individuals on whom public money should be spent most sparingly. The National Assistance Act seemed to turn its back on this doctrine, yet it failed to jettison the view entirely and it failed to provide financial resources sufficient to enable the Board to avoid having to distinguish between the claims made by applicants, particularly as regards their more unusual needs. Consequently the onus of distinguishing between the 'deserving' and the 'undeserving' poor tended to fall upon the officer dealing with the applicant in the field, just as it had fallen upon the relieving officer in the past. While the politicians and administrators who framed the Act would not have wished to have espoused the notion of the 'undeserving poor', they felt unwilling to risk the public criticism that would have resulted from an approach to poverty that involved ignoring the potential waste on the 'work-shy' and the fraudulent application in order adequately to meet the needs of the majority of applicants.   (Hill, 1969, pp. 85–6)

This has continued to be true of many aspects of social security policy.

This source of implementation problems is closely related to another of some importance. Sometimes the political ambivalence about a policy is reflected not so much in the policy itself as in the constraints that are set upon the implementation process. The simplest form of constraint here is, of course, the failure to provide the means, in money and staff, to enable a policy to be implemented properly.

Another example of a quite deliberately imposed implementation problem is the adoption of administrative procedures that are explicitly designed to affect the impact of a policy. Thus Deacon (1976) has shown how 'the genuinely seeking work test' was manipulated in the 1920s to make it difficult for unemployed people to establish their claim to benefit. He describes it as imposed as a quite explicit deterrent, without reference to the actual availability of work.

It is important, while acknowledging that many policies are made complex and ambiguous by the conflicts within the policy-making process, to recognize that it is intrinsically difficult to specify some policy goals in terms that will render the implementation process quite clear and unambiguous. This is one important source of discretion for implementers. Jowell (1973) has drawn attention to examples where the concern of policy is with 'standards' that are not susceptible to precise factual definition. He argues that standards may be rendered more precise by 'criteria', facts that are to be taken into account, but that 'the feature of standards that distinguishes them from rules is their flexibility and susceptibility to change over time'. Questions about adequate levels of safety on the roads or in factories, or about purity in food, are of this kind. So are many of the issues about need in social policy. Discretionary judgement is likely to be required by policy, alongside the more precise rules that it is possible to promulgate.

If a policy is a complex and ambiguous phenomenon, with aspects that go 'too far' for some people and 'not far enough' for others, it is important to acknowledge that the dissension that attends its 'birth' will continue to affect its implementation. It may therefore provide opportunities for some implementing agencies to develop new initiatives that were perhaps not originally envisaged. However, policies also often contain 'footholds' for those who are opposed to their general thrust, or who wish to divert them to serve their own ends. Bardach (1977) has developed an extensive analysis of the various 'implementation games' that may be played by those who perceive ways in which policies may be delayed, altered or deflected. While some policies contain few features that their opponents can interfere with – laying down, for example, a clear duty to provide a particular service or benefit – others, such as the Department of Health commitment to the development of community care for the mentally ill, depend heavily upon the commitments of implementers, and are relatively easily diverted in other directions or even rendered ineffective.

It is important to raise questions about the ways in which policies are expressed, and the evidence required to establish the extent of implementation. Policies may be conveyed to local implementors in a range of ways from, at one extreme, the explicit imposition of duties and responsibilities to, at the other end of the continuum, the very loose granting of powers which may or may not be used. We can contrast, for example, the comparatively strict ways in which regulations under the 1986 Social Security Act instruct local authorities in the administration of housing rebates, with powers given (originally in the 1963 Children and Young Persons Act, now in the 1989 Children Act) to local authorities to make money payments, in exceptional circumstances to prevent children being taken into care, where no attempt has been made to prescribe how this should be done.

In this discussion it has been hard to draw the line between issues that are essentially *characteristics of policy* that affect implementation, and points that are really observations about the characteristics of either the relationships between central policy-makers and local implementers, or of the organization of the implementing agencies. While it is helpful to make a distinction between policies on the one hand and the implementation process on the other, this must raise problems at the margin. Policies are formulated with the implementation process in mind, and often it is more realistic to see policies as *products* of implementation rather than as 'top-down' inputs into the process.

THE 'CENTRE–PERIPHERY' RELATIONSHIP

It is possible to some degree to distinguish between those implementation issues that arise essentially from the 'distance' between what we may describe as 'centre' and 'periphery' and those that are facets of other aspects of relationships within complex organizations. The latter, which will be discussed in the next section, are of course considerably complicated by the problem of 'distance', particularly when two or more separate organizations are involved.

In British public administration the 'centre' will generally have been involved in the policy-making process. But where implementation is delegated to other organizations the 'centre' generally maintains an interest in the implementation process. Equally, the 'periphery' has an interest in policy-making and can be expected to contribute to a feedback process from implementation into policy elaboration. However, there are several different kinds of centre–periphery relationships that significantly influence the implementation process. The simplest model is clearly that in which the centre and the periphery belong to the same organization. The most complex occurs where policy implementation depends upon co-operation between separate autonomous organizations, and particularly where responsibility at the periphery is (a) delegated to several organizations with separate territories, and (b) dependent upon co-ordinated action between two or more local organizations.

Recognition that there may be issues to consider about 'levels' emphasizes the importance of this dimension for the study of implementation where separate organizations are involved. It is clearly important to identify not merely the issue of the relationship between different levels of elected government but also the existence of a variety of organizations whose relationships to either central or local government, or both, is often ambiguous: the health authorities, the Urban Development Corporations, the Funding Council for higher education and the universities; the New Town Corporations and so on.

It is important to bear in mind the wide range of inter-agency linkages that may be necessary, without reference to the subject matter of those linkages. Pressman and Wildavsky (1973) have made a tentative attempt to draw attention to what may loosely be described as the mathematics of implementation, the way in which the mere quantity of agreements necessary may, even when all parties are committed to a policy, undermine or delay effective action. Hence it is necessary to give attention to the following issues about centre–periphery relations:

1 the relationship will be likely to involve two or more organizations at either the 'centre' or the 'periphery' or both. Effective implementation may depend upon co-operation not merely between the two 'levels' but also between different organizations at the same level;
2 the centre–periphery relationship may be mediated through one or more intermediary or regional body;
3 relationships between agencies will in practice involve a number of different issues, and the symmetry that it is possible to draw in an abstract model will not be the same for each issue.

In reality any organization will be involved in a web of relationships, which vary in character and intensity according to the issue. Hence, local authorities have to deal with a number of different central government departments, but the extent to which this is the case varies from issue to issue. Equally, some activities require considerable co-operation between 'peripheral' agencies while others require very little. However, it may be misleading to lose sight of the overall pattern since the outcome of one relationship will affect responses to another. Relationships are ongoing; each will have a history that conditions reactions to any new issues. Equally, each organization will have developed its own sense of its task, mission and role in relation to others. These will affect its response to anything new.

One issue deserving of attention, if only because of the importance it assumes in the American implementation literature, is the 'special' agency set up to concern itself with policy-making and implementation in a specifically limited policy field. Schon (1971) has described government agencies as 'memorials to old problems'. It has long been recognized in the United States that there are difficulties in getting old agencies to implement new policies. A crucial innovation strategy has therefore involved the creation of new agencies for this purpose. However, students of this process have pointed out that these new organizations then face problems about their relationships to older agencies (see Selznick, 1949; Moynihan, 1969). While new organizations may possess a strong commitment to a new policy, and may have powers that enable it to bring together the resources for its implementation that were not possessed by any single previous organization, it still has to relate to a world in which other agencies have a great deal of power to influence its success.

One of the crucial issues, to which the creation of *ad hoc* agencies in the United States is a response, is the problem, at all levels but particularly at local level, of 'overlapping governments'. There are so many ways in which different government agencies can veto or neutralize other agencies' initiatives that a new agency, with more precisely defined policies, is seen as offering, perhaps in desperation, a new way to 'get something done'. While it would be foolish to suggest that a comparable problem does not exist at all in Britain, it is important to recognize that ours is a more simple system in which individual agencies have more clearly defined powers and more definite boundaries to their responsibilities and sphere of influence. Only rarely, therefore, can we identify examples of agencies set up explicitly to circumvent problems of this kind. Moreover, when they do occur they are more often allowed to operate in territories (in both a spatial and a policy sense) in which others' intervention is limited.

The New Towns are examples of successful British innovations in this sense. What is interesting about them is that, while the development corporations acquired powers that gave them a great deal of autonomy within their own territories, there is today a variety of questions to be raised about the extent to which their 'success' was secured at the expense of other policies to which they 'ought' to have related. While the New Towns often built up relatively successful and prosperous new communities, they did little to relieve the problems of the least-privileged in the old communities from which they drew. Hence, while by providing for 'overspill' they have helped to solve some inner-city problems, they have exacerbated others.

While the use of the New Town device is now being discontinued, British governments still experiment with approaches to urban renewal which bypass existing agencies. The Urban Development Corporations are the latest such devices, spawned by a central government which sees the local authorities as likely obstacles to local economic development.

Three motives can perhaps be identified for the creation of special agencies in Britain, although there are of course dangers in taking ostensible motives as real ones: to create an effective separate and accountable 'management system'; to reduce political 'interference'; and to provide for the direct representation of special interests. In Britain today the last of these is clearly the dominant motive.

The removal of some aspects of the elaboration of policy from direct political influence, particularly when there are powerful special interests within the quasi-autonomous body, introduces complications that make it particularly difficult to distinguish policy-making from implementation. These agencies may be seen alternatively as implementers that affect the character of policy or as independent creators of policy forever in a relationship of tension with the 'centre'. It is this tension that can then sometimes be seen as leading to central efforts to curb the independence of agencies whose initial freedom was provided by government. The arena of quasi-autonomous agencies is a turbulent one, requiring regular revision of textbooks such as this one!

THE ORGANIZATIONAL CHARACTERISTIC OF IMPLEMENTING AGENCIES

In the study of agencies concerned with policy implementation two significant bodies of literature can be drawn upon. There are studies by organizational sociologists that suggest the limitations upon the formal control of subordinates by means of rules (see, for example, Crozier, 1964; Argyris, 1960), and the behavioural studies of law enforcement, which have emphasized the significance of bargaining and discretion in the activities of the police and other rule-enforcers (Bottomley, 1973; Gunningham, 1974). Both suggest that there are finite limits upon the prescription of subordinate behaviour. Very detailed rule-making is a difficult and time-consuming activity. If it has to be backed up by close supervision and control a point may be reached where such activities are self-defeating. If the subordinate has to be so elaborately controlled the supervisor might just as well undertake the task. Conformity to rules relies primarily upon compliance, upon a willingness to work within a regulated framework which Etzioni (1961) has suggested rests either upon acceptance of a 'utilitarian' financial bargain or upon a 'normative' commitment. A key point about the former is that it also invokes in practice some measure of 'tolerance' on both sides; some concept of 'trust' (Fox, 1974). This applies limits to the things the supervisor can require the subordinate to do, and involves acceptance by the superior of limited deviations by the subordinate from the activities that are expected.

It is not necessary to elaborate this diversion into industrial sociology unduly. The general point is that mindless conformist implementation is rare. More commonly, even in a wide range of situations in which subordinate staff are primarily motivated by 'utilitarian' rather than 'normative' considerations, there is some concern about the justification for the policy that is to be implemented. Indeed, as the recent concerns of trade unions in, for example, the health services and in social security suggest, there seems to be a growing 'rank and file' interest in policy. This extends beyond a tendency to influence policy delivery by the characteristic 'insubordinate' responses of evasion, delay and so on, into a desire to feed back views into the policy-making process.

The studies of rule enforcement in particular indicate that in most tasks, and especially in the more elaborate tasks, there will be a strong element of discretion. Earlier in this chapter three sources of discretion were identified, arising from (a) a deliberate recognition of local autonomy, (b) 'political' difficulties in resolving key policy dilemmas, and (c) 'logical' problems in prescribing 'standards'. This discussion has added a fourth: the inherent limits to the regulation of tasks (Jacques, 1967). In practice, prescriptions for policy implementation convey discretionary powers to field-level staff for reasons that are combinations of these four 'sources' of discretion. An alternative way of looking at this phenomenon is to see the field official as a 'street-level bureaucrat' (Lipsky, 1980). His or her job is characterized by inadequate resources for the task, by variable and often low public support for the role, and by ambiguous and often unrealizable expectations of performance. The official's concerns are with the actual impact of specific policies upon the relationships with specific individuals; these may lead to a disregard of or failure to understand the wider policy issues that concern those 'higher up' in the agency. The 'street-level' role is necessarily uncertain. A modicum of semi-professional training defines the role as putting into practice a set of ideals inculcated in that training. Yet the 'street-level' bureaucrat is also the representative of a government agency, one that is itself subject to conflicting pressures. In day-to-day contact with clients and with the community at large, he or she becomes to some degree locked into the support of individuals and groups that may be antipathetic to the employing agency. In such a situation of role confusion and role strain, a person at the end of the line is not disposed to react to new policy initiatives from above as if he or she were a mere functionary. New policies are but factors in a whole web of demands that have to be managed.

It is interesting how many of the social workers who regard themselves as identified with their clients, sharing some sense of oppression by the 'bureaucracy' that weighs upon them both and working therefore to help the clients receive resources from the 'system', have a view of social security field staff that is directly in contrast to their view of their own position. They see social security staff as biased and prejudiced against the poor and only too ready to evade their responsibility to help. They demand, therefore, that the social security bureaucracy should more effectively control and discipline its subordinates. Without taking sides on these views it can be acknowledged that there are 'two faces' to street-level bureaucracy. It may be seen as the effective adaptation of policy to the needs of the public, or it may be seen as the manipulation of positions of power to distort policy towards stigmatization, discrimination and petty tyranny. Which it does will vary according to the policy at stake, and the values and commitments of the field workers, but it will also depend upon the scope accorded by the organizational control system, for this phenomenon is not necessarily independent of 'biases' built into the policy delivery system. Social workers can manipulate their 'system' in favour of some clients because their agency grants them licence to deploy such commitments. Social security officers can discriminate negatively because they are encouraged to be vigilant to prevent fraud and abuse.

Consideration of discretion and of the roles of 'street-level' bureaucrats must also involve looking at the implications of professionalism for implementation. For Etzioni (1961) the compliance of professionals to their organizations rests upon 'normative' commitments. But policy-makers may be said to have to 'pay for' a lessening of day-to-day control problems with concessions in the implementation process; professionalism tends to involve participation in the determination of policy outcomes. In the health service, for example, doctors have been able to secure a very full involvement in policy-making within the service as one of the prices for participation. Three interrelated points may be made about professionalism:

1   that it may entail a level of expertise that makes lay scrutiny difficult;
2   that professionals may be, for whatever reason, accorded a legitimate autonomy;
3   that professionals may acquire amounts of power and influence that enable them to determine their own activities.

These sources of professional freedom clearly have a differential impact depending upon (a) the professional involved, (b) the organizational setting in which professionals work, and (c) the policies that they are required to implement. The importance of the level of expertise for professional power has led some writers to make a distinction between professions and semi-professions (Etzioni, 1961) with doctors and lawyers in the former category but social workers and teachers in the latter.

The second point has been the subject of controversy about the impact upon professional activities of organizational, and particularly public, employment, the conclusion to which would seem to be, in short, that 'it depends on the profession and upon the organization'. On the third point, once again, a good deal depends on the nature of the policy involved.

There is a large number of situations in which it is expected that professional judgement will have a considerable influence upon the implementation process. Clearly explicit in many policies is an expectation of this. This applies to many decisions made in face-to-face relationships between professionals and their clients. Many of the issues involved are increasingly the subject of controversy, involving arguments about 'rights' versus 'discretion'. Within these arguments disputes occur about the significance of expertise and about the scope for effective limitation of discretionary power. The effective resolution would also impose many difficult policy questions – about moral rights to choose (for example, with reference to abortion) and the best way to allocate scarce resources (for example, with regard to kidney machines) – which are at present partly masked by professional discretion. There are also some important questions here, which are very hard to resolve, about the way to link together professional autonomy in dealing with an individual relationship with a client, and a policy-based concern (or 'public concern') about the way in which professionals allocate their services as a whole.

A further important complication for the study of implementation introduced by the involvement of professionals is that some activities depend upon the co-operation of two or more professional groups. Studies of attempts to co-ordinate the efforts of various professions concerned to protect children from injury by their parents have suggested that particular professional practices, activities and terminology may intensify communication problems. There are also, clearly, some key problems about the boundaries between the various professional 'territories'.

It is important to recognize the extent to which professional involvement with policies implies not merely scope to influence implementation but also an impact upon policy itself. Within the health service the very direct influence of the doctors has been subjected to considerable attention by policy analysts (Ham, 1985; Klein, 1989; Harrison, Hunter and Pollitt, 1990). What has perhaps been accorded less attention has been the ways in which policy and implementation have involved a feedback from implementation as policies have been found inadequate to meet the demands of 'good professional practice'.

Packman (1975) has examined the way in which social workers in children's departments gradually found that good child-care practice required not merely the control and care powers possessed under the 1948 Children's Act but also preventive work to keep children out of 'care'. They innovated as far as possible under the 1948 Act but eventually secured a further Act, in 1963, which legitimated 'preventive' work. A similar concern to extend social work practice, to enable integrated work with whole families, led, as Hall (1976) has shown, to further legislation in 1970 which brought all local authority social work within one department.

The discussion in this section has developed the key points about inter-organizational practice by means of consideration of the rules–discretion dichotomy. But to end it three issues must be raised, which have been implicit rather than explicit within the argument so far: the relevance of the lack of clarity within much policy, the significance of value conflict, and the importance of rewards.

The first of these points does not require much further emphasis at this stage. A lack of clarity in policy has already been identified as one explanation for discretion. But equally when the relationship, within a system of rules, between means and ends is far from evident, then implementers may be more disposed to break, and their supervisors may be disinclined to enforce, rules.

A lack of clarity about policy goals and conflict about values, as already suggested, often go hand in hand. Burton Clark (1956) has written of 'precarious values'. Policies may have among their goals objectives that lack support in the community. Implementers will be aware of the controversial character of the policies and may not themselves subscribe to the goals entailed. The social security official required to secure the delivery of benefits to one-parent families, but also expected to prevent abuse, may well take the latter consideration more seriously than the former, letting his or her conception of morality and stereotypes about the social behaviour of the claimants influence behaviour (Marsden, 1973).

But the implications of Clark's analysis go further than this, seeing the problem of precarious values as affecting not merely day-to-day behaviour but also the way in which a whole organization may conceive its tasks. In particular, an organization that is given a task that is controversial and unpopular in many quarters, such as an organization charged to promote racial and sexual equality or one providing help to a stigmatized group such as vagrant alcoholics, may find that it is given an unclear mandate and is placed in a position in which it finds it hard to acquire 'legitimacy' for its activities. This may lead to the adoption of 'safe' and uncontroversial activities, organizational security being put before any movement towards potentially disruptive goals.

The problem of 'precarious values' may also be related to the problem of rewards. We return here to Etzioni's analysis of the distinction between 'utilitarian' and 'normative' rewards. Clearly, the official placed in a position of 'role-strain' between the demands of superiors and the expectations of the public, or of 'value conflict' between his or her own ideals and those embodied in policy, will be influenced by rewards of both kinds. Benefits now and hopes of advancement may curb an inclination to deviate from the requirements of superiors; a feeling that some parts of the job are 'worth doing' may be even more influential. But the substitution of 'unofficial' or 'official' goals may be a product of recognition that more 'worthwhile' activities may thereby be undertaken. The motivation of field-level staff is an important issue even within the most integrated organization. Where, however, 'control' is attenuated by a gap between those concerned with policy and the implementing agency, it may assume crucial significance.

THE SOCIAL, POLITICAL AND ECONOMIC ENVIRONMENT

Policies are evolved in a wider environment in which problems emerge that are deemed to require political solutions, and pressures occur for new political responses. Implementing agencies continuously interact with their environments. Much has already been said that has a bearing upon the underlying significance of the environment.

Whatever the relationship between state and society, policies may be interpreted as responses to perceived social needs. Government is concerned with 'doing things to', 'taking things from' or 'providing things for' society or for parts of it. Putting policies into practice involves interactions between the agencies of government and their environment. Those who do that are, of course, themselves a part of social environment in which they operate.

However, in looking at social policy we must also question whether the distinction between the policy system and its environment can be easily made. In chapter 1 it was established that it is misleading to see any single equation between the activities of the social policy system and the enhancement of social welfare. But just as the policy determinants of welfare are multiple, and sometimes unexpected, so individuals' welfare is influenced by phenomena that have nothing to do with the activity of the state. The determinants of an individual's welfare can be broadly classified as depending upon their own capacity to care for themselves combined with (a) market activities and relationships, (b) the behaviour of 'significant others' as providers of 'informal care', amongst whom family members are likely to be the most important, and (c) the role played by the state. To study welfare requires attention to all 'determinants', and changes in the way in which welfare is provided are particularly likely to involve shifts in the roles played by these 'determinants' and shifts in the relationships between them. In other words, the process of interaction between policy system and environment is a very active one, and those interactions occur across an ambiguous and shifting boundary. To give a concrete example, personal social services care is only one element in individual care systems in which family, neighbour and purchased care are likely also to play a part. A shift in the availability or character of any one of these care ingredients is likely to have an impact on the others. Day to day policy implementation in the state-provided sector involves the management, or indeed mismanagement, of its relationships to the other elements.

Accordingly studies of social policy have conceived of the system as a 'mixed economy of welfare' (Webb, 1985). Furthermore, 'social divisions of welfare' have been identified recognizing not merely that there are different sources of welfare for individuals, but also that individuals differ in the access they have to different welfare systems. Titmuss (1958), who originated the notion of 'social divisions of welfare', identified alongside mainstream 'public welfare' 'fiscal welfare', the system of relief from taxation (of which the relief for mortgage interest payments and pension contributions are among the most important examples); and 'occupational welfare' (the range of fringe benefits available to some employees). Titmuss, together with others who developed his work such as Sinfield (1978) and Townsend (1979), argued that these other welfare systems may provide large benefits additional to, or quite separate from, the benefits provided by the more central institutions of the welfare state. They may operate in a direction quite contrary to any egalitarian tendencies in the mainstream policies. The 'social divisions' theme has been taken up in another way by some recent feminist writers who have been concerned to show not merely that many welfare provisions discriminate against women, but also that female services within the family and neighbourhood form crucial separate welfare systems, enhanced in importance when other systems fail or are withdrawn (Rose, 1981; Land and Rose, 1985).

These points have been emphasized in this chapter because the implementation of many contemporary policy initiatives – privatization, the limitation of social expenditure, the extension of community care – involve changing the balance between the various ingredients in the 'mixed economy of welfare'. Where government withdraws or reduces its direct contribution to welfare it may still make an indirect contribution if the social security system subsidizes private provision, or it may have to acquire a new range of regulatory concerns about the quality of private services, or it may face increased problems in the other areas of concern because of the new pressures placed upon individuals and families.

Those who are directly affected by policies, the public, may be crudely divided into the unorganized and isolated public – who pay taxes, receive benefits, seek planning permission, visit doctors and so on – and the organized public, the organizations upon whom policies have an impact. These relationships may be studied with a view to ascertaining whether implementation proceeds in terms of the even-handed justice that Max Weber (1947) suggested is, or should be, characteristic of bureaucratic administration. Clearly, questions about bias in the behaviour of public officials, the mechanisms by which scarce benefits or services are rationed, the roles played by 'gatekeepers' and the problems of securing effective 'take-up' of some benefits are issues of concern for the implementation of policies (see Foster, 1983). In the study of these matters many of the issues about the motivation of implementers – about 'role-strain', 'precarious values' and the exercise of discretion – concern the interaction between the nature of policy, the implementation system and the characteristics of the public. Policy delivery is not easily made an 'even-handed' process; class, gender and race differences influence access to professional services, some social security applicants are less well informed and more easily deterred than others, and 'street-level bureaucrats' who may be regarded as highly responsive to local needs in a white neighbourhood may be seen very differently in a black one. Here the 'environment' affects the way the policy is received.

This chapter has portrayed the implementation process as a complex one, in many respects inextricably bound up with the policy-making process. It has suggested that in the study of social policy it is important to give attention to implementation problems that arise directly from the characteristics of policy, but to recognize also that there is a complicated interrelationship between these and a range of inter- and intra-organizational factors. Finally, all these complications interact with a complex environment.

An approach to the examination of social policy has been introduced here that has not been given much explicit attention in relation to the study of specific policies. One justification for this lengthy examination of policy implementation is that, while we all experience the effects of the implementation process, and many of us participate in various ways in it, very few of us are involved in policy-making. Yet it is this policy-making, often particularly that which occurs at the highest level, that receives very much more attention. It is hoped that in considering the detailed discussions of particular areas of policy, contained in the next section of this book, readers will bear in mind the importance of the implementation process for the actual impact of social policies upon the public.

SUGGESTIONS FOR FURTHER READING

The author has contributed to further discussions of the issues raised in this chapter in chapters 8 and 9 of his book with Glen Bramley,

Analysing Social Policy (1986) and in chapters 6 to 9 of his book with Chris Ham (1985). Susan Barrett and Colin Fudge's *Policy and Action* (1981) is also an important source. Other key works on implementation are those by Pressman and Wildavsky (1973) and Bardach (1977) and articles by Van Meter and Van Horn (1975) and Sabatier (1986).

The theme of discretion has been a particular concern of the author's work cited above. Those who want to follow up this issue should also look at the writings of Jowell (1973), Davis (1969) and Galligan (1986), and a collection of papers edited by Adler and Asquith (1981).

Specific Areas of Social Policy

Each of the chapters in this part of the book will contain the following:

1 an account of the policies involved, which deals with their scope and coverage in Britain at the present time, and examines their organization;
2 a consideration of the particular characteristics of the British system, which seeks to give some insight into the reasons why it takes the form it does and the general consequences of that form for the service provided for the public;
3 the more detailed examination of a selection of specific issues of contemporary importance: these will consider particular policy problems and interesting current policy innovations. New directions suggested for policy, and solutions to policy problems, will be related to the factors that will influence their chances of adoption and implementation. Readers should note that some of the sections of specific sub-topics may be relevant to more than one chapter. Hence, issues about the relationship between personal social services and both income maintenance and health services are discussed in the personal social services chapter, and the discussion of the education of ethnic minorities in the education chapter makes many points relevant to other policies.

CHAPTER 5

Social Security

INTRODUCTION

The expression 'social security' is used here to cover all the British state systems of income support. These fall into three categories: contributory benefits, non-contributory benefits which are not means-tested but are contingent upon the individual being in some specific category (a child or disabled), and means-tested benefits. The Beveridge plan for contributory benefits (Beveridge, 1942) envisaged that they should provide the main source of protection against the problems of old age, sickness, unemployment and widowhood. The legislation of the 1940s, picking up the main pieces from earlier contributory social security schemes, attempted to provide this coverage. The main contributory benefits date from that time but the system of contributions, the nature of the benefits and the character of the alternative benefits available to back up the contributory system have all changed a great deal since then.

The Department of Social Security is responsible for the main social security benefits, using a group of agencies. The main agency for the delivery of benefits, the Benefits Agency, operates through a network of local offices. There are centralized or concentrated computer systems for the main benefits. There are other agencies, including the Contributions Agency to deal with the collection of national insurance contributions and the Child Support Agency to collect contributions towards the maintenance of children in families dependant upon income support from absent parents. Housing benefit is administered by the lower-tier local authorities, under either housing or finance departments. The Department of Social Security lays down a strong rule structure for the whole system, including housing benefit. The only part of the system for which there now remains extensive local discretion is the Social Fund (see pp. 102–3).

CONTRIBUTORY BENEFITS

All employees, together with the self-employed, contribute on a weekly basis towards the national insurance scheme of sickness and unemployment benefits and pensions. They do so on an earnings-related basis, subject to a maximum contribution level. Normally these contributions are deducted by employers, who also have to pay additional contributions for their employees. These should not be confused with income tax deductions.

Since 1977 there has also been in operation a 'state earnings related pension' scheme that will provide earnings-related pensions; these will begin to reach a satisfactory level for those retiring in the 1990s. Individual employees must contribute either to this scheme or to officially approved private schemes. Those who 'contract out' in the latter way will secure only the basic retirement pension from the state, which is the main present form of income support for the retired.

The employee who is unable to work on account of sickness is initially dependent, since the enactment of the Social Security and Housing Benefits Act of 1982, upon his or her employer for support. The latter is, with some exceptions, required to provide sick pay at least up to minimum levels prescribed by Parliament for 28 weeks. After that anyone still unfit for work moves on to invalidity benefit, set at a flat rate level. There is also a state sick benefit scheme, providing benefits lower than invalidity benefits for people in the first 28 weeks of sickness who have recent insurance contribution records but were not in employment immediately before they became sick. Also those whose incapacity for work arises out of an industrial accident or a prescribed industrial disease may get special, higher, benefits after 15 weeks of incapacity for work.

There are similar systems of statutory maternity pay, payable for 18 weeks, backed up by a reduced state maternity allowance for women with recent work records who do not qualify for pay from their employers.

Unemployment benefit is available to the formerly employed after three days out of work, subject to complex previous contributions conditions. After a year on this benefit entitlement is 'exhausted', and recipients cannot re-qualify until they complete a period of 13 weeks in work. There are, for both sickness and unemployment benefit, rules designed to prevent abuse of the scheme. The rules with regard to unemployment benefits are, however, much more obtrusive. There are provisions for disqualification from receiving benefit for up to 26 weeks if individuals are judged to have left work voluntarily, lost their jobs through their own fault or refused a suitable vacancy. There are also rules to prevent persons involved in industrial disputes and seasonal workers from benefiting from the unemployment scheme.

Widows have an entitlement, based upon their husband's contributions, to widowed mothers' allowances if they have children to support and to widows' pensions if they are over 45. For the widows' benefits and for retirement pensions during the first five years after reaching pensionable age (60 for women, 65 for men), there are 'earnings rules' which reduce the income received, on the basis of sliding scales which allow some but not large amounts of earnings. These rules only apply to earned income; in this sense they differ from the fuller forms of means tests. Widows lose their benefits on remarriage; there is also a 'cohabitation rule' which may be operated to treat widows living 'as wives' the same as 'married wives'.

NON-CONTRIBUTORY, NON-MEANS-TESTED, CONTINGENT BENEFITS

Child benefit is paid to the parents or guardians of all children under 16, and children between 16 and 18 who are still at school. The only qualifying condition is a residence one. 'One-parent benefits' can be claimed as a modest addition to child benefits for single parents.

There are some non-contributory benefits available to the long-term disabled, which must not be confused with the industrial injury disablement provision or with invalidity benefit. Amongst these are the disability living allowance (a combination of the former attendance allowance and mobility allowance) set at various rates depending upon the need for care from another person; the disability working allowance for disabled people able to work; and the non-contributory invalidity pension, available to those among the long-term sick who have not been able to contribute to secure invalidity benefit. These are new benefits starting in 1992 to replace attendance allowance and mobility allowance (see Table 5.1). There is a range of detailed rules concerning these benefits which cannot be discussed in the space available here.

MEANS-TESTED BENEFITS

The 1986 Social Security Act, which was implemented by April 1988, radically altered the structure of means-tested benefits. The attention given in the Act to the rationalization of means tested benefits, although it did also make changes to the pensions scheme and to some

TABLE 5.1   Numbers of recipients of, and amounts of public expenditure on, the main social security benefits in Great Britain, 1989–90

	Recipients (thousands)	Expenditure (£ millions)
Contributory benefits		
Retirement pensions	9795	20,697
Invalidity benefit	1190	3837
Unemployment benefit	375	733
Widows benefit and		
industrial death benefit	405	911
Non-contributory, non-means tested benefit		
Child benefit	12,000[a]	4513
Attendance allowance	795	1159
Invalid care allowance	115	184
Mobility allowance	585	769
Means-tested benefits		
Income support	4155	7675
Housing and community		
charge benefit	3905	3805
Family credit	305	425

[a] Numbers of qualifying children

Source: Central Statistical Office, *Social Trends 22*, London, HMSO, 1992, p. 93.

of the contributory benefits of lesser importance, is indicative of the extent to which the government recognizes that means tests are now very central to our social security system. People dependent upon contributory benefits often need means-tested support as well, at least in respect of their housing costs. At a time of high unemployment a contributory scheme for those out of work, which has initial qualifying rules and the exhaustion of entitlement after a year, leaves many in need of means-tested benefits. In particular, young new entrants to the labour force are unprotected by the unemployment benefit scheme. In addition, many people in work earn insufficient for their needs, and have to apply for means-tested family and housing benefits to supplement their incomes.

The figures in table 5.1 give some idea of the extent of coverage of contributory and means tested benefits respectively. Bear in mind that many people can qualify for more than one benefit, and that, in particular, means-tested benefits may supplement contributory ones.

In setting out their objectives for reform, in the White Paper which preceded the 1986 Act, the government said:

> We believe that resources must be directed more effectively to areas of greater need, notably low-income families with children. We want a system that is simpler to understand and better managed. We want sensible co-operation between the social security and tax systems. And we want a system which is consistent with the Government's overall objectives for the economy. (HMSO, 1985)

As far as the means-tested benefits were concerned, the Act provided new schemes to take the place of supplementary benefit and family income supplement, and changed the housing benefit scheme. It also swept into the means-tested system two contributory benefits of previously near to universal availability: maternity grant and death grant.

The scheme which has replaced supplementary benefit is known as 'income support'. It operates a means test based upon a simple personal allowance structure, enhanced in some cases with 'premiums'. The specific personal allowance rates are for a couple, a single person over 25, a person between 18 and 24 and three age-related rates for children. Then there are different premiums for families, lone parents, pensioners under 80, pensioners over 80, disabled people, and seriously disabled people. The idea running throughout is that the determination of the appropriate overall entitlement for a household should be a simple and predictable process. Additions for special needs have been abolished. Then rules, not so dissimilar to those operating under the former supplementary benefit scheme, determine how any income should be taken into account. People in full-time work (defined as being 16 or more hours in employment per week) are disqualified from receiving 'income support', but part-time workers may obtain it. To deal with this an earnings rule is used, based on net income, which involves disregarding a small amount and then deducting the rest from any entitlement. Similar 'disregards' are used for some other kinds of income, but state benefits are taken into account in full. There are special rules dealing with savings, disregarding small amounts and then applying a sliding scale to reduce benefits for greater amounts to an upper limit at which they disqualify for benefit entirely.

Alongside the 'income support' scheme is a means-tested benefit available to low-paid full-time workers. This is 'family credit', and it has replaced 'family income supplement'. The calculation rules for this benefit are based upon those for 'income support'. The maximum credit is payable where net earned income is equal to, or below, the personal allowance available to a family on 'income support'. Hence, the government aim to ensure that most families where there is a full-time breadwinner are better off than comparable families on 'income support'. Above 'income support' level the credit is withdrawn at the rate of 70 per cent, that is for each £1 of income above that level 70 pence of credit is lost.

The housing benefit scheme has been designed to be compatible with these two other means-tested benefits. The 'income support' rules are used in the calculation of benefit so that any tenant whose income is at or below income support level gets the full housing benefit entitlement. Thus, an anomaly which occurred before, under which people on housing benefits but not supplementary benefit could be worse off than people on both benefits, has been eliminated. Housing benefit provides support for rent; it does not provide support for house buying. But people on 'income support' may get help under that scheme to enable them to keep up mortgage interest payments. Hence, low-income owner-occupiers can only get this help if out of work, whilst renters may qualify for housing benefit even if in full-time work.

The housing benefit scheme is, in effect, extended to local taxation. Thus, at the time of writing, low-income poll-tax payers may apply for a reduction in their payments, up to a maximum of 80 per cent, with the calculation based upon the housing benefit means test. It is envisaged that a similar scheme will apply when the council tax is introduced, whilst if rates are restored the equivalent help will come by way of the revival of the former rent rebate scheme.

Under the former supplementary benefit scheme there were provisions enabling single payments to be made to help people with exceptional expenditures – removal costs, furnishing, house repairs and so on. An elaborate body of rules dealt with these entitlements. The 1986 Act has swept away single payments. But it set up a Social Fund, to be administered by a specially trained group of Department of Social Security officers. Under the Fund there are two kinds of grants available as of right to people on 'income support' or 'family credit': a lump sum maternity needs payment, and a funeral needs payment (the amount of which depends upon funeral costs). There is also provision for grants to be made from the Social Fund to assist with the promotion of 'community care'. These may be available when someone needs help in becoming established in the community after a period of institutional care, to assist with travelling expenses to visit relatives in hospitals and other institutions, and to improve the living conditions of defined 'vulnerable groups' in the community. Elaborate guidance is provided to Social Fund officers to help them determine needs of this kind. They are expected to liaise closely about such matters with social services and health services staff, and to take into account powers these other departments may have to provide assistance in cash or kind. Apart from the grants, outlined in the points above, all other help from the Social Fund is by way of loans, normally repayable by weekly deductions from benefits. Again officers have been given elaborate instructions on the circumstances in which they may provide loans. The Social Fund, excluding the two items of benefit as of right, is 'cash limited'. Within this budget 30 per cent is available for community care grants and 70 per cent for loans. This means that local offices also have annual budgets, and will be expected to relate a set of rules about priorities to the total sum available. Claimants for help from the Social Fund, other than claimants for maternity and funeral payments, have no formal right of appeal against decisions, though there is an elaborate provision for internal 'review'.

This description of the new structure for the main-means tested benefits does not exhaust the list of benefits. One quite important means-tested benefit administered by local authorities, entitlement to free school meals, had its availability restricted under the 1986 social security changes. Free school meals are now only available to children whose parents are on 'income support'.

Other means-tested benefits include grants to students in higher education, relief from payment of National Health Service charges, and legal aid. Local authority social services departments also use means tests to determine charges for residential care and domiciliary services.

THE DISTINCTIVE CHARACTERISTICS OF THE BRITISH SYSTEM OF SOCIAL SECURITY

The British national insurance scheme today bears little resemblance to commercial insurance. There is no 'funding' and investing of contributions. Invalidity benefit continues for as long as the claimant is sick, assuming an initial fulfilment of the contribution conditions. It is impossible to relate flat-rate pensions to contributions; the rate of inflation of recent years has destroyed any correspondence between contributions and payments in terms of the face value of the money involved, and no inflation-proofing assumptions were built into the original scheme. When the state earnings related pension scheme (SERPS) was set up in 1977 some consideration was given to the future relationship between amounts to be paid out to qualifiers and amounts to be contributed by participants in the scheme whilst in work. Concern about the relationship between these groups in the early years of the next century, when the number of SERPS beneficiaries will increase rapidly but that of SERPS contributors seems likely to be comparatively low, was seen by the Thatcher government as a justification for reducing the benefits offered. This change, together with measures to increase the extent of contracting out of SERPS into private schemes, was included in the 1986 Social Security Act.

The unemployment benefit scheme maintains an insurance principle of sorts. Despite the fact that, as early as the 1920s, the scheme was rendered insolvent by the extension of protection to 'bad risks' and the lengthening of the period for which benefit was payable, the exhaustion of benefit after a year and the special re-qualification rules provide some limits to expenditure upon this benefit. It is these restrictions that have, at a time of high unemployment, substantially limited the extent to which unemployed people can avoid applying for 'income support'. In 1989–90 only 16 per cent of the male unemployed registering for benefits were getting unemployment benefit alone, while 65 per cent were only getting income support. The remainder consisted of 5 per cent getting both benefits and 14 per cent getting nothing (*Social Trends 22*, 1992, p. 94).

The presence in the British system of a 'safety net' group of means-tested benefits to back up the contributory scheme is by no means peculiar to this country. Such assistance schemes are very widespread, and in many countries they remain under local control and more closely resemble the British scheme's predecessor, the poor law. What is perhaps peculiar to the British scene is the complex overlap between the two systems. In Britain the contributory scheme appears to provide close to universal coverage but in fact has to be supplemented in a large number of ways.

The abandonment of the 'insurance' relationship for unemployment benefit, and some relatively slight increases in contributory benefit rates, would markedly reduce dependence on means-tested benefits. Yet these changes are open to objections. The main effect of increasing the availability of unemployment benefit would be to shift the support of a large group of people from 'income support' to contributory benefit with little change to their income, whilst a relatively small number of people with other sources of income (the early retired with private pensions) made actual income gains. Similarly, an increase in contributory benefits relative to 'income support' would produce income gains for a group not among the least poor (not on 'income support'), while merely altering the source of help for the very poor (who would then accuse governments of giving with one hand and taking away with the other).

On balance the shift in the British system in the early 1980s has been in the opposite direction. The ending of earnings-related supplement to short-term benefits, the introduction of the employer-based sick pay scheme, and measures which have reduced the value of benefits have reduced the contribution of contributory benefits to income support and increased that of means-tested benefits.

LEVELS OF BENEFITS

Clearly, it is important in assessing a system of social security not merely to look at the structure of the system but also to look at the level of benefits provided by it. There are examples, for instance, within the British system that look most impressive until one scrutinizes the levels of benefit available. This is particularly true of the various benefits for disabled people. For example, disability living allowance does not compensate for the substantial care costs implicitly occurring when someone gives up full-time work to care for a disabled person.

It would be pointless, in discussing the main social security benefits, to provide specific figures, which would be dated by the time many read this section. Instead, some of the general issues about the setting of benefit levels will be outlined. Reference has already been made to the relationship between contributory benefit levels and 'income support' levels. Any government setting these relative levels not merely has to look at its stance on means-tested benefits but also has to take into account that the costs of any shift away from the selective approach entails a cost made up of the extra benefit paid to those *not* already on 'income support'. If these include large numbers of people who have failed to claim the means-tested benefit, this will be a contribution to the reduction of poverty; but what if the new arrangement mainly provides a bonus to those already above the poverty line? This is a cruel irony for the commitment of egalitarians to universalism. The pragmatism of everyday politics leads away from a commitment to a more ideal system of social security.

Hence, a great deal of debate about poverty in Britain is concerned not about the contributory benefits as such, but about the means-tested benefit levels, and about the people and families whose incomes fall below those levels. There are three ways to try to assess the adequacy of this 'poverty level': in relation to absolute concepts of need; in relation to other incomes; and over time in relation to the movement of prices and other incomes. In the early years of national assistance studies which attempted to relate poverty to an absolute standard, based upon the cost of providing a basic minimum of necessities, were still regarded as providing a sound basis for the fixing of benefit levels. More recently this approach has been discredited. It has been pointed out, notably by Townsend (1979), that poverty is only a meaningful concept when individual standards of living are related to those widely taken for granted in a society. The British bare minimum would be quite a good standard of living for people in the more deprived countries of the world. At the same time, British views about what is necessary for an adequate way of life change over time. These changes are related to developments in living standards within the nation as a whole. When the national assistance scales – which today, much updated for inflation, form the basis for the 'income support' scales – were first set, in 1948, television was not even available; in the next few years it was regarded first as a luxury then as a necessity, and now colour television has moved in the same way out of the luxury category. If poverty is regarded as a relative concept, the key questions are, for example: to what extent should those on the official poverty line have incomes that make it difficult for them to share a way of life of the majority of the people? Or how large should be the gap between the incomes of those on the poverty line and average incomes? Or even, what should the relationship be between the lowest incomes in our society, most of which are provided by the social security system, and the highest incomes? In other words, the crucial questions are about relationships between the official poverty level and other income levels.

This has been effectively examined by Peter Townsend in his large study of poverty (1979). He persuasively makes a case for regarding large numbers of British people, including both people dependent upon social security and many on low wages, as being in poverty. A more recent study by Mack and Lansley (1985, but with an update expected at the time this book is going to press) lends support to Townsend's argument. This demonstrates the extent to which low-income people lack things which, according to a public opinion survey, are regarded as necessities.

A variant on this theme of considerable importance in contemporary political debate concerns the relationship between social security incomes and average earned incomes over time. After all, the real political questions are not so much about the setting of levels in the abstract as about the need for, or the amount of, benefit increases. The pressure groups regularly draw politicians' attention to the ways in which, over a period of time, those whom they represent are losing ground. Two important alternative kinds of yardsticks are used for these judgements: indices of earnings and indices of prices. The plural form is used in both these cases since there have been extensive arguments about the best ways of calculating them. In particular it has been argued that a price index for the poor should be rather different from a more general one, since the poor spend their incomes in rather different ways. However, the general problem of choice between earnings and prices as bases for judgements on benefit levels over time is that, while attention to earnings presumes relative positions, it may be important to protect the living standards of the poor at a time when prices are rising faster than earnings.

Before 1973 there was no statutory requirement for government to take specific notice of wages or price movements in determining benefit levels. *Ad hoc* political judgements governed uprating decisions. However, there was a tendency, over time, for the relationship between short-term benefit rates and wage rates to remain roughly the same (Barr, 1981).

In the Social Security Act of 1973 the Conservatives provided a statutory link between benefits and prices. In 1975 an amendment to the Social Security Act committed the Labour Government to uprating long-term benefits in line with prices or earnings, whichever was greater, and short-term benefits in line with prices. Heavy price inflation in the late seventies did produce some relative gains to social security recipients. In 1979 the Conservatives amended the statutory requirement so that long-term benefits were only to be linked to prices. Also, short-term benefits might be increased by up to 5 per cent less than the inflation rate. These rules relate only to the contributory benefits but, in most cases, means-tested benefit rates have been uprated on a similar basis.

The relationship between social security incomes and low wages is clearly important. Several studies of poverty have related incomes to the level provided by the main means-tested scheme. Apart from drawing attention to numbers falling below it because of a failure to claim benefits, they have shown that there is a significant group who fall below that standard because of low wages. Developments in the family benefits, and in housing benefit, have been designed to tackle this problem. However, there is an alternative way of responding to it. This is to argue not that something must be done to augment the earnings of the low wage-earner, but that means-tested benefit levels must be kept below the lowest wage levels. There was at one time a provision within the supplementary benefits rules – the wage stop – to enable individual benefits to be kept down. This was abolished soon after the introduction of family income supplement, which reduced the numbers of cases involved considerably. It has been argued that few of the unemployed are in fact deterred from obtaining work by benefit payments being above the levels they can obtain as earners. However, there is undoubtedly a relatively small gap between the benefits paid to some families, particularly large families, and the wages paid for low-skilled work. The deterrent effect of this will depend first upon the actual costs of going to work; secondly, upon individual views of the psychological costs and benefits of work; and thirdly upon the benefits still obtainable when in work. It is difficult to estimate the actual extent of deterrence at a time when jobs are scarce. However, there is a widespread public belief that this deterrent effect actually contributes to our high unemployment rates. Politicians share, or are sensitive to, this belief. It accordingly influences their attitudes to increases in the short-term benefits. However, the government see the 'family credit' scheme, which provides benefit to parents in work whose net income is at or below the 'income support' level, as dealing with this 'unemployment trap' problem. That, however, depends upon 'take up', an issue to which we will return.

As well as a concern about the relationship between benefits and other incomes there is also a concern about relativities within the benefit system. The 'income support' scheme rules make assumptions about the extent to which a couple may live more cheaply than a single person, about the extra needs of elderly and disabled people, about the different costs of children at various ages, and about the lower needs of single adults under 25. Some of these judgements are clearly controversial. In particular the low 'income support' rate for the single under 25, and the particularly harsh treatment of 16–18s who have left school, seem to be related to an assumption that such people can live with their parents, and not form separate households. The assumptions about the costs of children made by the rules have also been challenged as unrealistic about the costs of teenage children. It seems fair to suggest that considerations about the evidence on actual costs have been mixed with views about who are the most deserving amongst the poor in the determination of some of these rules.

SOCIAL SECURITY ASSUMPTIONS ABOUT FAMILY LIFE AND WOMEN'S ROLES

The assumptions about family life operated under the poor law involved a household means test under which all a household's needs were taken into account and also its resources, so that adult children of a needy couple were expected to contribute to their maintenance. The contributory benefits developed in 1911 treated the insured claimant as the sole beneficiary, providing flat-rate payments at the same level regardless of his or her family commitments. However, in the 1920s the principle of additions to benefits, taking into account the needs of wives and children, was introduced. The improved contributory scheme developed in the 1940s carried forward this principle, while means-tested assistance shifted from a household means test to a family one. Broadly, then, British social security policies have been developed on the assumption that the typical claimant is a married man with a non-working wife and dependent children. That is not, of course, to say that the system cannot cope with claims from single people, but that it has had difficulty in coming to terms with both female employment and with multi-person families constituted other than on the basis of legal marriage.

Until the 1970s, married women were required to pay lower contributions and received lower benefits than men. There was additionally an arrangement, now largely phased out, under which they could contract out of all the contributory scheme except the industrial injuries part. While this anomaly is being eliminated there are still others. Married women cannot claim contributory benefit increases in respect of dependent husbands and children. The continuation of provisions for non-employed wives to be treated as 'dependants' for whom husbands can claim additions to benefits implies that the return an employed woman receives on her contributions may in some cases be worth only the difference between the full pension or benefit and the addition for a non-working wife. In other words, there are difficulties in securing a fair balance in a scheme that tries, on the one hand, to make provision for 'dependent' wives and children and, on the other, to enable the married woman to be a contributor and claimant in her own right.

The position with regard to means-tested benefits is even more complicated when men and women live together, and perhaps have children, but are not married. A family means test requires judgements to be made about whether family situations exist. Generally this is straightforward; claimants agree with official interpretations of their situations. Indeed, it is to the advantage of a male claimant, living with a non-employed 'wife' and children (even if they are not his) to claim them as his family. However, difficulties arise where claimants, normally female, wish to be treated as independent but find that the Department of Social Security regards them as the 'wives' of male friends. The Department of Social Security has tried to develop a definition of 'living together as man and wife', which distinguishes stable relationships from more casual ones, but difficulties and disagreements still occur. It is, of course, only heterosexual relationships that are treated in this way – in all other cases claimants' needs are assessed separately. The issue here, which as was pointed out above also applies to widow's benefits, arises from the family-based approach to benefits. While it would be possible to treat unmarried 'couples' differently from married ones, the only fair way to avoid problems of this kind is to cease to make assumptions about family patterns of support, but instead to have a structure of *individual* entitlements (see Dale and Foster, 1986, ch. 6).

PROBLEMS OF MEANS TESTING

There is an extensive literature on the problems of means testing. Much that has been written on this subject comes from those who advocate, as an alternative, the strengthening of the contributory benefits system so that it becomes more universal in its coverage and provides better benefits. We have seen already some of the political objections to this approach. Alternative approaches to this issue are also found. One of these suggests that we could have a structure of 'basic income' in which all would be guaranteed a minimum income, and some of us would secure earned incomes (necessarily more heavily taxed) to supplement this state minimum (Walter, 1988; Parker, 1989). This would be a radical departure from our current system. It finds little support close to the corridors of power. Another alternative which has awakened a wider interest is 'negative income tax' (Minford, 1984; Dilnot, Kay and Morris, 1984). The British 'pay-as-you-earn' system for the deduction of tax would seem to be the ideal vehicle for the development of a system whereby additions rather than deductions could be provided in some cases. However, the basis for the assessment of tax would have to be shifted from an annual to a weekly one, arrangements would have to be made for the system to operate when people were both in and out of work, and some more-precise information on need would have to be available to the tax authorities.

When the Conservative government announced its radical review of social security in 1983 it seemed possible that the negative income tax idea would be adopted. In practice the 1986 changes have been influenced by this approach, in the adoption of a common set of rules to determine benefit rates and in the use of 'net' rather than gross income (that is, income after tax). But the income tax system itself remains 'untainted' by social security considerations. Hence the standard problems about means testing remain, albeit in a form much affected by the 1986 Act.

The general case against means tests is that they confuse, deter and stigmatize those who need help. People prefer benefits to which they have clear-cut rights, and about which they can obtain unambiguous information. Those who have to claim help are often already in trouble, about which they are ashamed or for which their neighbours criticize them; to have to reveal intimate details to an official in order to obtain benefits deepens the sense of 'stigma'. The low take-up of some benefits is attributed both to this 'stigma' and to the complexities surrounding the administration of means tests.

It is undoubtedly the case that take-up levels for the means-tested benefits are lower than for many other benefits. But there are marked variations between the various means-tested ones. Income support take-up rates are relatively high, particularly if the entitlement is likely to be large. Family credit and housing benefit take-up figures are lower. The Department of Social Security estimated that the take-up rate for family income supplement (family credit's predecessor) was below 50 per cent (Department of Social Security, 1991). The position with regard to family credit is not likely to be much better. Take-up of housing benefit is influenced by two things: whether the household is also on income support and whether they are local authority tenants. In a study by the Department of Social Security before the introduction of the 1986 Act changes, private tenants not on supplementary benefit were shown to have only a 64 per cent take-up rate, by comparison with a near 100 per cent rate for local authority tenants on supplementary benefits (ibid.).

The big disparity between take-up of housing benefit by public tenants and that by private tenants occurs because local authorities, as the administrators of those means tests, can much more easily publicize the former among their own tenants. Another factor that facilitates take-up of benefits is that 'income support' is regarded as an automatic 'passport' to others. This is most evidently the case with relief from NHS charges. However, this implies a cause for concern about the needs of those just above 'income support' levels, together with those who, in not claiming small amounts of income support, may also be shutting themselves out from ready access to other benefits.

One particular problem about the multiplicity of means tests is that, operating together, they may create a 'poverty trap'. This is a kind of income tax effect under which an individual whose earned income rises may find that tax and insurance contributions increase while benefit income decreases and together they diminish any gain to a very low level. The government stated that one of the main benefits of the 1986 Act was to be that, by using earned income after tax and national insurance deductions and having the main means tests operate with a common framework, they would eliminate the 'poverty trap' problem for most people. However, an individual gaining £1 in income may lose 34 pence from it in tax and insurance contributions. Then the remaining 66 pence will affect family credit entitlement, where a 70 per cent taper is applied. This will reduce the gain to 20 pence. But then the housing benefit taper is 80 per cent (60 per cent on rent and 20 per cent on poll tax) so that the eventual gain may be no more than 4 pence. An individual entitled to both these benefits will thus be subject to the equivalent of a 96 per cent tax rate on gaining £1 of earned income. This is the extreme case (based upon tax rates and benefit rates applying in the 1991–92 financial year), but even an individual without a tax and insurance change and with housing benefit but no family credit will experience an 80 per cent taper reducing the gain to 20 pence. These losses are much higher than the highest level of income tax!

This 'poverty trap' problem must afflict any unified means-testing system, including negative income tax. If the tapering-off effect is to be reduced, benefit receipt will logically spread further up the income distribution, adding to the cost of the scheme. In the last resort this can only be compensated by increasing tax rates, either across the board or through alterations to the higher-rate bands.

CONCLUSIONS

The British system of social security has been built up by the development of a contributory system together with a limited system of family benefits, which were conceived to minimize dependence upon means-tested benefits. However, the latter have not been reduced to the 'safety net' role envisaged for them by Beveridge and others. Indeed, in recent years an alternative strategy has been suggested, to confine expenditure on social security by placing an emphasis upon means-tested benefits. While the main issue for debate about the system seems to be the conflict between the case for a comprehensive system of non-means-tested benefits, probably founded upon contributory principles, and the alternative means-testing approach, this conveys an over-simplified notion of its character. In fact, the two approaches are mixed together in the system, and the overall picture is further confused by a range of *ad hoc* responses to special issues and problems – the needs of disabled people, the compensation of industrial injury victims, the requirements of support for students and schoolchildren, and so on.

The 1986 Social Security Act has simplified the means-tested part of the system. This eases administration, and limits the opportunities for errors, differential rule interpretation and outright discretion within the main means tests. It is an approach to reform around which a broad consensus might have formed were it not for the fact that the government was determined that the new scheme should be no more costly than its predecessors, and that it should make it easier for them to contain the future growth of social security costs. Therefore simplification inevitably implied rough justice, gainers being counterbalanced by losers. In addition, the very controversial Social Fund was introduced, with loans as its main form of aid and cash limits, to take up the strain on the system previously imposed by the complex single payments rules.

The growth of means-tested relative to contributory benefits since the 1960s, caused by political reluctance to increase the expensive contributory benefits, and the use of *ad hoc* measures to cope with problems of low wages and high housing costs, produced a great deal of turbulence in social security policy. Has the 1986 Act brought in a period of stability? Or will it lead to further attacks on the contributory system on the grounds of its irrelevance for the determination of most non-pensioners' incomes? Or will we see a future government attempting to turn back the tide and revert to a modernised version of the Beveridge approach?

SUGGESTIONS FOR FURTHER READING

The author has published an account of the British social security system (Hill, 1990). The Child Poverty Action Group (CPAG) annual handbooks on means-tested and contributory benefits are the key sources for details, including benefit rates which change at least annually (and have not therefore been quoted here).

The government's White Paper (Cmnd. 9517) outlining the proposals for the 1986 Act provides a good guide to their thinking. All but a few details of its proposals were enacted. A summary of the Act and a critique is provided in the Social Security Consortium's *Of Little Benefit* (1986).

CPAG pamphlets are useful critical sources of information on the system. Deacon and Bradshaw's *Reserved for the Poor* (1983) is an excellent review of the issues about means testing and the various alternatives to it, but was completed before the government proposed its changes. Parker (1989) provides a good critique of policy, coupled with advocacy of 'basic income'.

The best discussions of poverty and social security are Townsend's important poverty survey (1979), and Mack and Lansley's book (1985).

CHAPTER 6

The Personal Social Services

INTRODUCTION

This chapter will deal with those services which are the responsibility of the local authority social services departments in England and Wales. The decision to treat the personal social services sector as equivalent to that of the local social services departments is an arbitrary one, justifiable only in terms of existing departmental boundaries in England and Wales. In Scotland, for example, the relevant departments are the 'social work departments' and their responsibilities include duties carried out by the probation service in England and Wales. The justification for refraining from giving attention to the probation service is that a proper consideration of its role raises issues about its relationship to the courts and to other aspects of penal policy, which it is not intended to cover in this book. In England and Wales, before the creation of social services departments in 1971, a chapter like this would have had to deal with activities carried out within several public departments. There are still now some variations between authorities in the services that are the concern of the social services departments – a few departments have taken over the education welfare service, and child guidance remains an interdepartmental 'hybrid' service – but broadly the activities of these departments can be made the focus of attention.

One way of classifying the personal social services is in terms of their contributions to the needs of specific groups in the population: elderly people, physically handicapped people, mentally ill people, people with learning difficulties (a group which used to be called mentally handicapped), and children. An alternative classification is in terms of kinds of services: residential care, day care, domiciliary services, and fieldwork. These two modes of classification can, of course, be related to each other. A two-dimensional table could be drawn up, relating kinds of clients to kinds of services. This is difficult only where client groups fall into two or more categories – where elderly people are also physically handicapped, for example – unless the service is seen as being provided for families rather than for specific individual clients. It is the new integrated service's commitment to families that is seen as fitting unsatisfactorily with the various client-group classifications. However, in most cases the focal beneficiary of the service will be identifiable. It is field social work, rather than the provision of concrete benefits like residential care, that is most difficult to classify in these terms. However, even in this case the problem is not so much frequent doubt about the focal clients as a lack of clear information to enable social workers' activities to be clearly classified for the purposes of budget documents and planning activities.

In this chapter personal social services' activities will be discussed in terms of the kinds of services involved, treating their relevance for specific client groups as the basis for consideration within each service heading.

RESIDENTIAL CARE

There are two main groups of residential accommodation supplied by local authority social services departments: accommodation for the elderly, provided under Part III of the 1948 National Assistance Act, and accommodation for children who have been removed from parental care. The old people's homes have faced the problem, since 1948, of living down their heritage as 'workhouses'. While authorities have steadily replaced those institutions that were established under the poor law, putting in their places smaller and generally more homely institutions, they have faced difficulties in eliminating the public view that these are places to which people go only 'as a last resort'. The limited number of places available has emphasized the 'last resort' character of these homes, in more senses than one. It has been difficult to establish within them a mixed population of elderly people with varying degrees of frailty. Instead, there is very often a problem of maintaining a distinction between the population of these homes and the patients of the overburdened geriatric wards of the hospitals. The group the local authorities cannot readily refuse to help are those so frail that they cannot any longer manage in their own homes, whatever the level of domiciliary service provided. Many of these people require extensive nursing care but cannot secure hospital places.

About 100,000 elderly people were accommodated in these local authority homes in the United Kingdom in 1990 (*Social Trends 22*, 1992, p. 142). There is a widespread concern about the best way to use the supply of residential places for the elderly, and about the implications, for the future supply of these places, of an ageing population and of a diminishing capacity to provide family support. The distinction between the local authority's responsibility and the health service's responsibility is a difficult one, producing planning problems and 'boundary' conflicts over individual cases that are seldom in the old people's best interests. Local authorities would like to maintain a distinction between those for whom they supply domiciliary care and those for whom they supply residential care that is based upon individual preferences and needs and not upon a desperate attempt to spread scarce resources in the most economical way. A typical problem here is the desire to make temporary residential accommodation available to support family care within the community on an occasional 'holiday' basis; this comes into conflict with the pressing demand for all units of accommodation to be used for long-term accommodation.

However, an added complication for the determination of the local authority's responsibility for the residential care of the elderly is that there is a large, and growing, number of privately run homes available. About 160,000 people were accommodated in registered voluntary private homes in the United Kingdom in 1990 (ibid.). The number of places in this sector had more than doubled since the mid 1970s. By contrast, the number of public-sector places has gone down. Local authorities are responsible for the registration of voluntary and private homes, and have therefore to monitor their standards. They are thus placed in the anomalous position that they are the ultimate judges of the quality of services which relieve them of their own statutory responsibilities to provide care.

This rapid growth in private care has been stimulated by the availability of social security benefits to enable old people to pay charges. It has been an uneven growth. In some areas it has dramatically reduced the demand for local authority care. In others its impact has been quite slight. The greatest growth has been in the south and west of England, particularly in the seaside areas. An Audit Commission report on this issue has described this growth as a 'perverse effect of social security policies', distorting efforts to get the balance right between residential and community care and increasing regional inequalities. They point out that, for example, 'there are now nearly ten times as many places per 1000 people aged 75 and over in private and voluntary residential homes for elderly people in Devon and East Sussex than there are in Cleveland' (Audit Commission, 1986, p. 3).

An odd situation had thus developed by the end of the 1980s to which the government had to give attention. Local authorities had been seeking to extend forms of care within the community. The local authority burden had been reduced, relatively, in the 1980s, but not particularly through the evolution of community care. Rather, a private sector had grown, unconstrained by public authorities' concerns about the importance of maintaining people in the community and about confining the use of residential places to the most needy.

The government's response to this was contained in their White Paper, *Caring for People* (HMSO, 1989), and legislation was enacted in 1990 to try to deal with the situation. What was decided was that local authorities should be responsible for assessing need for care (for all who needed publicly supported care) and should then 'purchase' that care either from their own resources or from the private or voluntary sectors. Hence, they would be responsible for determining whether residential care was necessary, or alternatively whether some lesser form of domiciliary care should be provided (or, of course, nothing), and also for determining who should be the provider. In doing this the government was very concerned that private providers should be able to compete on a basis of equality with public providers. The subsidy of private residential care through the income support scheme was to cease.

This transfer of responsibility is complicated. It implies mechanisms to shift resources from the social security budget to the local authority social services budget. At a time when the government was in the middle of dealing with controversial changes in local government finance it was disinclined to rush this change. Hence, whilst it required local authorities to start to plan and reorganize for the new system after the beginning of 1991 they decided that it should not come into operation in full, and in particular the new arrangements for the residential care of elderly and handicapped people should not apply, until April 1993.

Despite the slight decline in the public-sector contribution to the residential care of the elderly, nearly a quarter of local authority personal social services expenditure is devoted to this item. That figure would be larger were it not that some of the cost of care is recovered by means of charges to residents. Charges are determined by means tests, with a minimum charge set by the secretary of state and recoverable from 'income support' where necessary. Local authorities cannot recoup all, or large parts of, their costs from social security as the private homes can!

The position with regard to residential care for children is complicated and rather confusing. A large proportion of the children who are in legal terms 'in the care of the local authorities' are not in fact in any kind of institution, indeed, a significant proportion of them are living in their parents' homes. There were about 68,000 children 'in care' in England in 1988. Of these, 54 per cent were boarded out in foster care, and 14 per cent were under the 'charge and control' of a parent, friend of relative. The remainder, 32 per cent, were in some sort of institution-alized care, about two-thirds of them being in local-authority run 'community homes' (Department of Health, 1991, p. 114).

Children may be taken into the 'legal' care of a local authority where parents are unable to care for them or are deemed to be unfit to care for them. In the first category there is also a group of generally older children, who are considered to be out of parental control. Care deci-sions are the responsibility of the courts, but most action to take chil-dren into care will have been initiated by social workers in the social services departments. Once a child has been taken into care the local authority will seek to ensure a settled future for him or her. In many cases this will mean return to parental care. Where this is not possible foster care is widely used. Hence, institutional care is likely to be regarded as a temporary expedient in many cases, while the situ-ation is assessed and longer-term plans are made.

Under the 1969 Children and Young Persons Act local authorities acquired increased responsibilities for the care of children brought before the courts for delinquent acts. The object of this legislation was to move further from the labelling of young offenders as criminals, and to make the issue for decision by the juvenile courts one about res-ponsibility for care rather than punishment for crime. Social services departments may now have to undertake the 'supervision' of such chil-dren, or they may be given legal custody of them under a 'care order'. They may fulfil the parental responsibilities entailed in a care order in a variety of ways, including the supervision of a child within a residen-tial institution. The former remand homes and approved schools be-came specially staffed 'community homes' under this legislation. Since many local authorities do not possess the residential resources to ful-fil responsibilities of this kind on their own, and in particular lack the necessary range of resources that must include (exceptionally) a 'secure' institution, there are regional planning committees to facilitate the use of homes by authorities other than the ones responsible for their management.

Where the care responsibilities of local authorities are discharged through the use of foster parents, payment will be made and the arrangements will be supervised by social workers. The cost of residen-tial care for children, including fostering, remains a significant element in social service department budgets, consuming around 10 per cent of the total.

This discussion of residential care has involved only two client groups: the elderly people and children. Mentally ill people and people with learning difficulties may receive institutional care within the public sector; this will be from a mixed range of facilities, some of which come under the direct control of the health service rather than social services.

There is, however, a growing local authority involvement in the provision of hostels and 'half-way' houses. Some of the most complex problems relating to the mix of funders which have to be sorted under the new legislation, discussed above, concern these groups.

DAY CARE AND DOMICILIARY SERVICES

Social services departments organize a variety of day-care services. For the elderly most provide day centres where people can go for company, social activities, occupational therapy, perhaps cheap mid-day meals, and maybe some aid or advice. Similar facilities are often provided for handicapped people. For the younger handicapped, and particularly for people with learning difficulties, local authorities provide centres where company and therapy may be accompanied by productive activities. In many cases these are more or less sheltered workshops, doing commercially sponsored work and paying pocket-money to handicapped people. There are some difficult distinctions to be drawn here between sheltered work, therapy and provision for some daytime life outside the home. The new 'community care' legislation relates to all these provisions as it does to residential care. The government's expectation is that local authorities will become more flexible about the range of help they provide *in the community*, and of course that they will make use of an increasingly wide range of non-statutory 'providers'. This use of non-statutory facilities will not be a new experience for many authorities but what will be new are the contractual arrangements which will have to apply.

The primary form of domiciliary care provided by social services departments is the home help service. This has developed remarkably from a service primarily conceived to help in maternity cases to a large enterprise serving predominantly the elderly, and thus playing an important part in helping old people to manage in their own homes. Local authorities in England and Wales provide around the equivalent of 63,000 full-time home helps. The development of the services is, however, uneven. According to the Audit Commission (1986, p. 24):

> home help provision varies by a factor of six or more among authorities – from under seven full-time home helps for every 1000 people aged over 75 (equivalent to less than eight minutes of actual help every week for each person aged over 75) to 44 full-time home helps.

This is another area of care where the public sector is accompanied by a large private sector. People may purchase their own help, and of course, where services are inadequate the gap is likely to be filled by large amounts of unpaid work by relatives and neighbours. Local authorities may charge for home help services, and may use means tests to determine the level of the charge.

Local authorities may also provide meals, taken to people in their own homes. This 'meals-on-wheels' service is often provided through a voluntary organization. Again, the extent of coverage by the service varies widely from area to area, from, at one extreme, a 'token' meal a week to, at the other, the provision of a comprehensive, seven-days-a-week service. Local authorities may set charges for this service; the extent to which they subsidize it is also variable.

Local authorities provide a range of other 'benefits in kind' to assist with the care of people within the community. The Chronically Sick and Disabled Persons Act of 1970 suggests a wide range of services that local authorities may offer to handicapped people. Despite the emphasis in that Act upon local authority duties, the word 'may' in the last sentence is appropriate. There are wide variations in the adequacy of the help provided. Authorities may provide, and pay the rental costs of, telephones; they may adapt houses to meet the needs of the disabled; and they are able to provide a variety of aids to daily living. They tend, however, to impose budgetary limits that ration quite severely the money available for such benefits. However, a further piece of legislation, the Disabled Persons (Services, Consultation and Representation) Act 1986, increases the rights of disabled people to be informed about provisions and consulted about their needs. This should have the effect of increasing the flow of services to the disabled.

Social services departments also provide day care for pre-school children. These day nurseries were largely developed during the Second World War, but this service has not since grown to a really effective level. Places are few, and are generally only given to children from very deprived backgrounds. In recent years there has been a considerable growth of private provision for day care for young children–daily minding, day nurseries and play groups–for which the social services departments have supervisory responsibilities. In 1990 there were 830,000 maintained or registered day-care places for children under five (not to be confused with nursery school places) in the United Kingdom. Only 36,000 (4 per cent) of these were in local-authority-maintained day nurseries or playgroups; 555,000 (67 per cent) were in registered day nurseries and playgroups and 238,000 (29 per cent) were with registered child-minders (*Social Trends 22*, 1992, p. 52). There are undoubtedly large numbers of unregistered child-minders!

FIELDWORK

The services provided by local authorities that were described above as 'fieldwork' include visiting by social workers, social work assistants, occupational therapists and volunteers recruited and organized by social services departments. The social work aspect of this is often emphasized; in Scotland the departments are called 'social work departments', and in England and Wales social workers are the dominant professional group and occupy many senior management roles. But it is important to recognize that the support of people in their own homes is carried out by a variety of workers, not all of whom are, or should be regarded as, social workers. The distinction here between the social work task and other tasks is a difficult one to make. The public often makes no distinction between social work and many other 'caring activities', yet social workers are increasingly preoccupied by a concern to define their task. This has implications not only for social workers' 'professional' aspirations, but also for the costs of various services since trained social workers are relatively expensive.

The activities of fieldworkers centre around a range of duties of social services departments. The responsibility for the care of children requires visiting where child abuse or neglect is suspected; the supervision of children both under directions from courts and under a duty to prevent harm and keep them wherever possible with their families; the investigation and supervision of adoption and fostering arrangements; and a general readiness to respond to cries for help from families under all kinds of pressure.

The whole body of law relating to the care of children was revised in the Children Act of 1989. The main thrust of this complex legal framework was to further enhance the involvement of families in the examination of situations where a public authority intervention seems necessary, and to minimize the likelihood of the removal of children from their family of origin. This Act also widened the range of ways in which authorities might spend money on preventative work with families, including the provision of direct material assistance to families. It remains to be seen whether the resources will be forthcoming to make this a reality.

Fieldworkers are required to help in various ways with the care of mentally ill people and people with learning difficulties within the community, and social workers have statutory duties under the 1983 Mental Health Act to assess and take appropriate action when mentally ill people appear to require compulsory hospitalization. The care of elderly and handicapped people in the community involves a need both for visiting to give support and advice, and for the assessment of special needs for services or aids. Where authorities employ occupational therapists they play an important part in assessing the needs of, and helping, disabled people. Authorities often also employ specialist social workers for blind people, and sometimes for deaf people. They may sub-contract these specialist services to voluntary agencies.

On the reorganization of the National Health Service in 1974 the local authority social services departments were given responsibility for hospital social work. This service evolved from two very different traditions. In connection with the more advanced mental hospitals a quite sophisticated psychiatric social work profession had developed, often leading the way in the provision of case work both within hospitals and among their out-patients. In the general hospitals, on the other hand, social work had its origins in the activities of the almoners required, before the coming of the National Health Service, to assess patients' capacities to pay fees. Once hospital treatment was free this group of social workers took on a variety of different jobs. In many cases they were regarded primarily as important links between hospitals and the community, and in particular therefore for arrangements with regard to the discharge of patients. Yet others, particularly in the more sophisticated hospitals, developed forms of case work and counselling, to help patients deal with the psychological and social problems that often accompany medical ones. Hospital social work therefore has very mixed traditions, and is very patchily developed today. Now an important issue for them is how to integrate with the community-based social work while remaining one of the professional groups involved in the hospital service (DHSS, 1974). They share this last problem with the social workers employed in the child guidance service, who are social services employees working alongside psychiatrists from the health service and psychologists from the education service, within administrative arrangements that are a product of local compromises between the three services involved.

Overall, fieldworkers are important 'gatekeepers' (see Foster, 1983) for a range of services provided by social services departments and related agencies. The new community care legislation is likely to enhance this role, with social workers and related ancillary staff designated as 'care managers' to determine access to providers.

FORWARD PLANNING, NEEDS AND PRIORITIES

The integration of the local authority social services occurred at a time when local government was becoming increasingly conscious of the need for forward planning, and for co-ordination between services by means of corporate planning. The new social services departments brought together services that had hitherto been poorly co-ordinated, and that had made relatively low demands on local authority resources. Clearly, the departments had to plan much more coherently for the future. Indeed, central government gave these new departments specific duties to carry out research and undertake forward planning. A similar increased emphasis upon planning was affecting the organization of central government. The Department of Health, which acquired responsibility for all the personal social services after their local reorganization, was required to assess the needs both of these services and of the health services, and to integrate the two.

The Department of Health initially required local authorities to prepare ten-year forward plans. Subsequently it was decided that such long-term plans could not be co-ordinated successfully at a national level. Moreover, the reorganization of local government, which followed only three years after the creation of social services departments, and the fairly dramatic change in public expenditure plans as a consequence of inflation and efforts to control it by curbing public spending, rendered these long-term plans comparatively irrelevant. They also had inevitable weaknesses as documents were prepared hurriedly, often with inadequate data and in advance of necessary research. In 1976 the Department of Health adopted a more limited but more systematic approach to forward planning. It required local authorities to provide figures on levels of provision and expenditure in the current year, estimates for the next year, and forecasts for two further years. This involved filling in a relatively straightforward form (which related well to the kind of information authorities were already assembling for their own budgeting needs) and supporting it by narrative comment. This exercise was sufficiently limited and precise to enable the Department of Health to assemble national data, make comparisons between authorities, and feed its observations back to local authorities. The new Conservative Government abandoned this exercise in 1980, probably largely because planned expenditure reductions would so limit growth as to make forward planning statements irrelevant.

An interesting feature of the abandoned exercise, and therefore of possible future ones, was the way in which the Department of Health tried to secure a more rational basis for loan sanctions based upon a balance between national and local priorities. The Department of Health expected local authorities to bear in mind its statements on national priorities (DHSS, 1976a) but to relate them to local ones. When it made decisions about the acceptability of new local initiatives, therefore, it endeavoured to relate its views about their compatibility with national policies to the evidence local authorities had provided about different local needs. Cynics within local government saw the planning system as a further Department of Health invasion of local autonomy. The Department of Health rejoinder was that, on the contrary, the system enabled it to be more sensitive to local needs. There was a conflict, of course, if local and national policies clashed, and there was no special evidence that local needs differed.

There were two important sources of complications for the planning process, both of which remain important despite the abandonment of a formal national system. One of these is the way in which the personal social services system under local authority control is inextricably bound up with the National Health Service. This issue will be explored further in a later section. The other is, as was seen when the relationship between public and private residential care was discussed, that the assessment of needs for social services is bedevilled by the fact that in many areas of this work the statutory services provide only a small part of the total care and support within the community. The total need for statutory residential or domiciliary services depends upon the other ways in which these needs, or their equivalents, are met. This means in fact that there is a confusing relationship between needs and the availability of services. The scarcity of social care produces not only heavy demands on the local authorities, but also extensive efforts to meet the need for it in other ways.

The new community care policies once again require local authorities to engage in planning exercises inevitably bringing in some of the considerations set out in the last paragraph. At the same time the increased central control over local authority finance (discussed in pp. 56–7) requires the centre to make clearer what it considers social services needs to be at the local level. There is an inevitable conflict, given that the grant to local authorities is largely non-specific, between this and local government autonomy.

The increased recognition in the 1980s of the limited funds available for public services, and the relationship between this and the growing needs for social care (as a result, for example, of the growth in numbers of the elderly) has sharpened concern to find ways of balancing the respective contributions to the 'mixed economy of welfare'. While this is sometimes presented as a new issue, social care has always involved some combination of care within the family and community, care which is bought, care which is provided by voluntary and charitable agencies, and care which is provided by public agencies. What is perhaps new is acceptance that the contribution from the last source is inherently limited. Hence the development of a lively debate about the roles of the other forms of care.

An important part of that debate concerns the search for ways of defining need, and identifying how public agencies should respond to it.

Economists have an approach to this issue. They tend to relate need to demand, and stress the virtue of the price mechanism as a means of adjusting services to demands. If there is a high demand for a particular thing then this will be reflected in a willingness to pay higher prices. Higher rewards will attract more suppliers, and may ultimately bring down the price. Always, however, an equilibrium is maintained in which supply and demand are balanced by the price mechanism. To what extent does this offer a solution to the problem of needs in the social services? Clearly, it does not if the local authority is the only supplier of a particular service or the controller of access to that service. Equally, it does not if that authority is the funder of the service for low-income people without the resources to purchase it themselves. Conditions of monopoly or near-monopoly then exist in which, in theory, the supplier can determine the price and those unable to pay must go without. The attempt to identify real needs regardless of ability to pay is the hallmark of the public service here. Rationing according to the capacity to pay is quite widely regarded as a bad way to distribute many such services. The price mechanism solution is also inappropriate where is it arguable that people who need particular services are unlikely to recognize the need and translate it into an effective, money-backed demand. Social work services designed primarily to protect children from their parents will fall into this category. However, there remain services, such as the home help service, that are provided both by the statutory authorities and by the private market. In some senses the need for these services can be regarded as fairly limitless – most of us would like our domestic chores to be done by someone else. The price mechanism seems to offer a basis for distinguishing this absolute need from effective demand, and of allowing for the existence, side by side, of a public and private sector.

This is all fair enough in theory, but what about those with high needs, in some absolute sense, but a low capacity to pay? There are two possible answers to this objection to the use of the price mechanism. One is that social affairs should be arranged in such a way that what are really income-maintenance problems do not have to be solved by the provision of subsidized services. This is an attractive argument, but one that matches poorly the real world. The other is that means tests should be devised to enable cheaper services to be given in some cases. The trouble with this latter solution is that it can cope with situations in which only a minority have to be helped outside the market place, but it quite destroys the market concept when it has to be very widespread. The reality is, for many of the personal social services (including the home help service), that some more fundamental way of defining need is required: a minority can buy the services on the open market; there remains a large group who appear to need them free or at a reduced price, only some of whom receive them. The problem remains of determining how much the service should expand to meet the unmet needs (see Judge, 1987; for a strong pro-pricing line, see Harris and Seldon, 1976).

This digression into the market approach to need was necessary, first, because it has significant advocates, and second, because it offers an approach to the definition of need. The alternative is to ascertain some more absolute way of determining need. In some cases this does not seem so problematical; in relation to some diseases, for example, there may be a finite group whom it is generally agreed are in need of treatment. But in other cases the problem is one of making a distinction between 'absolute need' and some more limited concept. While I may contend that I need my house cleaned in order to free me to write books, you may argue that I am still physically capable of doing this work while others are not. They, you will say, are the ones really in need. But would this be a disagreement about needs or about priorities?

For the personal social services, then, the determination of needs is complicated: (a) by the fact that the departments do not have the sole responsibility to meet certain kinds of needs, and (b) because their views of needs must be determined by their views of priorities. Neither of these problems are ones that can be solved by more and better research. Research may be required once they have begun to answer the more fundamental questions, but first they have to resolve difficult questions about the limits of the statutory social services' contribution to the solution of the social problems, and about the importance of any specific service relative to others.

These are dilemmas for all public policy, and particularly for all social policy. Finite resources require choices, in the last resort, between more education and more health services, for example. Within specific departments, and particularly within personal social services with their very mixed collection of services to various client groups, the weighing of priorities is a particularly difficult political exercise. This discussion of issues about the determination of need has been included in this chapter because of some particularly intractable problems about need for personal social services; it is, however, applicable to some degree to all the services discussed in this book.

These, then, are the fundamental problems for forward planning. But it would be misleading to suggest that departments, and committees, necessarily spend a great deal of time worrying about these issues. They are more likely to give attention to what are, in effect, second-order problems. How many people are there who are not getting help despite the fact that they are at least as disadvantaged as those who obtain services? To what extent does the authority's level of provision fail to meet the needs of people who are helped in other areas? Is it possible to identify specific consequences of help, or failure to help, in terms of family breakdown, hospitalization and so on? What alternative sources of help are there in the area and can these be supported as well as supplemented? Is the composition of the population who are helped changing in ways that will make the present package of services inappropriate in the future? The importance of questions like these should not be minimized, but they take place against a background of extreme uncertainty about needs, about the roles of social services departments in relation to those needs, and about the difficulty of what seem to be invidious judgements concerning the relative priorities to be accorded to various groups of needy people. These fundamental questions seem to call for political solutions. But politicians are reluctant to try to answer them: they often respond by providing roughly the mixture as before. In chapter 3 it was suggested, moreover, that the British form of democratic politics does not provide very satisfactory mechanisms for settling issues of this kind. Often the key issues are pushed back to the administrators and professionals, and believed to be matters for expert judgement. This is an issue that will be raised again in chapter 7 on the health service.

THE PLACE OF SOCIAL WORK IN THE SOCIAL SERVICES DEPARTMENTS

One of the most difficult elements for forward planning and priority determination within social services departments is that part of the service that is provided by social workers and related staff. It has already been suggested that many of the needs for social work help are seldom expressed, at least not in any straightforward sense. The pressures that lead to calls for more social work come from the anxieties of the public and politicians about child abuse, the deterioration of old people who live alone, or the disturbance caused by aggressive, mentally ill people, for example. These are issues of social control as much as of service. Pressure also comes from the many requests to social services departments that are not so much for specific services as for help with a wide range of problems of poverty and deprivation. Social work is seen as having a contribution to make to the problems of underprivileged communities in many different ways; indeed, often these expectations go far beyond the profession's capacities, particularly when political and economic problems are perceived as social or individual ones.

There is a wide but essential diffuse demand, therefore, for the services of social workers. Forward planning exercises in social services departments find it difficult to categorize the actual contribution made by social workers. Social workers, inasmuch as they seek to protect their day-to-day activities from hierarchical scrutiny and control, contribute to this imprecision. It is also fostered by their own uncertainty about their work, and by controversy within the profession about the essential ingredients of the social work task.

There has been an extensive debate about what social work is, and a related one about whether it can be practised within local authority social services departments. This seems to have various interlocking dimensions. There is a concern about the relationship between social work and a variety of, perhaps more mundane, supporting tasks that may be performed. Thus Butrym (1976, pp. 10–11) distinguishes between:

1   'provision for the quality of inner life', which she regards as the social work task, above all;
2   providing 'support and containment', which is partly a social work task but may also be performed by others including volunteers;
3   dealing with 'matters of right and entitlement', where social workers need to know of the services available but should not be concerned with the day-to-day administration;
4   dealing with other agencies, where the social worker's task is to transmit relevant needs 'to appropriate institutions and to press for necessary changes to policies'.

A British Association of Social Workers working party has similarly published an elaborate attempt to distinguish some of the more complex tasks which require special skills, including in particular skills in dealing with interpersonal relationships, from more mundane activities (BASW, 1977). A quasi-official investigatory committee which looked at this issue in response to growing criticism of social work broadly endorsed, in a report published in 1982, these attempts to distinguish a core of social work expertise from the wider activities surrounding it (Barclay, 1982).

But critics of social work have condemned the quasi-psychiatric emphasis in some of this theorizing, suggesting that above all social workers should give relatively straightforward and practical help to people trying to cope with problems of deprivation (Wootton, 1959; Sinfield, 1969). The significance of this debate is, first, its implications for the balance to be achieved by departments between the use of trained social work staff and the use of less-trained personnel (including perhaps volunteers). Secondly, if at the core of the social work task lies intensive work with individuals with special problems, to what extent can such work be done in public authorities and, if it can be done there, what arrangements need to be made to protect this case-work from the other pressures upon social work time? Thirdly, and alternatively, if a wide range of work with problems of deprivation is to be performed by social workers, how are the boundaries to this work to be determined, and what are its implications for relationships between social services departments and other agencies?

A related debate has concerned the extent to which, in working with an individualistic model of social pathology and a concern about deviation from 'normal' behaviour, social work may reinforce the status quo and encourage models of behaviour which are class- or race- or sexual-orientation-specific (Corrigan and Leonard, 1978; Williams, 1989).

The traditional model of social work, with its concern with individual problem-solving, sees as its key method 'case-work', requiring intensive relationships with individuals and families. But two other approaches to social work receiving increasing attention these days are 'group work' and 'community work'. To these should be added a fourth, an 'integrated' approach embracing all the other three approaches according to the demands of the situations (Specht and Vickery, 1977). Group work clearly has a place within the statutory framework for local authority social work. It has particularly taken the form of 'intermediate treatment', involving help to delinquent children through shared activities with others. The position of community work is more controversial. It involves working with the communities to help them solve their own problems. There is, however, a radical school of community work which stresses the importance of the mobilization of groups against the power structure in the community. There is scope for argument, first, as to whether this really is social work and, secondly, whether it has a place within the framework of the local authority social services department. Schools of social work offer community work training, or a community work option, to their students, but community workers are also trained in other ways. Local authorities employ community workers to some extent, and some authorities tolerate relatively radical activities. They vary in the extent to which they see a need to integrate this work with social work. This case for a more radical approach to social work is particularly pertinent where traditional case work methods come up against cultural differences, as in ethnic minority communities.

There is one further dimension to the debate about the social work task which must be mentioned here. Before the integration of local authority social services departments, many social workers specialized by client group; indeed, this specialization was determined largely by the department in which they worked. Part of the case for integration of the personal social services was the argument that social work involved skills usable with, or transferable to, varying client groups. The new generic departments matched a generic concept of social work. The initial problem for most departments was to get social workers from different backgrounds to work together. To this end the generic approach was emphasized. Once the achievement of integration was no longer an issue, social workers began to explore the scope for specialization within the generic department. This specialization may be in terms of methods of work, or in terms of kinds of problems tackled; but it may also be a return to client group specialization.

At the same time, however, an informal, *de facto* kind of specialization has developed within departments. Child-care work is particularly seen as deserving of expert attention. This may be attributed to a variety of things: the clear statutory requirement about visiting and reporting where the courts are involved with child-care problems; the very high anxieties raised within social work and the public at large by child abuse and neglect; and the importance within the departments of staff with children's department backgrounds. Mental health work is also seen as important in some areas, and its underlying significance is emphasized by the emergency powers possessed by social workers and by the recognition, in the 1983 Mental Health Act, of the need for special additional training for this work. Work with people who are handicapped or elderly, on the other hand, is seen as less pressing and more routine. The consequence is that child-care work and mental health work is regarded as requiring the attention of the most experienced qualified staff, while the other activities are more readily delegated to others, where social work teams contain both qualified staff and some social work assistants (or social service officers). Matching this division of 'skill' there tends to be a division of work on the lines suggested above. Often social work assistants are the only 'specialists' in work with elderly people.

Recently, attempts have been made to ensure that real specialization occurs in social services departments as opposed to this *de facto* specialization with its unfortunate assumptions about kinds of clients and levels of work. However, the argument for and against specialization continues to be a live one. One movement back against specialization has emphasized the need for social workers to relate to small areas or 'patches' (Hadley and McGrath, 1981). This derives its strength from the concerns with community work or with 'integrated' work discussed above.

THE RELATIONSHIP BETWEEN THE PERSONAL SOCIAL SERVICES AND INCOME MAINTENANCE

Some of the functions that today are within the social services departments have at earlier times been within local authority health, education or even housing departments. However, further back in time, before 1948, there was a strong association between the personal social services and income maintenance within the poor law. It is worthwhile to look a little more at the separation that exists today between these two services, and at some of the factors that partially undermine that separation, particularly because they have important implications for some of the dilemmas about the social work role.

The political commitment, in the 1940s, to separating income maintenance from the personal social services was influenced by a hatred of the poor law. It was seen as possible to develop services for all freed from the stigma of the means test and the workhouse if the National Assistance Act of 1948 gave all income-maintenance responsibilities to a national body and the duty to provide residential and domiciliary care to the local authorities. The services for children were given a quite distinct identity by the Children Act of 1948, and developed their own special approach to community care within the children's departments of the local authorities. A concept of social work was able to develop, very different from that within the American welfare departments where income maintenance and social work are closely linked. Social workers, regardless of their political persuasion, have come to see it as very important that they are able to give aid, advice and support to their clients without at the same time having responsibility for their incomes. What this implies is that, whereas personal social services under the poor law were essentially for the poor and were very involved in the control of the lives of the poor, today in the British system it is possible to conceive of the benefits of the services as available to all without discrimination.

That, then, is the ideal; the reality is a little different (Jordan, 1974; Hill and Laing, 1979). It is clearly the case that a very high proportion of the users of the personal social services are low-income people. It is quite hard to envisage a situation in which it could be otherwise. The peculiarity of the personal social services is that they are concerned with a range of benefits that is also provided in other very different ways, by both commercial enterprises and voluntary activities. The very existence of a statutory group of services of this kind poses some delicate questions about the nature of the balance between this and individual, family and community provisions. The assumption is that the statutory provisions are necessary when the others fail. Politicians get worried about the possibility that private responsibilities will be abandoned in favour of public ones. This is possible; it is in the nature of statutory intervention into areas generally the realm of private action that it may alter behaviour. However, the evidence is that typically those who seek help from the personal social services do so when other possibilities no longer exist. An absence of other ways of meeting such needs is particularly associated with poverty.

Several connections between income maintenance and the personal social services therefore exist. Many of the services are rationed by means of charges, motivated at least partially by that political concern to keep down the expected volume of demands upon the service. If charges are not to deter the poor, however, they must be abated through means tests. These need to be related to the other means tests within the social security system. That is one connection; the other is more complicated and more clearly explains the social work concern about separation of their services from income maintenance. There is a correlation between the forms of pathology that come to the attention of social workers – delinquency, child abuse, even publicly threatening mental illness – and poverty (Holman, 1978). It is difficult to summarize here a very complex, and deeply value-laden, debate. Strands within it include arguments about the extent to which the rich can hide their pathology, or seek help from sources other than social services departments; about the extent to which poverty *causes* social pathology and vice versa; and about the extent to which this 'deviancy' simply involves a labelling of the non-conformity of the poor. The fact is, however, that it is primarily low-income people who become the clients of publicly employed social workers.

It is this fact that leads many who have written about social work to stress the importance of a relationship with the poor that does not include responsibility for their incomes (Jordan, 1974). Yet at the same time many social workers recognize a need to help clients with their income-maintenance problems. There is a power under the 1989 Children Act (carried forward and enlarged from earlier legislation dating in the first place from 1963) and under a related but rather more all-embracing provision in Scotland, enabling money payments to be made to help social services clients where these might assist in keeping children out of care. Here, then, is a statutory recognition of a connection between lack of money and social pathology. Yet this power is comparatively little used, and several writers have drawn attention to the danger that it might be used to reward good behaviour and become a social control device within social work (ibid.; also Handler, 1973). In general, an alternative approach is preferred in which social workers assist clients to claim benefits from other agencies. Such work is generally described as 'welfare rights work'. To some degree, in many authorities, specialist workers, who are often not social workers, have been taken on to do this sort of work. There has also been a considerable growth of aid and advice work on welfare benefit problems in voluntary agencies and advice bureaux. However, social workers are bound to have to take on some of this work; some do with great commitment while others feel it will distort their activities and pull them away from 'real' social work.

The character of welfare rights workers has changed as the social security system has changed. Before 1980 the concern was to get supplementary benefits officers to exercise their extensive discretionary powers. After 1980 the complex structure of apparent 'rights' required that poor people secured help in finding their way through the regulations, identifying things to which they were entitled and getting the increasingly hard-pressed social security administration to grind into action. The social security changes brought in by the 1986 Act has thrown the social workers and welfare rights specialists into turmoil. Rights to single payments have more or less disappeared. The new Social Fund scheme seems to require social services personnel to replace the conflictual pattern of behaviour required to secure rights by collaboration with social security officers to determine need for 'community care' grants. The loans provisions for other forms of help, administered by officers with high levels of discretion, similarly suggest a need for a very different approach to getting resources for clients. The position is further complicated by the fact that social services departments retain their power to make grants described above. In practice this power is little used, and most departmental budgets for this item are limited. If this were to change, or if social workers are co-opted into helping determine needs for Social Fund grants and loans, social workers could be back to money-rationing responsibilities in a big way. This development was feared when the Social Fund was introduced; in practice social workers seem to have coped with the conflict, very often by turning a deaf ear to material needs.

THE ROLE OF THE VOLUNTARY SECTOR

Reference has already been made to the 'mixed economy of welfare'. In this voluntary agencies are, alongside family, community and private enterprise, an element of considerable importance. Voluntary organizations carry out many functions on behalf of social services departments. These entail large grants, and in some cases the voluntary component of the work is small. Thus some departments use a voluntary agency to provide a range of services to blind people. A service widely provided in this way, but involving a large component of voluntary work, is the 'meals-on-wheels' service. The Women's Royal Voluntary Service is often responsible for this. Social service departments also help to support the activities of voluntary organizations. These range from large organizations offering special forms of residential and domiciliary care to quite small local community ventures. While some of this work may be meeting needs that would otherwise be met by the departments, in many cases the voluntary ventures that are subsidized undertake tasks that are quite distinct, and perhaps innovatory. As noted above, the new community care legislation will inevitably further enhance this voluntary organization involvement.

There is a variety of ways in which individual volunteers are used in the personal social services. They may be deployed under the auspices of voluntary agencies. They may be organized under schemes requiring community services of convicted offenders, or schemes to provide work for the unemployed in return for special allowances (should those in these two categories properly be called volunteers?); or they may be individuals who undertake, by direct arrangements with the departments, to help with particular tasks. A wide range of tasks may be involved: supportive visiting of clients; taking people from residential homes out in cars; helping social services clients with decorating or gardening; helping to run clubs and day centres, and so on.

All this voluntary input into the personal social services may be seen as helping to multiply the amount and range of services available for a given amount of public expenditure. It may also be seen as adding a community dimension to a service that is in danger of becoming too bureaucratized and professionalized. Some of it is a logical extension of the way in which the personal social services are called in to replace or buttress independent caring in the community. It may be seen in this way as helping to put back a community support system that, in the best of all worlds, should have been there.

However, there are problems about this balance between statutory effort and voluntary effort. It may be seen as a way of achieving personal social services 'on the cheap', with departments helping to provide partial and inadequate voluntary services instead of meeting their obligations to provide more comprehensive, direct ones.

While above it was suggested that volunteer services may be better than bureaucratic or professional ones, they may alternatively be worse. Social workers who are reluctant to make use of volunteers suggest that they may be unreliable, they may be indiscreet, they may give gratuitous advice where none is desired, and they may give bad advice and interfere in problems they do not understand (Holme and Maizels, 1978). Voluntary help often comes from people who are very unlike the people who need help – groups such as middle-class, middle-aged, married women are prominent among the ranks of volunteers.

It may be argued that what is needed in many situations is the development of community-based self-help activities, not the importation of volunteers from outside. On the other hand it would be rash to suggest that this form of voluntary activity is without its problems. Some of the points about reliability and discretion certainly apply to it. Equally, encouraging situations in which communities help themselves may also be seen as providing social services on the cheap. If it is not to be seen like this then another problem must be confronted: that community self-help may also entail making demands for new services from the departments. This form of voluntary activity may therefore imply situations in which departments subsidize their own pressure groups. Some social services departments have been able to accept relationships with the voluntary sector that involve this. However, many others have been unwilling to see volunteers in other than traditional, supplementary, service-giving roles.

The Relationship between the Personal Social Services and the Health Service

In many respects the concerns of the health service and those of the social services departments overlap. The following are a few key examples. In the planning of services attention has been given to the way in which people are likely to require mixtures of health care and social care. In this example what is particularly relevant is the modern concern to maximize care within the community rather than inside institutions. What this implies is a combination of medical care from general practitioners and community-based nursing staff, on the one hand, and social care, from home helps, social workers and so on, on the other. Deficiencies on either side may have to be made up by extra services on the other.

The discharge of patients from hospital in itself has substantial implications for personal social services provision. It is important that social support services are readily available at this stage. Hence day-to-day co-ordination between the two services is crucial. Reference has already been made to the extent to which discharge of people from geriatric wards will have implications for residential homes. Conversely, when old people's homes can no longer cope with their sickest inhabitants hospital services need to be readily accessible.

A very different example of the need for inter-service co-ordination and co-operation is supplied by the problem of child abuse. Non-accidental injury to children is frequently discovered by doctors and health visitors, yet it is the social services departments that have the responsibility for preventative and legal action in these circumstances. On the other hand, where social workers suspect child abuse they may need medical confirmation of their suspicions. Once child abuse is suspected continued vigilance is necessary. Sometimes it is a health service worker who is best placed to maintain a watching brief, sometimes it is a social worker. In many cases both departments accumulate evidence on this problem; it is important that they share that evidence both formally through case conferences and informally (Hallett and Stevenson, 1979).

These are just a few examples of situations in which the relationship between the two services is significant. Many others could be given, both where joint planning of services is important and where joint action and cross-referral is required. Their importance has led the Department of Health to encourage, and the local agencies to adopt, a variety of means of developing links.

At the service planning level the Department of Health has led the way by emphasizing the need to look at the health service and personal social services together. Within individual localities they have encouraged the development of formal joint planning activities. A particular stimulus to this has been provided by 'joint financing'. Money from within the health service budget is made available to social services departments to help finance projects to meet needs that might otherwise have to be met by the health service. In the long run social services departments are expected to take over the full cost of these ventures. However, where positive progress can be made in shifting people from institutional to community care a more direct transfer of resources from health to personal social services may occur.

There is nevertheless still concern about the extent to which the boundaries between the NHS and local government hinder the development of integrated community care. Hence the highlighting of this theme in the government's new approach to community care.

CONCLUSIONS

The responsibilities of the social services departments, in England and Wales, involve a wide collection of activities. These range from the provision of relatively precise benefits, through a variety of residential and day-care facilities, to a number of very personal and individualized services. They include a high proportion of the social work practised in this country.

This mixture of activities has grown rapidly. This growth is perceived with quite considerable anxiety by the public, since most of the activities were hitherto undertaken outside the statutory sector, within the family and the community. One interpretation of this growth is that public services can now be provided to help to strengthen family and community life. If this view is taken then residential care replaces the neglect of the isolated old, and social work helps families to cope with crises that would hitherto have destroyed them, and so on. But there is an alternative view that the growth in these services is in itself an index of social pathology, that people are not coping so well with aspects of life that in the past were of little concern to public services. This ambivalence is compounded by widespread uncertainty about what social services departments do (indeed, they are often confused with social security departments), a very vague conception of the social worker's role (shared, it seems, by many social workers), and a deep uncertainty about the circumstances under which help may be sought from the various specific services.

In the 1990s will the implementation of the new community care policies clarify the position, or will the complexities of the notion of the purchaser/provider split, together with increases in the range of occasions in which resource constraints force the denial of services, heighten the confusion?

Suggestions for Further Reading

Two general books on the personal social services which are recommended are Christine Hallett's *The Personal Social Services in Local Government* (1982) and Adrian Webb and Gerald Wistow's *Social Work, Social Care and Social Planning: The Personal Social Services since Seebohm* (1987). Books by Judge (1987) and Booth (1979) also deal with many of the financial and planning issues in this area of policy. At the time of writing, with the community care changes still being implemented, there will be a need to await for a while yet an account which will fully take them on board. The White Paper (HMSO, 1989) offers a clear official version of its objectives.

The Barclay report (1982) on the social work task gives a portrait of the activities of fieldwork teams, as does Goldberg and Warburton's *Ends and Means in Social Work* (1979). A variety of different perspectives on what the social work task should comprise are provided in the books by Butrym (1976), Specht and Vickery (1977), Jordan (1974) and Corrigan and Leonard (1978).

The issue of the 'mixed economy of welfare' is explored in an article by Judge (1982). Issues about community care and public expenditure in the social services have been explored in Webb and Wistow's *Planning, Need and Scarcity* (1986) and in Glennerster's *Paying for Welfare* (1985).

CHAPTER 7

The Health Service

THE ORGANIZATION OF THE SERVICE

By contrast with the beginning of chapter 6 on the personal social services, the first part of this chapter needs to be less concerned with what the service does – people are relatively clearer about this – but more concerned with how it does it, and particularly how it is organized. Clearly, the ingredients of the health service are hospitals, the family or primary care practitioners (doctors, dentists, pharmacists and opticians operating outside the hospitals), and other community-based services (community nursing and health visiting, and preventive medicine). One of the most confusing aspects of the health service is the structure that has been designed to contain, and hopefully integrate, these various activities.

The basic structure of the system within England can be represented diagrammatically, as in Figure 7.1. At the top the health service is the responsibility of the Secretary of State for Health who is assisted in this task by a Policy Board, which he or she chairs. Then, to deal with operational matters there is a Management Executive chaired by a Chief Executive. In this way the government has departed from the normal top civil service control structure and created a system which seems to mimic a private company.

England is divided into fourteen regions. In addition to planning and advisory responsibilities, the Regional Health Authorities (RHAs) have a range of executive responsibilities for the health service: the appointment of specialist medical staff (except in the NHS Trust hospitals, see below) and the planning and management of capital expenditure in particular. The District Health Authorities (DHAs), of which there are 192 in England, have overall responsibility for the planning and provision of comprehensive services in the territories they cover. It will be seen from the diagram that at that level there are also separate

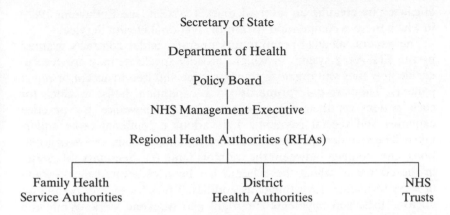

FIGURE 7.1   Basic structure of the health service in England

Family Health Service Authorities (FHSAs) responsible for primary care.

The Districts are concerned with day-to-day running of the hospital and community services (but not general practitioner services). Within the districts there are sub-divisions for administrative purposes, known as units. In addition, in many districts, there are, since the legislation of 1990 which modified the structure of the health service, National Health Service Trusts. These are semi-autonomous bodies, ultimately answerable to the Secretary of State through the relevant RHA, able to manage their own finances, appoint their own staff and plan a package of services which they 'sell' to DHAs. They may also engage in private work. Most of these are hospitals or groups of hospitals, but in some cases community units have become trusts. Since 1991 there has been a steady growth in the numbers of trusts, and it is possible that this will become the pattern for the service as a whole. The Labour Opposition has attacked trusts as the thin end of the wedge of privatization (we will return to this theme below). Meanwhile the current mixed structure of operational units and trusts is managed on a basis which is described as a purchaser/provider basis. What this means is that the DHAs are required to enter into specific contracts with units and trusts to secure the services needed for the patients in their area. The providers engaged in this way need not necessarily be in the DHA's geographical patch. In addition, general medical practitioners are allowed to apply to become 'fund holders' who can make independent arrangements with hospital providers for the needs of their own patients. This last aspect of the new scheme is, at the time of writing, but little developed. Overall, the government's aim is to enhance efficiency by creating an internal market system (see Enthoven, 1985) in which there is competition within the National Health Service.

The general medical practitioners operate, under contracts granted by the FHSAs, a system in which, broadly speaking, they are free to decide how they will organize their practice and free to accept or reject patients. They are paid primarily on a 'capitation' basis, so much for each patient on their list together with an allowance for practice expenses and special payments for various exceptional tasks undertaken. The system of payments has been the subject of extensive negotiations and conflict between the doctors and the Secretary of State, in the course of which the scheme has been elaborated in a variety of ways to include such things as additional fees for elderly people on doctors' lists, and payments for night and weekend work. While the doctors have clearly been eager to secure maximum rewards but to remain within a system that preserves their freedom, the government's objectives in these negotiations have included the encouragement of forms of group practice, the development of health centres and an increase in the number of doctors practising in some areas. In the last few years the general practitioner service has grown much more sophisticated. Isolated independent practice has declined, and health centres, providing a wide range of medical services, have multiplied.

Opticians and pharmacists are paid on a fee-for-service basis. The complications over maintenance of lists do not apply in their cases. However, there are some problems, particularly as far as dentists are concerned, about setting up a system of remuneration that rewards most adequately the best practice, is administratively straightforward and can be supervised without detailed surveillance of day-to-day activities.

The dental, optical and pharmaceutical services are, like general medical practice, administered by the FHSAs. These have responsibilities to see that the various services are available in their district, to help patients obtain practitioners and to deal with complaints.

Prior to reorganization in 1974 the local authorities provided some of the community health services, under the direction of the medical officers of health. They were responsible for community nursing services, running maternity clinics, measures to prevent the spread of infectious diseases, and a range of public health responsibilities (controls against impure foods, insanitary living conditions, and so on). There was also a separate school health service, although usually the medical officer of health was also in charge of this. Reorganization left the district councils with the public health responsibilities, but shifted all other services under the wings of the health authorities.

The service reorganization of 1982 and the introduction of the changed system of management has rather dispersed this 'community health' group of activities. In 1974 one possibility was that community medicine would assume a key role in the planning of the service, extending concerns about preventive medicine. Now such specialists are rarely found in key management roles. The community nursing services remain in some areas within district management units, but in others have been dispersed into units also containing hospital staff. At local levels there has been some scope for the development of 'primary care teams', groups of health service workers based upon a health centre and sharing a common clientele. But at that level community teamwork is made more difficult by the independence of the general medical practitioners. However, the latter may employ nurses in their surgeries, and recently the government has provided them with incentives to provide health checks for their patients.

In Scotland and Wales responsibility for the service is that of separate ministers (the Secretaries of State for Scotland and Wales) and separate departments. This devolved structure enables the omission of the regional tier in the system. In Scotland the next tier authorities are called health boards, and most of them have another tier of districts under them. In Northern Ireland there are four health and social services boards with 'area' responsibilities, each responsible for a number of units. Overall, in the other countries of the United Kingdom, the service and management arrangements are broadly the same as those for England.

Until the 1980s the managerial arrangements for the NHS could have been described as broadly 'collegial', that is, the various professionals within the service were represented in the management structure. Then, after 1983, each region, district and unit was required to appoint a general manager, on a fixed term contract. Many of these general managers were already health service administrators, but there were appointments from outside and in a few cases senior professionals, particularly doctors but occasionally nurses, have received these posts. These managers were accountable to the relevant appointed authorities. Then, under the changes enacted in 1990, the RHAs and DHAs themselves were restructured to comprise up to five 'executive members', who include the general manager and the finance director, and five non-executive members (including a non-executive chairman). FHSAs were given a similar structure.

Hospital doctors have traditionally exercised a considerable degree of autonomy. Crucial for this is the concept of clinical freedom, which can be effectively extended from a right to determine the treatment of individual patients to a right to plan the pattern of care as a whole. The new managerial arrangements, and the significance of the contracting system for patterns of work, seem to threaten that freedom. It is hard to say how significant that threat is; a great deal will depend upon the arrangements made to involve the doctors in management within the units and trusts.

Consultants may be part-time appointees, enabled to combine private practice with NHS work. Junior hospital doctors, below consultant status, are organized in consultant-led teams. Many of them are in short-term appointments, which are seen as building-blocks of trainee experience leading up to consultant status. There are problems of relatively low pay, heavy duties and insecurity for junior doctors, enhanced by difficulties in advancing to consultancies.

The access of patients to the hospital system is normally by way of a general practitioner referral, though direct self-referral is acceptable in the event of accidents and emergencies. Once under hospital care individuals may be treated as in-patients or out-patients. The general notion here is of a hospital-based service for problems that are beyond either the expertise or resources of general practitioners and the 'primary care' teams. However, the lines are sometimes blurred. Modern health centres can often provide services that are elsewhere provided by hospitals. The arrangements for general practice budget holders may further encourage this development. Community hospitals provide, in some areas, limited service of a kind traditionally provided by 'cottage hospitals', and they may involve general practitioners in their work.

The NHS is financed out of national taxation. In 1990–1 (HMSO, 1992), in the United Kingdom it cost about £7.7 billion (after the recouping of charges). Of this, 76 per cent was spent on hospital and community services, 20 per cent on family practitioner services and the remaining 4 per cent on a miscellaneous group of centrally run services. Throughout its history the growth of the cost of the health service to the Exchequer has been a matter of political concern. Demographic changes, affecting need, technological changes, affecting the quality of treatment, and rising staff costs mean that the cost of the NHS increases without there necessarily being any improvement in the service it provides. Attempts have been made to estimate how much expenditure has to grow each year merely to maintain a consistent level of services to the public. A conservative estimate puts it at 2 per cent, but many suggest it is nearer 4 or 5 per cent (Robinson and Judge, 1987; see also the discussion of this difficult and controversial subject in Hills (ed.), 1990, ch. 4). This is important in explaining how, in recent years, we have found both the public and NHS practitioners complaining of falling standards, supported by concrete evidence from increasing waiting lists for operations, whilst governments claim they are spending more, in real terms, than ever before on the health service. This is a theme to which we will return when we look at trends in public expenditure in the final chapter.

Charges to recipients of services bring some money back to the health service. The figure above of £27.7 billion spent on the service is a net figure, the gross figure was £29.1 billion. All receipts thus account for about 5 per cent of the health service's gross budget, and a little over three-quarters of these are charges to patients. Charges cover part of the cost of the supply of drugs, medical appliances, spectacles, and dental treatment. They are not applied to hospital in-patients or to children and the elderly. There are means tests that enable low-income people to secure the remission of charges.

NEED AND THE RATIONING OF THE HEALTH SERVICE

The British health service is thus, broadly speaking, free and universally available. The general issues raised by the absence of a price mechanism to convert needs into effective demands was discussed in chapter 6 on the personal social services. One of the political preoccupations ever since the founding of the National Health Service has been the apparently limitless character of need.

There seem to be two crucial problems that were given insufficient attention by those who forecast a decline in need for health services. One is that everyone whose life is saved lives on to become ill again. More precisely, increases in life expectancy bring with them the likelihood of increased work for the service in dealing with the chronic illnesses that particularly affect the elderly. Even without the benefits of the health service the elderly would be a growing proportion of the population during the last decades of this century. The other is, again, the difficulty about defining need. There is a growing understanding that the relationship between having a medical need and seeking medical attention is complex and obscure. Individuals may experience considerable suffering from a condition that manifests no pathological abnormality. Conversely, they may have serious medical problems and yet experience little suffering. Perhaps more significantly, in quantitative terms, minor deviations from 'good health' are tolerated by many people for long periods of time without medical attention being sought. This applies, for example, to problems like indigestion, recurrent headaches and skin complaints. The evidence is therefore that:

> As a result of several epidemiological enquiries, using many different methods and many different definitions, we have become aware (surprising as this may seem) that the medical services deal with only a rather small proportion of the symptoms of disease experienced by members of the community. (Tuckett, 1976)

There is a choice between the policy conclusions to be drawn from these findings. One is that a great deal more should be spent on the health service, and in particular many more efforts should be made to screen for unidentified illness in the population. The quite opposite view is that the fact that many people manage without medical treatment for many complaints suggests that those who do 'bother' doctors about similar problems should be encouraged to become more self-reliant and to make more use of self-medication. A less extreme version of this view suggests that, since medical resources are clearly limited, it is important to control access to the services in such a way that the more serious complaints are treated, while doctors are not overburdened with the trivial. At the moment the system depends primarily on general practitioners' judgements for this necessary filtering process. Are there ways of pushing the responsibility for it back to the patients? This provides one argument for the exploration of the case for a charging system to control demands upon the service.

A case for health service charges is also argued in terms of the desirability of choice and competition. This has been made most cogently in the United States by Eliot Friedson (1970), who sees the power of the consumer as enhanced by a relationship with the doctor in which he or she has the capacity to 'hire or fire'. For Friedson the English model of health service organization places individuals in a very weak position in dealing with doctors, and provides the community at large with an absence of weapons for bargaining with a medical profession that would not be so united were doctors in competition with each other. The new purchaser/provider system is designed to try to come part way to solving this problem, but of course it does not give the 'hire or fire' power directly to the consumer.

The fundamental point in favour of a free service is that charges may deter people from seeking necessary help (Abel-Smith, 1976). This is, as suggested in the previous chapter, particularly likely to be the case when incomes are low. Moreover, one of the effects of ill health is naturally to reduce income and to increase other costs. The issue at stake is not simply therefore one of inequality in general, but specifically of inequality between the sick and the well (regardless of other determinants of their income and expenditure). Clearly also, while in other areas of life people may be expected to make choices between different ways of spending money, serious illness leaves little choice. Individuals will bankrupt themselves to save their lives, and those of their loved ones.

Where much of the health service is still 'in the market place', as for example in the United States, the issues are rarely actually as stark as these. There are two reasons why they are not. One is that many people insure themselves against sickness. The other is that a 'safety net' means-tested medical system exists for the poor. Arguments in favour of a free service must therefore deal with the weaknesses of these two alternative forms of provision.

The key problems with insurance schemes are that they will not insure the 'bad risks', they often exclude some conditions (especially preventable ones, for example pregnancy), and they may collapse. While it is true that these schemes may reduce the powers of doctors, who are dependent upon the patronage of the insurance agencies, they do not necessarily curb trivial demands since subscribers may be determined to obtain their money's worth. It is however the exclusion of certain groups from insurance cover that is the main problem. In the 1980s the case for an insurance-based approach to health care re-emerged on the political agenda. Private insurance schemes had grown rapidly, facilitating the growth of private hospitals (Higgins, 1988). Debate developed, therefore, about the extension of these schemes nationwide. The case for such a new approach involves suggesting that individuals might be required to insure themselves privately, and that the state might underwrite such schemes and make special means-tested provision for those for whom they cannot cater. It was given very serious attention by the Conservatives in their review of policy before their 1990 changes to the system.

The problems with a means-tested health service are: the requirement of a test of means before treatment; the likelihood of situations in which individuals will have to abandon resources – or wait to 'hit the bottom' – before they can get treatment; and the probability that (as was the case in Britain when such a system operated) two classes of health service will exist. In the last resort, as implied above, the case for a free service is not that it helps to distribute resources from the rich to the poor, but that it enables the healthy to support the sick. If it is believed, on the other hand, that it is in the interests of the evolution of society that the 'weak should go to the wall' it will of course be comparatively easy to take an alternative view.

EQUALITY OF TREATMENT WITHIN THE HEALTH SERVICE

In the atmosphere of concern about rising health service costs and advocacy of privatization by the New Right there is considerable concern in Britain on two related issues: the most appropriate relationship between the health service and the residual private medical sector, and the extent to which the health service provides equality of treatment to all the population.

These two issues are related, since the diversion of medical resources into a private sector, largely accessible only to the better-off, reduces the resources available to other sectors of the population. However, the defenders of private medicine argue that the resources involved are, in a sense, extra ones, which would not necessarily be diverted into public medicine in an entirely nationalized sector. Particular bones of contention, however, have been not so much the right of the private sector to exist, as the support that sector receives from a variety of special links with the health service.

Both general practitioners and consultants are able to take on private patients as well as health service ones, and now National Health Service Trusts may venture even more boldly into private services for patients from home or abroad. This enables health service resources to be used in various ways in support of private medicine. It facilitates the undertaking of public and private work side-by-side, the use of public resources (such as expensive equipment) for private patients, and 'queue-jumping' when public beds are scarce. Moreover, situations arise in which it is possible for doctors to say to people that, while health service treatment will be inadequate, or long delayed, they may secure a better deal by becoming private patients.

The growth of private insurance raises the question of the overall impact on the state service of alternative ones. Is there scope here for desirable competition? Is it a valuable addition to consumer choice, enabling people who are so inclined to pay a little extra for a superior service? Or does it threaten the basic service, and reduce its capacity to meet the needs of all?

The health service's capacity to meet need has been subjected to extensive scrutiny. Epidemiological studies of the differential impact of mortality and morbidity have been of importance here. These show considerable differences in the experience of ill health between different regions of the country, between different social classes (Townsend, Davidson and Whitehead, 1988), and between different ethnic groups. The statistics on infant deaths have been given particular attention. Twice as many children of unskilled workers die in the first month of life as children of professional workers. The infant mortality rate (deaths in the first year of life by 1000 live births) varies widely from region to region. The Royal Commission on the NHS quoted figures on this for 1977. The highest rates were 17.2 in Northern Ireland, 16.1 in Scotland, and 15.5 in the Yorkshire region. The lowest were 11.2 in East Anglia and 11.6 in South West Thames region (HMSO, 1979). Statistics for districts would have shown even greater disparities. Similar evidence can be adduced from studies of illness experience in other age groups.

The policy question this evidence raises obviously concern, first, the extent to which these differentials are attributable to differences in the availability of health services; and, secondly, inasmuch as they are attributable to other factors (low income, poor housing and so on), to what extent better health services can and should offset these disadvantages. On a narrow interpretation of the first of these questions there is evidence of differences between different parts of the country in terms of the availability of health care. There are variations both between and within regions. Similar disparities may be noted in numbers of doctors and other health service practitioners per head. It should, however, be stressed that these figures do not clearly correlate with the data on mortality. Expenditure on health care and numbers of doctors needs to be related to the differential incidence of needs, taking into account such factors as the age structure of the population.

The government, after the first reorganization of the health service, set up a Resource Allocation Working Party (RAWP) required to develop a formula to facilitate comparisons between the resource needs of different regions. This has used population estimates weighted to take into account differential mortality and different utilization rates based upon differences in the age and the structure of the population (DHSS, 1976b). Allocation of new money to the regions has been based upon the RAWP formula, and allocations by regions to districts are based upon similar principles.

This has proved a difficult and controversial exercise in the light of the inadequacy of the statistics available, the difficulties in relating such data to needs and the uncertainty about the relationship between costs and effectiveness.

While this effort to tackle some of the problems of 'territorial injustice' that have beset the National Health Service since its foundation has been widely welcomed, there are some other issues about the availability of services that require attention. Social class differentials in the use of health services suggest that efforts need to be made not only to ensure that adequate resources are available in underprivileged areas but also to facilitate access to those resources by all in need. This raises policy questions about the siting of surgeries and hospitals, the arrangements made by doctors to enable patients to secure appointments, the extent of the use of health service personnel – such as health visitors – who actively seek out those in need of health care, the extent of health education, and the significance of screening services (such as in industry).

Finally, these questions lead on to the other question raised: the extent to which there might be an expectation that health services should be better in some areas, or for some people, to help to compensate for other social disadvantages. The opposite is generally the case in Britain; there is a correlation between poor health services and other social, economic and environmental deficiencies. To what extent should the concept of a state health service embrace a responsibility to point out how other social factors contribute to ill health?

These last questions have led some critics of the National Health Service to say that it is really a 'national illness service' (HMSO, 1979, p. 15). Academic studies of the health progress of the nation have suggested that changes in the environment and in behaviour have been more important than medical advances (McKeown, 1980).

There is a number of interrelated approaches to the prevention of ill-health. Healthy lifestyles may be regarded as a matter of personal choice. It is evident that many people have become aware of the need for exercise and the need for a healthy diet. Yet lifestyle options may be influenced by income and environment, constraining choices. They may also be influenced by the practices of the food and drink industry, the additives they use and the things their advertisements promote. Other aspects of our living and working environments may be quite outside our control. It may be argued that governments have important regulatory responsibilities to help protect our health. The limited list above of points about this vast subject indicates that the health of the nation depends upon much more than the efforts of the NHS.

THE REPRESENTATION AND PROTECTION OF THE PUBLIC

When the formation of the National Health Service was debated in the years before 1948 many doctors made clear their opposition to local government control. While some community services were kept within local government between 1948 and 1974, the main forms chosen for the local control of the health service were hybrid organizations in which ministerial appointees served alongside local authority nominees. Since 1991 these arrangements for direct local government representation on health service governing bodies have disappeared. Public representation is therefore only at the national government level.

An interesting innovation in 1974 was the setting up of community health councils (CHCs) to enable the public viewpoint to be expressed. But the status of these bodies is as officially recognized and subsidized pressure-groups, with rights to make representations and to seek information. Such power as they have primarily rests upon their capacity to embarrass health authorities. Even in relation to this weapon, they have an awkward choice to make between seeking a close day-to-day working relationship which may inhibit its use, and remaining more aloof but losing opportunities to secure information and to make informal representations. One other point not to be forgotten about CHCs is that they are not themselves representative bodies in any of the senses in which that term is used in democratic theory. Half their members are appointed by local authorities and one-sixth by the

RHAs; the remainder are elected by relevant voluntary organizations (by means of rather haphazard election processes which do nothing to ensure that they are representative of the patients in their areas).

This, then, is the pattern of public representation within the health service. Those who advocate bringing the service under local authority control are unlikely to secure a shift now, both against professional opposition and against a structure of organization that fits ill with the pattern of local government in many parts of Great Britain.

However, for many members of the public what matters more than representation is protection from abuse and malpractice, and the chance to be heard when dissatisfied with the service provided. Apart from the general opportunities to make representations, which apply to all the public services, there is, for the health service, a number of special procedures available. Practitioners and hospitals may be sued for tort damages, and professional malpractice may result in debarment from practice by the relevant professional organization. Patients may complain to the FHSAs that practitioners have acted in breach of their terms of service, and penalties may be imposed including, at worst, 'sacking' from health service employment. Complaints against hospitals may be formally investigated by the DHA, and exceptionally the Secretary of State may order an inquiry. Examples of the latter have thrown important light upon weaknesses in the hospitals for mentally ill and handicapped people. Finally, a patient may complain to the health service commissioner, though the powers of this official broadly preclude investigations in areas where other forms of investigation or litigation are available.

There is thus no absence of avenues for further action by individuals with grievances. However, the multiplicity of procedures is confusing to patients; and all involve very formal approaches which deter action. This formality is regarded as important for the protection of vulnerable professionals from frivolous complaints. But the general problem here is that evidence that things are going wrong in particular parts of the service, particularly the family practitioner parts, does not come to light easily, and thus attract corrective action, when complaints involved are insufficiently serious to activate the formal machinery. Community health councils may contribute to the correction of problems of this kind, through the accumulation of evidence on grievances brought to their attention or through surveys of patients' experiences. Their lack, however, of formal powers implies that they must then seek to influence the behaviour and practices of staff who see themselves as accountable to no one. This is a challenge to CHC subtlety and tactical skill.

There is one other source of influence upon day-to-day practice within some parts of the health service. This is the Health Advisory

Service, accountable to the Secretary of State and staffed by seconded professionals. It is required to conduct a limited audit of the operation of particular services. This body is concerned with the overall performance in specific areas, particularly where institutional care is involved, and not with the scrutiny of individual professional decision-making. It clearly could be developed into a more all-embracing, and perhaps more public, medical audit system.

CONCLUSIONS

An American student of the British National Health Service described it as 'something magnificent in scope and breathtaking in its implications'. He went on to say:

> In the light of past accomplishments and future goals, the Health Service cannot very well be excluded from any list of notable achievements of the twentieth century. So much has it become a part of the British way of life, it is difficult for the average Englishman to imagine what it would be like without those services that have contributed so much to his physical and mental well-being.   (Lindsey, 1962)

That expresses rather well the peculiar mixture of utopian expectations and of taking the service for granted that gives a slightly exaggerated quality to British discussions of policy issues in the health service.

We have expectations of the service that often go quite beyond any capacity to deliver results. We oscillate wildly therefore between pride in our system and disquiet about its waiting lists and overcrowded wards. We put doctors on a pedestal as the magnificent experts who dominate the system, and we get angry about their arrogant presumptions. We demand more and more from the service, and we get worried that we are perhaps becoming a nation of hypochondriacs who can too easily make demands upon it. These mixed emotions colour the reactions of both politicians and the public to the main policy dilemmas that inevitably confront the service.

Undoubtedly a public approach to medicine involving disproportionate expectations about its capacity to solve the problems of suffering and death lies at the root of some of our difficulties in putting health policies in context, and coming to terms with the strengths and weaknesses of our health service. There are signs however that the 'demystification of medicine' is beginning to occur. This is helping us to assess much more realistically decisions about the allocation of resources between the hospital service and the community services, and between the health service and other public policies. Some of these issues have been considered in this chapter. Others were given attention in the discussion on 'forward planning, needs and priorities' and on 'the relationship between the personal services and the health service' in the previous chapter.

We are beginning to ask whether we have not so far been too ready to delegate decisions involving moral questions as well as medical questions to professional practitioners. We are beginning to achieve a better understanding of the extent to which many of the determinants of the health of the nation have little to do with the quality and nature of its clinical medical services.

SUGGESTIONS FOR FURTHER READING

Two good textbooks are Christopher Ham's *Health Policy in Britain* (1992) and Rudolph Klein's *The Politics of the NHS* (1989). A further recent contribution on this subject is Harrison, Hunter and Pollitt's *The Dynamics of British Health Policy* (1990).

The Black Report on *Inequalities and Health* and Whitehead's *The Health Divide* (1988) are vital sources on the activities and performance of the health service. They are published together in a book cited in the bibliography as Townsend, Davidson and Whitehead (1988). Glennerster's book (1985), recommended at the end of the previous chapter deals with many of the finance and public expenditure issues. Issues about finance and performance are well examined in the relevant chapter of Hills (1990).

CHAPTER 8

Education

EDUCATION POLICIES AND THE ORGANIZATION OF THE SYSTEM

The state's role in education is a dual one; it is the major provider of education, and has also assumed a responsibility to supervise it in the sector for which it is not directly responsible. This chapter will confine its attention largely to the publicly maintained education system, but some consideration will be given to the private sector inasmuch as some key policy issues concern the relationship between the two sectors. About 7 per cent of the United Kingdom's schoolchildren are in private schools.

As in the health service chapter, it can be taken for granted that readers will be aware of the basic services provided by the system. Furthermore, the organizational structure of the education system is relatively simple and relatively well-known.

The provision of state schools is the responsibility of the counties, the metropolitan districts and the London Boroughs in England and Wales. In Scotland it is the concern of the regions, while in Northern Ireland it comes under appointed education and libraries boards.

Higher education is outside local authority control. A government-appointed Funding Council deals with the financing of universities and polytechnics, and therefore in various respects controls them.

At the end of the 1980s the government substantially reduced local government control over education. It took higher education entirely out of their control, set up City Technology Colleges, on an experimental basis, to provide some centrally funded secondary education; and the 1988 Education Act enabled the governors of county and voluntary maintained schools, with the support of parents, to apply to the Secretary of State for maintenance by grant from central government instead of maintenance by local education authorities. It also imposed a set of rules relating to the government and management of local authority schools which forced local authorities to fund schools on the basis of a centrally determined formula and to delegate significant management responsibilities to their governing bodies.

In Scotland, Wales and Northern Ireland, education, other than higher, is the responsibility of the Scottish, Welsh and Northern Ireland Offices respectively. In England the relevant central government department is the Department for Education.

The school system can be identified as involving three sectors: a very small pre-primary sector, primary education and secondary education. In most cases these sectors can be identified respectively with the education of children under five, between five and eleven, and between eleven and the school leaving-age of sixteen (with many pupils continuing at school until eighteen). However, some authorities have developed systems that deviate from the strict break between primary and secondary education at eleven-plus. These have generally introduced an intermediate, middle-school system, for children in two or three of the year bands between nine and thirteen. A few have developed separate schools to split the secondary age group.

One innovation of the latter kind has been the introduction of 'sixth form colleges' for the over-sixteens. The educational arrangements for those over the minimal school-leaving age is further complicated by the fact that some further education colleges offer both practical and academic courses for children in the sixteen-to-eighteen age brackets.

The arrangement for starting compulsory education at the age of five differentiates Britain from many other countries, which do not make it compulsory until six or seven. However, the concomitant is that public pre-school education is ill-developed. Despite considerable public pressure, and considerable emphasis by educational experts on the importance of the preparation for education that may be provided in nursery schools and may thus particularly assist those children who receive but limited help from parents, the pre-school system has remained small.

The main point of note about policies for primary education has been the extent to which, very often on the basis of local initiatives, innovatory approaches to education have been developed. Many primary schools have been transformed over the last 20 to 30 years from formal institutions in which uniformed children sat in straight rows in classes that were streamed on the basis of tests of educational ability, to very informal places where pupils move about freely to work together in little clusters drawn from mixed-ability classes. The gradual elimination of selection at eleven-plus has clearly contributed to this 'liberation' of primary schools. It is an interesting example of a change that developed from the bottom and has never required any formal recognition in legislation, but which may nevertheless be regarded as a major policy development. Its implications are now beginning to receive attention. Politicians are starting to ask whether this largely professionally motivated innovation has gone too far. There is a growing concern about levels of literacy and numeracy, and responsibility for their alleged inadequacy is sometimes attributed to this educational revolution. The increased controls, involving testing and a national curriculum (see below), under the 1988 Act were a response to this concern.

In chapter 2 it was shown how the idea of the comprehensive secondary school gradually replaced the bipartite or tripartite system envisaged at the time the 1944 Education Act was passed. In 1989 about 86 per cent of secondary school children in the public sector in England were in comprehensive schools. The percentage was 99 per cent for Wales and 100 per cent for Scotland (*Social Trends 22*, 1992, p. 50). The growth of the idea of the comprehensive school may be identified with that same development in professional educational thinking that created the 'progressive' primary school. But this change in policy required much more positive decision-making by local politicians. The internal organization of a school may be changed gradually and subtly over a period of time by its head-teacher and staff. Change in the organization of the local education system requires more centralized and publicly apparent decisions. Comprehensivization received an impetus not only from new ideas on education but also from increasing Labour Party opposition to the divisive character of the old system. Popular support was forthcoming largely, it may be suspected, because of discontent about the inaccurate and necessarily arbitrary distinctions that had to be made between children by tests conducted at the age of eleven.

By 1979 the development of comprehensive education was nearing completion. The Labour Government had, in the 1976 Education Act, required local authorities to develop plans for comprehensivization. A minority of authorities were holding out on this. But on coming to power the Conservatives repealed this law. This had the effect of stemming the tide, but – as the figures above indicate – not reversing it.

One aspect of the resistance to comprehensive education has involved the argument that the abandonment of selective schools leads to a lowering of educational standards and to the neglect of the needs of the most able children. This view seems to have been taken increasingly seriously in recent years. It has also inhibited the extension of the educational changes going on in the primary schools into the secondary schools. In particular it has contributed to the maintenance of ability-based 'streaming' in many comprehensive schools. This phenomenon, which can have the effect of creating a divided education system within an apparently integrated school, is further reinforced by the imminence, in the teenage years, of the public examinations. These involve a sixteen-plus examination, the General Certificate of Secondary Education, and the Advanced ('A') level examinations normally sat at eighteen-plus.

Two further current government initiatives under the 1988 Act have strengthened the hands of those who stress the need for formal, and probably 'streamed', education. These are the proposals for a national curriculum, and the testing of children at seven, eleven, fourteen and sixteen. The curriculum consists of three 'core' subjects of English, maths and science (plus Welsh in Welsh-speaking areas) and seven 'foundation' subjects: history, geography, technology, music, art, physical education and another modern language (for over-elevens). There is also a requirement to provide a programme of religious education, which reflects the 'dominance' of Christianity in Britain. Curriculum Councils have been set up to keep these developments under review. The testing system involves setting attainment targets and is carried out under the supervision of the School Examinations and Assessment Council. It is the government's intention that collective test results should be published.

These two measures represent a marked departure from the philosophy of the 1944 Education Act, which left most education under local government control and left issues about the determination of the curriculum largely in the hands of teachers, operating with an eye on the entrance requirements for higher education and the expectations of employers.

At the time of writing the first results from the testing of seven-year-olds has just been published for each local authority in a form which encourages their presentation by the media in a 'league table' form without regard to differences in social class or ethnic origin. Sociological studies of education have suggested that many social factors determine school performance. They have particularly suggested that as children approach the school-leaving age there are many factors, often out of the control of the schools, that contribute to the divisions between the school-oriented 'academic' pupils and the anti-school group, who increasingly see their education as irrelevant and who drop out of all school activities (Ford, 1969; Willis, 1977). An increasing concern, therefore, in secondary education is not so much the fate of the brighter pupils – the comprehensive schools have been eager to 'prove themselves' by doing justice to the needs of this group – as the difficulties entailed in providing a relevant education for those at the other end of the ability range. There are related problems here, of course, of absenteeism and delinquency. Overall the issue concerns the relationship of the education system to the needs of underprivileged groups in our society – for example, the children of low-skilled workers and racial minorities. Since, moreover, such groups are located in specific areas, there is a geographical dimension to this problem. One of the arguments advanced in favour of the comprehensive school is that it is able to take all the children of a limited geographical community. But suppose such a 'community' is manifestly not truly 'comprehensive', and worse still, suppose atypical residents in that community take steps to get their children educated elsewhere; then new distinctions arise between schools in which their catchment areas rather than their selection policies influence, or are believed to influence, their characters. This is a growing problem for comprehensive secondary education in Britain. It is one which has been intensified by government efforts to ensure that parents have maximum opportunities to choose schools for their children, an issue to which we will return.

The education of handicapped children requires the system to develop certain special resources. However, the trend is to try to integrate the education of the handicapped as far as possible into the ordinary system. There is a significant group of children in each authority who are classified as experiencing 'learning difficulties' as a result of the possession of various kinds of physical or intellectual handicaps. They are required to be carefully tested, and a 'statement' has to be prepared setting out their needs. They may then either be allocated to a normal school, which may secure some teaching or support staff enhancement to enable the child to be given extra attention, or sent to a school where there are special facilities and staffing arrangements.

The concepts of further and higher education embrace a number of different activities: vocational education, further academic education (both of a kind provided generally in schools and at higher levels) and non-vocational adult education. Education for degrees and for postgraduate qualifications is provided in universities, in polytechnics and in colleges of higher education. In 1989–90 there were about 616,000 full-time students (not counting students from abroad) in higher education. About half were in universities, as then defined (*Social Trends 22*, 1992, p. 61).

There is a number of non-teaching activities that make contributions to the overall performance of the education system. Schools may provide meals and milk to children. The former may be available free to the pupils whose parents are on 'income support'. The extent to which these should be subsidized for others has been something of a political football, and extensive cuts have been made recently to these services. Means-tested grants are also available towards the cost of school clothing, and towards support of children in the sixteen-to-eighteen group who are still at school. These are among the benefits that complicate the social security system.

The welfare of schoolchildren is also given attention through the school health service and the education welfare service. Exceptionally the latter is a social services department responsibility (in Cheshire and Somerset for example); more typically it comes under education departments. Historically the main concern of this service has been truancy. Today its objectives have been widened to embrace the whole range of problems that may affect educational performance. In this it has the support of the child guidance service, which was described earlier in relation to the personal social services, as an inter-departmental hybrid. The relationship between social workers and educational welfare officers is a delicate one, since the latter are a relatively untrained group who are anxious to upgrade their skills and abandon the 'attendance officer' image (Ralphs, 1973). An established ethos and working style is, however, hard to change, and truancy does remain a central problem for the service.

PAYING FOR THE EDUCATION SYSTEM

Public education in Britain is, broadly speaking, free. There is a system of fees for higher education but nearly all British students, regardless of parental income, are able to obtain grants for undergraduate courses that cover at least these. Some further and non-vocational education has to be paid for by students, but generally these fees are subsidized. Hence the provision of education in Britain makes heavy demands on public funds. Most of this money has to be provided by the local authorities, but of course a high proportion of local expenditure is actually covered by central government grants. In 1989–90 education in the United Kingdom cost £23,956 million. Of this, £20,456 million (85 per cent) was spent on the local authority sector (*Social Trends 22*, 1992, p. 67).

The gradually falling numbers in the school age groups has, since the mid-seventies, encouraged government and local authorities to see education as a target area for expenditure cuts. Places in teacher education have also been dramatically cut. In 1981, in advance of the fall in the numbers in the eighteen to twenty-two age group, the government also identified higher education as an area in which they might apply disproportionate expenditure cuts. Subsequently, the continuing high demand for places led them to change their minds on this, but cuts were only partially restored and staff/students ratios worsened substantially.

Whilst the government has made the quest for greater efficiency in the use of diminishing resources the central thrust of its education policy, right-wing ideologues have also raised questions about the case for free education. The only practical inroad into this principle has been that schools tend to be forced to charge for extra benefits not seen as strictly part of the curriculum – musical instrument lessons, educational trips and so on. There has been some dispute about the legality of some of these charges under the law as laid down in the 1944 Education Act, but the 1988 Act legitimated them. It should also be pointed out that expenditure restraints have also increased the extent to which parents, individually or collectively, have needed to purchase textbooks and equipment for their children's education.

Another idea for change to the education system which has come from the political Right is that an education voucher system could be developed which would enable parents to place their children within either the private or public sector, paying supplementary fees to private schools where necessary. The Conservative Government encouraged a local experiment to explore the feasibility of vouchers. They have also enabled local authorities to provide 'assisted places' in the private sector for selected children. Expenditure constraints have kept the latter development to fairly modest levels.

The other major area in which there is serious controversy about the use of public funds is in relation to grants to university students. In this case it is not the basic tuition fees that are at issue but the grants provided to pay students' living expenses. The present system involves means-tested grants which, unless the student has been self-supporting for three years before restarting full-time study, take parental income and other commitments into account (there are also special and rather anomalous arrangements for the means-testing of married students, which cannot be explored properly here). The National Union of Students would like to see the means test abolished. They draw attention to the many anomalies involved, and to the problems faced by the many students whose parents do not pay their contributions towards the grants.

But there is an alternative line of criticism of the British system which has involved the advocacy of a loan system, as operated in many countries, as a preferable approach to the maintenance of students (Blaug, 1970). It is argued that students receive public funds whilst delaying their contributions to the national income. Nevertheless, by studying they enhance their own future earning potential. It is therefore suggested that it may be reasonable to expect students to repay all or some of the benefit bestowed upon them in this way. A number of schemes have been suggested. The more sophisticated attempt to avoid heavy demands on resources in early career, and to allow for the possibility that individuals may go into low-paid but socially useful work (Barnes and Barr, 1988). There are various special problems, such as the appropriate treatment for a woman whose career and earning power is affected by marriage and child-rearing. Administratively sophisticated schemes might become complex and costly. Critics of loan schemes point to the benefit the nation gains from its educated people, and warn that loan schemes might deter some people, particularly people from low-income families, from entering higher education.

In 1990 the government started a loans scheme. It decided that grant increases should be frozen and that in their place loans should be offered. The amount available in the form of a loan would be increased year by year as the grant fell in value. Interest is charged, but at a comparatively low rate. The government refused to consider any way of taking future income into account in determining repayment rates.

The existence of a comprehensive means-tested grants system for entrants to universities must be compared with the rather unsatisfactory situation with regard to some other students, and particularly with regard to schoolchildren between sixteen and eighteen years of age. It is mandatory upon local authorities to pay grants to university and polytechnic students. Other higher education grants are discretionary; this clearly has unfair consequences from time to time. Local authorities may pay limited means-tested maintenance awards to the parents of schoolchildren who are over the school-leaving age. These again are discretionary and are not very extensive in coverage. Children who have left school cannot even claim social security benefits. Except in exceptional cases financial help for sixteen-to-eighteen year olds is conditional upon entering training schemes. In some cases places on these schemes are not even available.

CONTROL OVER THE EDUCATION SYSTEM

The control of education in Britain involves what has been described as a 'partnership' between central and local government. Yet clearly that partnership is under threat. At a time when central government is trying to curb local government expenditure the fact that education accounts for around half this expenditure inevitably puts it in the spotlight. Furthermore, politicians at national level take a great interest in the way education is organized and conducted. The development of comprehensive education and the elimination of direct grant schools were issues that fundamentally divided the parties. Governments have also felt it important to take stands on such matters as literacy, the core content of the curriculum, the role of nursery education and the future of higher education. Strong commitments in national politics have been met by equally strong ones in local politics. Hence battle-lines have been drawn up, particularly on the comprehensive issue. Local authorities have even had recourse to the courts to resist what they see as central government interference. The main example of this was the battle in Tameside in 1976 when, after a local election victory, the Conservatives reversed a Labour plan to 'go comprehensive'. The Secretary of State sought to intervene, arguing that the change was too far advanced to be reversed. The court upheld the local authority's position. The change of government ended this particular battle.

The uneasy balance between central and local government is not the only delicate balance of power in the British educational system. At the local level the running of the system involves a number of different groups which are contending for influence or protecting their prerogatives. Each local authority appoints an education committee, consisting primarily of councillors but including some other representatives of groups interested in education, such as teachers, churches and local universities. It is a generally accepted convention that on contentious political matters the non-councillor members should restrain their intervention. The committee is served by a chief education officer who leads a team of officials who generally have teaching qualifications. There is thus a strong professionally orientated administrative group at the centre of the system.

Schools are required to have governing bodies. They are required to consist of an equal mix of local education authority nominees and parents. As pointed out above, these bodies are now responsible for delegated budgets guaranteed by the Secretary of State. They have significant controls over appointments. They can also apply for the school to opt out of local authority control. Even if they do not do this, the government has handed them a weapon they can use against a local authority that adopts policies with which they disagree. It is worth noting, for example, how this weapon has been used by schools threatened with closure in rationalization exercises.

In the schools themselves head-teachers expect a considerable measure of freedom in determining the way the school is run and the way subjects are taught. They operate, of course, in consultation with their teachers, but vary extensively in the extent to which they allow staff participation in decision-making. In the last resort, however, the class teacher clearly has some autonomy in determining his or her input and relationship to pupils.

An issue which has received considerable attention is parental choice of schools for their children. Whilst there were high pupil–teacher ratios and pressure upon school numbers in many parts of the country, the scope for parental choice was fairly limited. But as school rolls have fallen the situation has changed. In urban areas, in particular, variations in the popularity of schools have often become very clear. In the

Education Act of 1980 the government tried to provide parents with some measure of choice over schools. The Act requires local authorities to give information which will help with choice, and it lays down an appeal procedure for those whose wishes are not granted. Parental choice seems to be operating as a curb on innovation by teachers; it may also be helping to determine where cuts will fall. Inasmuch as it is more likely to be exercised by middle-class parents, it may be enhancing the tendency for there to be a hierarchy of schools, under the influence of geographical location. Patterns of social and racial segregation may thereby be enhanced.

Overall, the government is squeezing local authority powers both by increasing central controls and by extending governors' powers. Glennerster and his colleagues (1991) have seen this as a key example of a number of processes where, despite the rhetoric of decentralization, extensive centralization is occurring since in the last analysis an individual governing body is in a much weaker position than a local authority to resist the power of the central state.

EDUCATION AND THE DISADVANTAGED

Education plays a significant role in relation to the distribution of occupational opportunities in our society. On the Left there is considerable concern about the extent to which education contributes to upward mobility. There are two versions of this preoccupation. One of these involves a commitment to equality of opportunity, and therefore a demand that the able children of 'lower-class' parents should have access to educational openings. The other is a concern about equality in a more absolute sense. A naive version of this places faith in the possibility of an education system that can help to create a more equal society. A more sophisticated approach recognizes that education cannot be, by itself, an engine of social change but stresses that it must play a part by ensuring that children are not socially segregated and that schools attempt to compensate for other sources of inequality.

'Equality of opportunity' is a slogan that finds political support beyond the ranks of the Left. A rather mixed commitment to both forms of equality has informed the evaluation of education policy. Differential education opportunity and achievement has been extensively studied by sociologists and psychologists. The evidence accumulated by research in the 1950s and early 1960s (Douglas, 1964; Floud, Halsey and Martin, 1956; Jackson and Marsden, 1962) was used in making the case for comprehensive education and for the abandonment of streaming. Later attention shifted to those problems of underachievement in the education system that cannot be directly attributed to the way that system is structured. Two particular themes have been emphasized: the significance of home background for educational success, and the extent to which the 'culture' of the school system is alien to some children.

It has been shown that poverty and poor housing conditions militate against educational success (Douglas, 1964; Central Advisory Council for Education, 1967). There is little the education system can do about these problems, but it can try to compensate for them with extra efforts to help deprived children. Home backgrounds are relevant in another sense, too. There are wide variations in the extent to which parents help with the education of their children. Such help takes many forms, involving not only the more obvious forms of encouragement and the provision of books and study facilities, but also a great deal of implicit 'teaching' through interaction with children. The latter starts when babies are very tiny, and one of its most significant ingredients is the learning of language. The children who are most deprived in these respects are often those also most deprived in a material sense. But parental educational levels and abilities are also relevant. There is a variety of practical ways in which the education system may help to compensate for these less straightforwardly material disadvantages, both before and after children reach compulsory school age (Halsey, 1972).

The issue with regard to the 'culture' of the schools is a more difficult one. Partly the problem is one of identification of the needs and special interests of children whose backgrounds differ from the white educated middle-class males who dominate the system. There is a variety of ways in which stories, educational situations and examples can be devised that seem relevant to these children. Hence there is ample scope for change here. However, there must be limits to the extent to which this issue can be fully met, if only because of the extent to which it implies a conflict with the objective of facilitating social mobility through education. If a key concern of education is to prepare children to operate in a middle-class world, even perhaps to join that world, then it may not be particularly functional for it to be too obsessed with relating to working-class culture. There is a terrible dilemma here, very relevant to the alienation of some children from an education system in which they are becoming the 'failures'. You cannot eliminate the concept of failure so long as you still have the objective of enabling some to 'succeed' through the education system. It may be desirable to eliminate the more invidious aspects of competition within the system – to recognize, for example, that progress *relative* to ability may be as important as the easy success of the advantaged and talented – but notions of achievement, and consequently non-achievement, are fundamental to the role of education in our kind of society.

There are some special, and slightly different, issues about the 'culture' of education and the needs of racial minorities. These will be examined in the next section in relation to the whole range of problems, and therefore policy dilemmas, about the education of immigrant children and the children of immigrants.

The idea of attempting to compensate for disadvantage by providing special resources for the schools in some areas was suggested in a report of the Plowden committee (Central Advisory Council for Education, 1967). Many of the measures adopted did no more than attempt to redress the imbalance of educational resources between run-down inner-city areas, where the schools were old and facilities were limited, and newer suburban areas. Additional money was made available for capital projects and current expenditure in areas where there were high levels of deprivation. But in addition the government provided for extra teachers, above the normal quotas, and special additional allowances for teachers in those areas. Areas were designated on the basis of statistics on the socioeconomic status of parents, the extent of absence of housing amenities, proportions of children receiving free school meals, and proportion of school children with serious linguistic difficulties.

Some action research projects were initiated to monitor special compensatory education ventures in some of these 'educational priority areas'. They gave particular attention to the value of pre-school education, along the lines of the American 'Headstart' programme. In 1968 the government developed a special 'urban programme' of social policies for deprived urban areas. Under this programme local authorities could receive grants to expand nursery education and to support pre-school playgroups. The emphasis upon this stage of education led eventually in 1973 to the easing of limitations upon the development of nursery education.

The issues with which this section has been concerned have received much less attention in the political climate of the 1980s. With diminishing work opportunities for school leavers there has perhaps been less room for a generous concern about educational under-achievers. However, the public use of indices about examination results and tests has tended to obscure the extent to which a school's results are determined by the social backgrounds of its children. The emphasis upon standards and upon parental choice has been to the advantage of the relatively privileged schools. New resources are tending to follow the most successful parts of the education system, rather than – as demanded by an emphasis on compensatory education – the least successful. Comprehensive schools are nearly universally available, but in a system in which the gaps between the successful (in terms of conventional results) and unsuccessful schools are widening.

THE EDUCATION OF THE ETHNIC MINORITIES

Britain has a non-white population of around two and a half million. About 40 per cent of these are British born. The remainder are predominantly migrants from the West Indies and the Indian sub-continent. There is thus a substantial non-white school population, concentrated in urban areas. Most of these youngsters are the British-born children of migrants, as immigration has been tightly controlled since the 1960s. Of the non-white population 90 per cent under 15 were born in Britain.

When many non-white children were themselves immigrants the system saw their language problem and cultural difference as the main issue. Some of these are still evident. Many Asian children are encouraged by parents to make the most of educational opportunities, and many have made remarkable progress within the British system. They face problems, however, in coming to terms with strong contrasts between patterns of home life and school life. This is particularly an issue for girls coming from homes that cherish traditional ideals of feminine behaviour, expecting daughters to remain close to the family, to have no career ambitions, and perhaps to accept an early arranged marriage.

Some Asian groups have begun either to make demands for new developments in the education system in tune with their cultural needs (appropriate religious education; courses in Asian languages) or to call for separate state-subsidized schools for their children on the lines of Catholic schools. A look across to Northern Ireland, where a division in education on religious lines has many of the characteristics of a division on cultural lines and contributes to the division of that community, gives pause for thought on this model of education for a culturally diverse society. Such misgivings are reinforced by the extent to which there has also been interest in independence from white parents eager to minimize the Asian influence upon certain schools.

At one time in the late sixties and early seventies a number of education authorities bussed children to other areas to try to prevent certain schools having high concentrations of Asian children. Since this bussing was a one-way process applied only to Asians it was rightly abandoned as discriminatory. Now, the imposition of rules about having regard to parental choice means that local authorities cannot even manipulate catchment areas in the interests of any kind of racial 'balance', and choices may enhance tendencies towards segregation.

West Indian immigrants come from a society where European cultural models have a strong influence and are reinforced through the education process. It is precisely this bias in West Indian society, and in

American black society, that has been attacked by those concerned about the development of black consciousness. It is argued that this dominance of a white cultural model contributes to the maintenance of a subordinate self-image. Black leaders in Britain have become deeply concerned about the under-achievement of children of West Indian origin. They attribute this to a variety of factors, but see the white racial and cultural bias in the education system as reinforcing other aspects of disadvantage.

Hence, whilst the education system continues to see the issues about non-white children as ones about *their* characteristics, it may alternatively be suggested that the central issue is *its* racial and cultural assumptions, the phenomenon which is described as 'institutional racism'. In 1985 an official committee, chaired by Lord Swann, reported on its 'Inquiry into the Education of Children from Ethnic Minority Groups' (see Department of Education and Science, 1985). In a brief guide to the report Lord Swann, whilst not using the expression 'institutional racism' made it very clear that the issue of society and the education system's response was of central importance in explaining the problem of under-achievement by non-whites. He argued:

> on the evidence so far there is at least a dual problem. On the one hand, society must not, through prejudice and discrimination, increase the social and economic deprivation of ethnic minority families. On the other, schools must respond with greater sensitivity, and without any trace of prejudice, to the needs of ethnic minority children.   (HMSO, 1985, p. 9)

Lord Swann saw the latter being achieved through the concept of 'Education for All'. This meant that:

> The fundamental change needed is a recognition that the problem facing the educational system is not just how to educate the children of ethnic minorities, but how to educate *all* children. Britain has long been an ethnically diverse society, and is now, mainly because of her imperial past, much more obviously one. All pupils must be brought to an understanding of what is entailed if such a society is to become a fair and harmonious entity. (Ibid., p. 10)

Some Afro-Caribbean groups have set up weekend supplementary schools. In these, children receive a mixture of teaching that emphasizes the black cultural heritage, correcting the European biases of history teaching, for example, and help with the learning of basic skills. The fact that such a development seems necessary poses a different sort of challenge to the education system from that posed by Asian 'separatism': it suggests a need to tackle the biases in the system through the encouragement of culturally relevant studies, and the acceptance that there is a problem about the white view of society. It calls for a sophisticated understanding of the issues by all teachers, and special efforts to recruit black teachers. The very ethnocentric biases in the new national curriculum (for history, for example) threatens to set back this aspiration.

This last problem about the education of black children links up very closely with the issue of the place lower-class white children find themselves occupying within the system, and with the quite concrete disadvantages of children from lower-income homes. Inasmuch as black entrants to Britain have generally been forced to accept many of the poorest jobs and worst houses, children find that the 'inferior' stereotype of the black person seems to be reinforced by their, and their parents', experience. Moreover, the fact that many black parents have had relatively little education themselves, and use a dialect form of English very different from that used in the schools, means that, like comparable lower-class white parents, they are ill-equipped to help their children tackle the education system. There is a web of reinforcing disadvantages here which makes the development of compensatory education particularly important for this group of children.

Readers may observe that this is the first time a section in this book has explored at any lenght the issue about the impact of an area of social policy on ethnic minorities. Many of the points made here are relevant to other policy areas. In particular the chapter on the personal social services could have discussed some of the issues about the inadequacies of services for minorities; and explored them in terms not unlike those used about educational separation, for example the issue of trans-racial adoption. Similarly the chapter on the health service could have dealt more fully with the extent to which there is an ethnic dimension to inequalities in health, and explored some of the communication difficulties which arise when white health professionals pay insufficient regard to cultural and language problems. Lack of space prevented those discussions; it has been interposed here because of the salience of the issue for education. Readers are urged to think about the relevance of the points made here for those other policy areas.

CONCLUSIONS

The state system of education had roots in a mid-nineteenth-century concern with the training of an effective workforce able to operate in an increasingly complex industrial system and society. Its growth has been inextricably bound up with the development of a democratic

society. The original view that the newly enfranchised should be liter-
ate has been answered by a belief by the electorate that education
holds the key to social advance. This may be in part an illusion. The
opportunity structure is determined by the economy and by the political system. Increased education does not in itself increase the supply of
'top jobs'; it merely increases the competition for them. The fact that
educational qualifications are widely used as a basis for discrimination
between applicants for jobs emphasizes the link between education and
social and economic advancement, regardless of whether or not those
jobs require education at the level, or of the kind, possessed by those
deemed best-suited to fill them. Hence, the nature of the education
system and the opportunities it provides is of central political importance in Britain.

In this sense demands that 'politics should be taken out of education'
are based upon a total failure to comprehend what either politics
or education are all about. A study of education policy controversies
in the past 30 years demonstrates a great deal about politics and
administration in British society. Perhaps some of the demands for
politics to be taken out of education come from a sense of individual
frustration, by parents and pupils, about conflicts in which they feel
fairly impotent.

Education is perhaps the sector of social policy that people feel they
understand best; they try hard to influence it but find that many of the
key problems elude their grasp. The educational system's elusive quality should not, however, be explained simply in terms of the reluctance
of political and professional elites to accept participation. Its very sensitive relationship to the economy and society makes controlling its interaction with social change very difficult.

SUGGESTIONS FOR FURTHER READING

For a discussion of education policy with a particularly sociological
slant readers should look at Finch's *Education and Social Policy* (1984).
Regan (1977) has provided a very sound factual introduction to the
organization of the education system, while a book by Kogan (1978)
provides a lively discussion of the key political issues. However, the
events of the 1980s have seriously dated both. The 1988 Act will surely
be fully analysed in due course, meanwhile Simon (1988) has provided
a powerful polemic against it.

While it is also now very dated, the literature on education and social
class (Douglas, 1964; Floud, Halsey and Martin, 1956; Jackson and
Marsden, 1962), particularly the last-named, provide excellent insights

into underlying issues that are still with us despite the near-demise of the grammar schools.

Stone (1981) provides a useful examination of the issues surrounding the education of racial minorities, as does chapter 6 of Rex and Tomlinson's (1979) study of race relations in Birmingham. To them should be added the Swann report, discussed in this chapter (Department of Education and Science, 1985).

CHAPTER 9

Employment Policy

INTRODUCTION

Britain's manpower policies are the responsibility of the Department of Employment. In the financial year 1989–90 about £3400 million was spent on employment and training services (HMSO, 1992, p. 36). However it is not entirely satisfactory to see the sum total of government employment policies as a set of explicit employment services. Social security benefits play an important role in employment policy and, even more importantly, employment policy is in many respects a part of wider economic policy.

This is the first of the two chapters in which, as was pointed out in the introductory chapter, a considerable amount of attention has to be given to economic issues. In the next chapter, on housing, it is the fact that a great deal of the provision is through a private housing market which requires attention. In this chapter, while it is true that employment services are provided by both public and private agencies, what forces particular attention to be given to the interaction between social and economic policies is that employment services represent a form of public intervention in the economy and that job opportunities are determined primarily by the working of that economy rather than by the specific interventions of the employment services. Effective employment services may contribute to the creation of a healthy economy, but they cannot in themselves 'cure' an unhealthy one.

Many discussions of employment services give little attention to their social role. They are seen as concerned with the effective working of the labour market, and not as services which provide social benefits. There are two reasons for disagreement with this approach to the study of employment services. The first of these is simply a dissatisfaction with the conventional distinction between social and economic policies, as suggested in chapter 1. Economic policies have social effects, and clearly the social effects of a service designed to help people secure satisfactory jobs as quickly as possible are most important. The second is that considerations other than concern to make the labour market operate efficiently enter into the employment services. The alleviation of unemployment is as much a social issue as an economic one. Indeed, economic 'realism' may involve unconcern about unemployment and even a desire to maintain a 'reserve army of labour'.

THE CHARACTERISTICS OF THE BRITISH APPROACH TO MANPOWER POLICY

A government may manage the economy without making any use of employment services, and the case for employment services as necessary for either economic or social ends is less easy to make than the case for, for example, health services or education. The employment services date from the early years of this century, and have played a fairly low-key role until recently. Even to-day employment services expenditure, at about 2 per cent of public expenditure, is dwarfed by that on the other services discussed in this book.

In his book *Why Some Peoples Are More Unemployed than Others* (1986), Goran Therborn analyses the applicability of various theories explaining unemployment to the marked differences in its incidence in 16 advanced capitalist countries. His conclusion is that one can only explain the differences in terms of 'the self-fulfilling tendency of deeply institutionalised policy orientations' (Therborn, 1986 p. 30). The five countries with records of low unemployment in his sample – Switzerland, Japan, Sweden, Norway and Austria – differ from each other substantially in terms of their political systems and political ideologies but, Therborn argues, all have developed distinctive labour market policies even if, as in the case of Switzerland, such policies only consist of limiting the *supply* of labour.

Britain is one of the cases in Therborn's sample of countries with a recent record of high unemployment. Its policy response to this has been slow, limited and very much *ad hoc*.

In the early twentieth century British governments gradually rejected the view that the economy, and accordingly the labour market, should be left to work 'naturally'. At the end of the nineteenth century adherents of 'classical' economic theory began to acknowledge that it was perhaps necessary for government to play a role in assisting the 'natural' market system to operate more smoothly. In particular, the problems of adjustments, in the short run, began to be regarded as sufficiently serious to justify interventions. One such problem concerned the linking of 'sellers' of labour with the 'buyers'. To this end, after 1908, systems of Labour Exchanges were created.

Between the two World Wars continuing evidence that the economy could not readily absorb all who wanted work kept the issue of unemployment on the political agenda. There were strong pressures that forced the erratic development of income maintenance measures for the unemployed (see discussion in chapter 2), but manpower policies developed very little. A few very limited job-creation and training schemes were developed, but economic orthodoxy was against the heavy public expenditure on the creation of work that, by the middle of the 1930s, began to characterize the policy response in the United States. Only as preparation for war began to alleviate unemployment did official thinking begin to come to terms with its structural character. This change of approach is primarily associated with the Keynesian revolution in economic thinking which linked unemployment with under-consumption and urged governments to spend, and if necessary to unbalance budgets, to get out of a recession. The primary policy response required was in this case a macroeconomic one, rather than a form of manpower policy *per se*. However, at the same time, the special problems of certain regions, particularly those where employment had depended upon declining heavy industries, also began to be recognized.

The unexpected success of economic policies in preventing high unemployment from 1945 to 1970 enabled British governments to continue to adopt a comparatively passive stance on manpower policies. Then, in 1970, the incoming Conservative government led by Edward Heath decided to restructure the public employment service as part of its efforts to make public administration more dynamic. A consultative document *People and Jobs* (Department of Employment, 1971) declared that the employment service needed to be modernized. The Employment Exchanges were too identified with a limited service to the unemployed.

In modernizing the service the government was clearly influenced by the Swedish concept of 'active manpower policy', in which the employment service was seen as playing a crucial role in preserving full employment without high inflation. Britain's own problem in swinging rapidly from situations of economic stagnation when unemployment began to rise into problems of an 'overheated' economy bringing inflation and balance of payments difficulties were seen as at least partly attributable to problems of labour supply. 'Overheating' was associated with difficulties in securing adequately trained skilled labour. It was felt that a more sophisticated employment service, dealing with a much higher share of the job placings and able to give more expert attention to training problems, would much more effectively match supply and demand in the labour market and thus contribute much better to the maintenance of a balanced economy.

A new active service would seek to have a real impact upon the working of the labour market. In practice the British manpower initiatives of the early 1970s were brought into operation in a context not just of high inflation but also of rapidly rising unemployment. The modernized employment services had to operate in an economy about which many economists had abandoned the orthodox 'Keynesian' belief that there is a direct and simple relationship between unemployment and inflation. While it is easy to sneer that Britain's conversion to active labour market policy came too late, it is indeed hard to discern whether or not the new service contributed to the mitigation of problems in a very troubled labour market. Certainly, the system succeeded in ensuring that it was notified of a better proportion of vacancies than was the case in the past.

However, while *People and Jobs* saw the future of the service in terms of a lesser concern with the unemployed, and therefore a greater degree of assistance to those who sought to move between jobs, in fact the stagnation that occurred in the labour market forced the system to give a great deal of attention to the issue of unemployment.

On coming to power in 1979 the Thatcher Government inherited various special measures to deal with the problem of unemployment from its Labour predecessors. Its initial inclination was to curb these activities as part of its general attack on public expenditure. But it quickly came to recognize that the special programmes, particularly those for the young unemployed, offered the cheapest way of providing a response to the problem of growing unemployment. So instead the early 1980s saw a growth of expenditure on special training schemes and temporary job-creation measures (see Moon and Richardson, 1985).

Certainly, some of the measures adopted – in particular job creation and the use of subsidies – seem to have been influenced by the more active manpower policies of countries like Sweden. Ironically, in Sweden in the 1950s and 1960s such measures were seen as ways of helping the very small minority of the population unable to secure work on the open market when employment was as full as possible. They take on a rather different character in an economy characterized by a seriously deficient demand for labour. They have been criticized as inadequate alternatives to the effective management of the economy. One distinguished economist, Lord Vaisey, argued:

> The sum total of these schemes seems to me to be cosmetic rather than genuine in its economic consequences. What they do in effect is to push employment around a bit without much net effect. They are in no sense a

substitute for the substantial regeneration of British industry.... (House of Commons, 1977, p. 147)

In economic terms the official answer to Vaisey's argument was that these schemes provided or protected jobs with minimal inflationary effects, by comparison with the more direct ways in which the economy might be stimulated. But there is also an interesting social issue here: such policies may be used to influence the impact of the recession on particular groups of people. While they may do little or nothing to affect the overall level of employment they may help to ensure that particular people – the young, the previously long-term unemployed, the residents in certain areas – experience the ill effects of worklessness rather less than other people.

Politicians, when they justify special measures to provide employment, deliberately obfuscate these issues. They want to be able to claim jobs saved, or created by government intervention, as contributions to the alleviation of unemployment as a whole. The actual macroeconomic effect of these interventions is, happily for them, profoundly obscure.

The special programmes evolved, during the 1980s, from a mixed group of training and job-creation schemes for all ages towards a more focused approach to a form of training. First, the system was rationalized so that efforts were concentrated on a training system for under-18s – the Youth Training scheme – and a work creation system for over-18s – the Community Programme. Then later the latter was also replaced by a training scheme with a particular emphasis on the long-term unemployed in the 18–25 age group – Employment Training. These now seem to have become such permanent features of the, British employment policy scene that the expression 'special programmes', used to describe them in an earlier edition of this book, is no longer appropriate.

In arguing the case for its training schemes, the government laid a heavy emphasis upon the case for a trained work-force to meet the needs of British industry (Department of Employment, 1988a). To further this aim it set up, in 1990, a network of Training and Enterprise Councils led by local employers 'to contract with Government to plan and deliver training and to promote and support the development of small businesses and self-employment within their area' (Department of Employment, 1988b, para. 5.7). The two existing training schemes for the unemployed, already mentioned, the Youth Training scheme and Employment Training, are very central to this training initiative. The expectation is that training will focus upon the needs of the young unemployed, will be relevant to the needs of the private-sector and will be largely funded by that sector.

What is involved here is an approach to employment creation and training measures in which the emphasis is on the needs of the existing economic system, and control is very firmly in the hands of private-sector employers. Many of the special short-term job-creation measures which were developed in the late 1970s and were elaborated in the early 1980s have been abandoned. There is a strong emphasis on the training of the young, and many of the concerns of the middle-aged and elderly long-term unemployed have been disregarded.

Whilst all this activity has been going on the government has obviously had to spend considerable sums upon benefits for the unemployed. It has done this with great reluctance, and has increasingly found ways to reduce benefits and prevent individual access to such help.

Britain has moved from a situation in which there was little done at all to try to plan to prevent unemployment in the 1930s, through an era between 1945 and 1971 when regional policies were quite prominent but generally the health of the labour market seemed to make planning unnecessary, into a brief phase where it was recognized that some of Britain's economic problems stemmed from a lack of 'active labour market policy' in the 1970s. The rise of unemployment from 1975 onwards then 'hi-jacked' active labour market policy, concentrating the efforts of the Manpower Services Commission upon special measures for the unemployed. Responses to the problem of unemployment have pre-occupied the system ever since, but by the end of the 1980s training measures for the young had come to dominate.

THE PROVISION OF BASIC HELP, ADVICE AND TRAINING FOR THE UNEMPLOYED

The Jobcentres are the modern successors of the Labour Exchanges that were set up in 1908 to do just what their names suggests: to link employers seeking workers with employees. In the 1970s the Jobcentres were seen as replacing the large institutional Exchanges, with modern shop-front offices in commercial and shopping centres. There was an emphasis on self-service, individuals being able to select jobs from open display advertisements, only turning to staff when advice was necessary. The hopes for this approach have, however, been somewhat dashed by the rise of unemployment. In this context, notifications of vacancies are low and the system is concerned to use those it gets to ensure that unemployed people are making adequate efforts to seek work.

The Jobcentres have been seen as needing to operate very like private employment agencies. One area of employment work where that principle has been taken to its logical conclusion is in the operation of the Professional and Executive Recruitment service. This charges employers for its services, and is required to 'break even' financially every year.

There is also a specific employment service for disabled employees, set up in the 1940s with assistance to injured ex-servicemen very much in mind. This service employs specially trained staff who give advice and help with job placement. Individuals may register as disabled workers, and employers have a statutory obligation to ensure that disabled people form at least 3 per cent of their work forces. This quota has been poorly enforced throughout its history. In the contemporary context of high unemployment the disabled have fared badly, and the quota has become so irrelevant that there has been some debate about repealing the legislation.

Before 1974 the provision of unemployment services to those under 18 years of age was the responsibility of a separate youth employment service. The split between the youth service and the adult service was widely criticized. The government considered the option of abolishing the former, but in the end decided that the youth service, renamed the careers service and run by local education authorities, should continue to operate as a source of vocational and employment assistance for school-leavers and should be available to continue to help them for a time if they preferred to keep in touch with it. At about the same time the limitation of the service to help for the under-18s was abandoned. The new system requires close liaison between the local staff of the employment service and the careers service.

Until the late 1970s the training activities of the employment service concentrated upon re-training adult workers to enable them to move to new employment. Since that time the training side of the employment service's work has been increasingly concerned with the provision of training for young people who are unable to move directly into the labour market on account of the lack of jobs.

In 1990–1 there were about 350,000 entrants to the main youth initiative, the Youth Training scheme (YT). Just over 310,000 were on it in March 1991 (Unemployment Unit, January 1992, p. 12). YT involves public subsidy to a wide range of schemes – provided by private employers, voluntary organizations and public bodies – offering a mixture of work experience and training. They can last for up to two years and participants may secure qualifications whilst on the schemes. The achievement of qualifications is now strongly emphasized within YT as a whole. These schemes vary enormously in quality from elaborate skill training at one extreme to what are little more than 'make work' schemes for lower-ability young people in high unemployment areas at the other. The better the local demand for young workers the better the quality of the schemes – both in terms of the training they offer and the real labour market opportunities they lead on to. But it must be recognized:

1 that Britain has (by contrast with most of continental Europe) a very high proportion of young people ending their full time education and training at the age of 16;
2 that it used to have a strong pattern of apprenticeship into skilled work in industry which has now largely collapsed; and
3 that before the rise of unemployment in the mid-1970s the labour market for young people aged 16 to 18 was a thriving one which has now more or less collapsed.

The Youth Training scheme may be seen as a necessary means of filling a vacuum in the British education and youth training system, but it has also contributed to the creation of that vacuum by undermining the incentives to employers to provide at their own expense work or training for young people. The state now pays for most of this, through the Youth Training scheme.

It is important to note that, while in the early stages of the development of the Youth Training scheme the government was happy to make use of self-help initiatives and projects stimulated by social workers and community workers in order to enable the scheme to grow rapidly, in the longer run projects which were not seen as linked to the 'regular' economy have not been encouraged.

If the Youth Training scheme is the success the government claims it to be, why then is there a need for another training scheme targeted principally at the 18–25 age group? This is Employment Training which offers government subsidies to enable (a) trainees to be supported by a grant which amounts to the social security benefit rate plus a small amount; (b) firms to cover most of their training costs. Hence, enterprises taking on these 'trainees' can use them for up to 60 per cent of their time on 'practical training' – meaning, to all intents and purposes, *work*. The average number of people in training under this scheme during 1990–1 was about 200,000 (ibid., p. 3).

Whilst there is a variety of smaller training ventures run by the Department of Employment-funded Training and Enterprise Councils, YT and ET dominate the system.

OTHER MEASURES

It was remarked above that the expression 'special employment initiatives' is no longer an appropriate way of describing YT and ET.

This is less clearly true of some of the other measures which were developed over the last 15 years. Nevertheless, some of them, too, are showing signs of becoming permanent, hence this section is just titled 'other measures'. There are in fact so many of these now that it is impossible to cover them all.

There is a job-release scheme which helps to promote early retirement, providing subsidies which then create new jobs. There are various small-scale subsidy schemes: for young workers, for temporary jobs and for jobs created in small firms. The Community Industry scheme provides temporary employment for very disadvantaged young people. The Enterprise Allowance Scheme helps unemployed people to set up in self-employment, through initial subsidies.

In 1991 a scheme was launched which plans to provide job experience for 60,000 people a year, with payments at their social security benefit rates plus £10, on a variety of community and environmental projects. This has some resemblances to the Community Programme which was important in the late eighties.

There is a whole package of interrelated measures for the long-term unemployed – Restart, Job Clubs, Job Interview Guarantees and so on – which, for reasons which will be made clear, will be discussed in the next section.

THE POLICING OF THE UNEMPLOYMENT BENEFIT SYSTEM

In chapter 5 it was shown that the unemployed are supported by the state, according to their previous work records and length of unemployment, on either flat-rate unemployment benefit or means-tested 'income support' or some combination of the two. It was pointed out there that unemployment benefit could be stopped for up to 26 weeks where individuals had lost employment unnecessarily or had failed to take employment opportunities. It could have been added there that there are also powers to make deductions from 'income support' when these things occur.

There has been extensive controversy in recent years about the impact of the social security system upon the behaviour of the unemployed. High benefit levels are alleged to deter efforts to find work. Arguments centre upon two issues: the levels of income acquired by the newly unemployed, and the phenomenon of long-term unemployment.

It has been suggested that the introduction, in the mid-1960s, of earnings-related benefits and redundancy pay contributed to an increase in unemployment at that time. Economists have sought to test this hypothesis, by comparing other evidence on the state of the economy with data on unemployment. It seems possible that these new benefits did have a slight effect upon employment durations among the short-term unemployed. They were, in a sense, designed to do this. They reduced the impact of redundancy and helped workers to avoid hasty relocation into inappropriate jobs. However, the difference they made was marginal, and in the long run the only effect of any particular cushioning of the newly unemployed may be slightly to increase the job prospects of rather longer-unemployed people. Since they have their maximum effect near the beginning of a spell of unemployment they have no effect upon the phenomenon of long-term unemployment, which is of great significance at the present time. Earnings-related additions were abolished in the early 1980s so the argument would now only apply to the comparatively rare recipients of large amounts of redundancy pay.

However, it has also been suggested that unemployed people on means-tested benefits have been deterred from seeking work by the high levels of benefit relative to the lowest earnings levels. This has been used as an argument for ensuring that the unemployed gain less than any other group from the benefit system. The introduction of the 'family credit' scheme has been seen by the government as ensuring that people with family responsibilities will be better off in work than on benefit. The particularly harsh treatment of the under-25s under the 'income support' scheme helps to ensure that young people without family responsibilities cannot achieve benefit levels comparable with even exceptionally low wages.

In 1986 the government introduced the Restart Programme. This was designed for unemployed people who, according to them, 'need special help to return to work'. It involves interviewing people who have been unemployed some time. They may then be offered a variety of things. This may include a job, of course, and in this case if it is a low-paid job then there may also be a temporary Jobstart Allowance of £20 per week. It may include reference to some other special scheme. All that many are offered is attendance at a Restart course 'which re-motivates and re-equips people to get back into employment' or at a Jobclub, 'which helps people in their own job searches with expert advice and free facilities'.

In 1989 the government introduced a 'pilot' 'job interview guarantee' scheme; it extended this into a national programme in the winter of 1990–1. The aim is to break down employer resistance to recruiting the long-term unemployed. At the time of writing, the scheme seems to have met with some success. In the six-month period April–October 1991 66,000 people were sent to interviews and about a quarter of them were placed in jobs.

In many ways these ventures are an extension of the helping services outlined in the last section. Why then include them under a section on the policing of the benefit system? There are two answers to this. One is simply to ask, why should government be so concerned to develop a specific technique for reviewing the circumstances of the long-term unemployed at a time of very high unemployment? The other is to observe that at the time the government introduced Jobstart it also tightened the provision enabling the stopping of, or reduction of, benefits to those seen as failing to take employment opportunities so that the rejection of a specific job no longer has to be proved. In fact, failure to attend a Jobstart interview or accept recommendations made or actions taken after such an interview can lead to the stopping of benefit.

The government's statements at the end of the 1980s about the importance of the Jobcentres for the surveillance of the unemployed (Department of Employment, 1988a, p. 28) illustrate their resolve to operate the system in the way described above. What is more, there has been a persistent rejection of the other more logical move to integrate the administration of benefits for the unemployed with the rest of benefit work, to get away from the inefficient arrangement under which 'income support' for the unemployed is calculated by Department of Social Security but paid on their behalf by the Department of Employment.

CONCLUSIONS

For many years policies for the relief of unemployment, apart from macroeconomic ones, were confined to the provision of benefits and the availability of a relatively passive employment exchange system. The rise of unemployment in the 1970s was met by revitalized public agencies committed to 'active' manpower policy. This has led not only to extensive consideration of the case for intervening in the labour market on behalf of specific groups within the unemployed, but also to the development of job-creation measures. These measures have proved difficult to operate because of strong inhibitions upon competition with the 'regular' labour market. In Britain today policies have been designed to maximize removals from the unemployment register while minimizing their inflationary effects.

These policies have been conceived as temporary expedients. They are beginning to look rather permanent. Pessimism about the future prospects for employment is primarily based upon the British economy's diminishing capacity to absorb labour as high-technology industry grows in importance and Britain competes inadequately with the rest of the world.

Nevertheless, in December 1988 the government brought out a new report on employment policy, *Employment for the 1990s* (Department of Employment, 1998b). This document took a stance on the future of employment which was quite sharply at variance with what had gone before. It boasted of its 'great success in creating new jobs and reducing unemployment' and suggested that problems of labour shortage lie ahead for the British economy as the demographic trends which had led to a growth of the labour force begin to be reversed. In the depth of a recession in 1992 this seems an implausible position. However, there will in due course be a recovery from the recession. Will it be plausible then?

There are in fact still a number of reasons for scepticism. One is that the growth in the labour force was fuelled as much by increased female labour market participation as by a general demographic trend. It is not clear to what extent female participation is at its maximum, particularly given the complications which arise from the extent to which it has involved amounts of part-time work which may increasingly be regarded as insufficient.

The second reason is that accompanying predictions of a falling labour force there have also been statements about the burden of the growing elderly population, and some policy changes have taken place to reduce the value of pensions in the future. Since the period of very high unemployment saw the development of a range of measures to encourage ageing workers to leave the labour force, a changing job market would see the reversal of those measures. Furthermore, if job opportunities are good, our increasingly healthy elderly population will be encouraged to stay in the labour market.

In general, our unemployment data are very unreliable. The changes made to the method of counting the unemployed during the 1980s have been multiple and complex. The most important of the changes involved ceasing to count as unemployed people registering with the Department of Employment for work but not able to claim social security benefit. If the aim of the changes was to ensure that only the *real* unemployed were being counted, this was particularly inappropriate since anyone registering with no hope of financial gain was manifestly not cheating the system or seeking aid without any interest in getting work! Other changes involved eliminating from the count people temporarily on work-creation or training schemes, and people whom the government wished to encourage to withdraw from the labour force (particularly women and elderly people). Whilst the government's rationale for changing the counting method was to avoid exaggerating the problem of unemployment (a proposition that its opponents would turn the other way round) it must be recognized that any change to the counting basis tends to lead to the misinterpretation of trends. Elimination from the unemployed count of groups of people whose future labour market behaviour is more than normally difficult to predict – that is, groups such as women, the young and the old, whose behaviour in this respect is changing – does tend to make the statistics more difficult to use for planning purposes. In its 1988 paper the government seemed to be using its own statistics to arrive at peculiarly complacent predictions about the future of unemployment.

SUGGESTIONS FOR FURTHER READING

This is another topic on which recent policy change has rendered many books rather dated. There has been a large number of books on unemployment, but few have dealt with the measures for the unemployed in any depth. Quite an old book which nevertheless sets out the issues about unemployment and policies for the unemployed very well is Sinfield's *What Unemployment Means* (1981). Up-to-date analyses of policies are contained in the Unemployment Unit's regular *Unemployment Bulletin*; and one of the staff of that unit has examined policies for the young: Dan Finn in his *Training Without Jobs* (1987). Considerable use has been made in this chapter of the government's two publications on employment and training policy (Department of Employment, 1988a, 1988b). They do set out the rationale for current policies, but, as suggested in the chapter, they should be consulted with a sceptical eye. Some more-independent up-to-date books on employment policy are badly needed.

CHAPTER 10

Housing

INTRODUCTION

In Great Britain in 1990 the housing stock comprised 22.8 million dwellings. 5.1 million of them (22 per cent of the stock) were rented from local authorities, 0.7 million (3 per cent) were rented from housing associations, and 1.7 million (8 per cent) were privately rented. Owner-occupation accounted for 15.3 million (67 per cent) (Department of the Environment, 1991). We will see, in this chapter, that public policies influenced all these sectors, if not directly through public provision then indirectly through tax subsidies (in the case of the owner-occupied sector) or rent regulation (in the privately rented sector).

From the end of the First World War until 1979 the owner-occupier and publicly provided sectors grew dramatically at the expense of the privately rented sector. Since 1979 the former has continued to grow but the latter has significantly declined (it contained 29 per cent of the stock in the late 1970s) as a result of the sale of council houses to their occupiers.

These developments have been enormously influenced by government interventions. There have also, inevitably, been complex interactions between the sectors as the system has changed. For example, increased opportunities for owner-occupation have both diminished the demand for private renting and been partly created by landlords' desires to sell houses that seem no longer to offer a satisfactory return if they are let. We will return later to give more attention to some of the interactions of this kind that have policy implications. However, it is clearly simplest to introduce this discussion of policies by examining each sector separately.

THE LOCAL AUTHORITY SECTOR

While there had been a small amount of public housing built earlier, the effective growth of this sector dates from the enactment of legislation after the First World War to enable local authorities to receive central government subsidies towards the provision of housing 'for the working classes'. A long succession of subsequent Acts of Parliament have elaborated this initiative, encouraging both the building of large estates designed to meet basic housing needs and the adoption of substantial slum clearance schemes. While the housing no longer has to be specifically 'for the working classes', this sector has become the main provider of houses for those unable to buy their own.

The history of the subsidy system developed in this sector is complicated. For many years the government used, but regularly changed, a system under which local authorities secured a fixed sum per dwelling annually over a fixed period of years. In the 1960s the Labour Government adopted a new approach, without terminating the older subsidies, under which percentage subsidies were paid to, effectively, subsidize the rate at which authorities borrowed money. However, in the 1972 Housing Finance Act the Conservatives sought to sweep away all the continuing older systems of subsidy. The objective was to move to a system in which general-purpose subsidies were eventually eliminated. They recognized the need to continue to subsidize certain particularly expensive forms of development, and in particular slum clearance. They also acknowledged a case for subsidizing low-income tenants by requiring authorities to operate rent rebate schemes which received an element of national subsidy. Otherwise they expected local authorities to move towards balanced housing budgets by raising rents. A national system of 'fair rents', at higher levels than existing rents, was to be developed that might leave some authorities, whose housing commitments were particularly costly, with deficits that would be partly met out of central government grants. But most authorities should reach a position at which general subsidies would be unnecessary, and some would achieve surpluses which they would have to hand over to central government.

Naturally this new scheme was designed to be phased in gradually. Rents were to be increased in stages, and a 'transitional subsidy' was paid. Before the transition could be completed the Conservatives lost power, and the new Labour administration suspended the operation of the Housing Finance Act. They had, however, to put something in its place. In 1975 the Housing Rents and Subsidies Act was enacted as a temporary measure, pending a thorough review of the system. This gave back to the local authorities back their power to fix rents. It also maintained the subsidies to the local authorities at the levels operating under the transitional arrangements for the implementation of the 1972 Act, and added the following:

1   Subsidies towards new investment costs, and towards increases in the costs of servicing old debts (interest rates were rising fast at the time);
2   Special subsidies to help high-cost areas;
3   Subsidies to enable rents to be kept down as part of the counter-inflationary policies of 1974–6.

The promised review of the system was completed in 1977 and a 'consultative document' on housing policy was published (HMSO, 1977). This proposed a system that had some features in common with the Housing Finance Act but did not directly interfere with the authorities' power to fix their own rents, and did not entail a gradual phasing out of general-purpose subsidies. The general approach offered a potential for manipulation in a variety of ways determined by the ideology of the government operating it. The consultative document described the approach as follows:

(i)   The starting point of the calculation of subsidy would be an authority's entitlement to subsidy in the previous year;
(ii)   each year a basis for calculation of the extra expenditure admissible for subsidy – including extra costs of management and maintenance assessed on an appropriate formula – would be settled for the coming year in consultation with local authorities;
(iii) each year an appropriate level of increase in the 'local contribution' to costs, from rent and rates, would be determined for the coming year, also in consultation with local authorities;
(iv)   if the extra admissible expenditure of an authority exceeded the increase in the 'local contribution', subsidy entitlement would be increased. If on the other hand the extra local contribution exceeded this extra expenditure subsidy entitlement would be correspondingly reduced.   (Ibid., p. 83)

The Labour government fell in 1979 before it could enact this system, but the Conservatives' Housing Act of 1980 essentially took it over. Then, what became crucial, since the new government was committed to reducing as far as possible the central government subsidy to council house rents was the annual assumptions made, under point (iii) above, about appropriate levels of rent increases.

Therefore, during the 1980s large numbers of local authorities ceased to be entitled to subsidy from central government, other than contributions to pay the cost of rent rebates (housing benefit). By the middle of the decade only about a quarter of all local authorities were still getting this subsidy, and over three-quarters of the total sum being paid out went to London boroughs (Malpass, 1990, pp. 147–8). After this the numbers of authorities getting subsidy increased a little.

Under the arrangements described above, rents could still be subsidized from local resources (the rate fund). What in fact happened in the early 1980s was that there was an increased divergence between authorities. The sharp withdrawal of central subsidy meant than, in aggregate, local subsidies to rents exceeded national subsidies by 1983. However, it was once again only in a small number of authorities, mostly in London, that such contributions were of any significant size (ibid., p. 168). In around half of all authorities there were no contributions made at all. At the other extreme an increasing number of authorities were making contributions *to* the rate fund from rents – that is, council tenants not on housing benefit were subsidizing rate payers! Malpass describes the situation as follows:

> The total number of authorities making transfers to the rates increased year by year, from 84 in 1982–3 to 130 in 1988–9. English non-metropolitan and outer London authorities were more likely to make transfers than metropolitan, inner London or Welsh authorities. And amongst the English non-metropolitan districts, southern ones were more likely to make transfers than northern authorities.   (Ibid., pp. 152–3)

In a measure enacted in 1990 the government set out to force local authorities to phase out these exchanges between housing accounts and their general accounts. This measure was widely described as 'ring-fencing' the housing revenue accounts. Local authorities were forced to raise rents to replace local contributions. A further complication was that in determining the rules for these accounts the government started taking into account a notional income from housing benefit subsidy. What this implies is that authorities may find that they are in effect required to partly subsidize the benefits to low-income tenants from the rents of other tenants. This new regime is gradually being phased in; as before, the actual situation depends upon the government's application to each authority of the formula described above.

As suggested above, as general subsidy has disappeared and general rents have gone up so housing benefit has tended to become the dominant form of 'subsidy' going to local authority tenants. This is paid not by the Department of the Environment but by the Department of Social Security. As its costs went up the latter department reduced the availability of housing benefits by steepening the rate at which they tapered off with income increases.

The determination of capital expenditure, that is primarily the building of new houses, is also based on a system devised in the late 1970s by the Labour government. Before 1977 local councils determined their house-building programmes without consulting central government. However, to implement those programmes they had to secure central acceptance both to enable them to undertake such extensive investment and to obtain subsidies (inasmuch as subsidies were linked to specific building projects). Local government proposed and central government would dispose. The whole system was relatively haphazard since central government tried to link its decisions to national, and relative local, priorities but was dependent upon local initiatives, and did not necessarily have an overall view of national housing needs. Under the system established in 1977 local authorities are required to submit for annual central scrutiny their 'Housing Strategies and Investment Programmes'. These include not only their plans for the provision of new local authority housing, but also their plans to make loans for house purchase, to give grants for housing improvements, to improve their own stock, to clear unfit houses, to purchase houses and to assist housing associations. Statistical returns from the authorities are required on their own current and future activities, and on their intelligence on local housing needs and problems of private sector building. On the basis of these submissions the local authorities then, after a process of negotiation through the regional offices of the Department of the Environment, receive annual expenditure allocations, not in the form of specific permission for particular projects but in the form of a broad block.

The Thatcher Government's impact upon this system in the early 1980s was simply to limit expenditure, particularly on new building. From 1985 onwards, however, there was some relaxation to allow for the improvement of the council housing stock. New building remained low. In the late seventies local authorities in the United Kingdom built a little over 100,000 dwellings each year. In the early 1980s it was down to a little over 30,000 a year, and at the end of the decade it was about 17,000 (Department of the Environment, 1991, p. 47).

These changes in public housing policy in the 1980s, towards the reduction of subsidies and the restriction of new building, need to be seen together with the government's stimulation of the sale of council houses. Local authorities' role in the provision of housing was beginning to be restricted. A Housing Act passed in 1988 seemed to be going very much further in marginalizing the local authority role. In a measure, misleadingly presented by the government as enabling tenants to choose their landlords, opportunities were presented to housing associations and other independent buyers approved by the government to acquire local authority properties. Initiatives of this kind were bound to come from the potential buyers, encouraged by Conservative local authorities who wanted to sell their stock, rather than from the tenants exercising 'choice'. Such moves could only be blocked if a majority of the tenants concerned vetoed them. Another section of the Act proposed to set up a number of Housing Action Trusts in areas where, according to the government, substantial estate improvements needed to be made. These Trusts would take over local authority properties, spend government money on improvements and could then pass on the property to new owners.

The Housing Action Trust idea was opposed by tenants in several of the areas where they were planned, and the government backed down or gave pledges that after improvements the properties could be restored to local authority ownership. The 'tenants choice' proposal has so far only led to a limited number of housing association acquisitions from small southern authorities. All this part of the 1988 Act seems already a rather dated product of the high point of Conservative faith in privatization, at a time when the finance industry – having gone as far as it possibly could to sell mortgages to individuals – seemed temporarily to see acquisition of local authority assets as a good outlet for their profit-seeking.

In the 1970s the Labour Government had argued that: 'There is no longer an absolute shortage of houses. Whereas in 1951 there were about 750,000 more households than houses in England and Wales, by 1976 there were 500,000 more houses than households' (HMSO, 1977, p. 10). It went on to acknowledge that this did not imply a straightforward 'surplus' of houses. A considerable number of houses are temporarily vacant at any time and some people own two houses. However, it particularly emphasized the need to give attention to a range of special housing problems: regional and local imbalances in the supply of houses, the continuing presence of unfit or substandard houses (again unevenly spread across the nation), and the existence of specific groups in the population who have difficulties in securing access to houses adequate for their needs.

The Conservatives have more crudely reduced the supply of council houses so that in the area of population pressure around London the numbers of the homeless show that a straightforward quantity problem still exists. In other places, however, the central problems often concern the deteriorating quality of the housing stock and the existence of local authority dwellings that are difficult or impossible to let.

The whole picture is inevitably complicated, in ways which official housing need assessments do perhaps not adequately consider, by increases in rates of household formation – as young people leave home earlier and couples break up. Characteristic of recent policy has been the explicit disregard of these phenomena and indeed social security policies which attempt to prevent them happening.

These issues about homelessness and about the deteriorating local authority stock will be discussed further below.

OWNER-OCCUPATION

It has already been suggested that the examination of housing policy raises difficulties for any distinction between social policy and other areas of public policy. It might be imagined that the private market for owner-occupied houses had very little to do with social policy or indeed with government interventions in society. However, such an impression can be readily removed by an examination of the attention housing has been given in the policies of the major parties in the years since the Second World War. A central issue in the general elections of 1950 and 1951 was the performance of the Labour Government in 'building' houses, and the claim of the Conservative Opposition to be able to 'build' more houses. The argument was about the building of houses, but public authorities were not the only builders. The Conservatives came to power in 1951 committed to 'building' 300,000 houses a year, but many of these were to be built by private enterprise for owner-occupation. Indeed, the Conservatives increasingly encouraged the development of this sector during the 1950s. Both parties have been concerned, though in rather different ways, to assist the development of owner-occupation. They see an aspiration towards owner-occupation as having considerable electoral implications.

How then do public policies influence the owner-occupied housing sector? Of central importance is the large public subsidy to owner-occupiers that is given through the fact that interest payments on mortgage loans up to the first £30,000 attract income tax relief which reduces them by the standard rate of tax. There has been some political debate as to whether it is appropriate to call relief from taxation a subsidy. What is indisputable is that an allowance of this kind reduces the actual rate of interest paid by mortgage borrowers by a quarter (at the standard rate of tax operative in 1991).

The value of the tax allowance on mortgage interest is dependent on the rate of interest. The higher that is, the more valuable the tax concession. This is what has made it so significant in recent years. High rates of interest have enormously increased the sum of money lost to taxation. Indeed, the amounts are now so large that they far exceed the subsidies to public housing. In 1990–1 tax relief to owner-occupiers in the United Kingdom cost about £7700 million (Inland Revenue, 1991).

Mortgage interest relief was originally given when owner-occupied houses attracted a tax called Schedule A tax. But Schedule A tax was abolished in 1963. Now, therefore, owner-occupiers are securing help to purchase an asset the real cost of which is, so long as there is inflation, falling throughout the period of the mortgage. The peculiarity of owner-occupied housing today is that considerable financial sacrifices may be necessary to secure a house, but over time initial purchase costs, which of course determine mortgage size, become less and less in real terms. Owners have acquired assets that normally depreciate very much more slowly than money. Indeed, the very existence of tax relief contributes to their appreciation.

Governments support the aspiration towards house ownership. They therefore want to help more people to become owner-occupiers. However, the peculiar evolution of our system has left them with a device which, while it does help first-time buyers, continues to yield great advantages to owner-occupiers long after they have first started to borrow, and concentrates its help not upon low-income but high-income house-purchasers. Various ideas have been canvassed to reduce what has been called the problem of 'front-loading' of mortgage costs. All require government subsidy to shift the balance of expense. Logically such government expenditure could be offset against some withdrawal of the indiscriminate mortgage subsidy. However, there is a political objection to that (voiced quite plainly in the Labour Government's 1977 consultative document). This is that people make decisions to borrow money on the basis of certain expectations of tax relief. In other words, any sudden change would be sharply redistributive, would have its most severe impact upon those whose calculations left least margin for variation, and would therefore be very unpopular in a society where over half the householders are owner-occupiers and most of these are still repaying mortgages. The government has developed a number of special ways of helping first-time buyers (which space does not allow us to examine in any detail) but it seems unlikely to upset the basic structure of mortgage-lending and related income tax relief.

It is not merely through subsidies that the government has influenced opportunities for individuals to secure owner-occupied housing. In the period immediately after the Second World War the government maintained tight control over building through control over access to building supplies. As it relaxed these controls it stimulated private building. Then, in the 1950s, as it began to reduce the amount of local authority building, it thereby encouraged a shift of resources into building for sale. During that period of management of a fully employed economy along Keynesian lines the government came to recognize that one of the ways in which it could most easily influence the economic climate was by influencing the demand for building. While the direct controls of the immediate postwar period no longer exist, there remains a series of factors that influence the scale of building of houses for sale: the extent to which alternative – particularly public sector – opportunities exist for the building industry; the availability of credit – particularly cheap credit – for building enterprises and land speculators; the supply of building workers – particularly skilled workers; the availability of building society funds for home buyers; and the availability of land.

Until the 1980s the main suppliers of finance for house purchase were the building societies. These were comparatively cautious financial institutions, whose activities had grown slowly. Their origins lie in nineteenth-century self-help and charitable ventures, and they remain in some sense non-profit-making institutions. They depend for their operation on being able to attract funds at rates of interest, influenced by the general range of opportunities open to savers, to lend to house-buyers.

Government encouragement of home ownership naturally entailed, once the proportion of the population with their own houses was very high, ways to make it possible for those who were regarded by the building societies, who have been naturally cautious in these matters, as 'bad risks' to borrow money. Hence there has been governmental pressure upon these 'private' organizations to lend to more 'marginal' people or on more 'marginal' properties.

During the 1980s the government deregulated the financial market. Restrictions on building societies' activities were removed and other lenders, including banks, discovered opportunities to move into the domestic mortgage business. There was a boom period when lenders saw the housing market as an ideal source of profits. Mortgages were sold aggressively, and the customary caution about the creditworthiness of borrowers was abandoned. This further fuelled the boom to which it was a response, owner-occupation expanded and house prices moved up rapidly. This boom, pushing up house prices well beyond the overall rate of inflation, eventually collapsed in the recession at the end of the decade. House prices started to fall, the housing market became exceptionally static and, with rising unemployment, many recent borrowers found themselves in difficulties with their mortgage repayments. At the time of writing, the government faces political difficulties, with the frustration of individual expectations and the dispossession of impoverished borrowers. In their search for a solution they have turned to the lenders, seeking to persuade them to sustain the partly abandoned approach of the building societies of concern for the welfare of their borrowers. Devices are being sought to prevent widespread dispossessions.

Government intervention in the land market also has an impact upon owner-occupation – both by affecting the availability of building land

and by affecting its price. Of course, these two are interrelated, and one of the problems for intervention in the land market has been the relative unpredictability of these two effects. A concern about profiteering from land speculation has influenced legislation by all the postwar Labour governments, while the Conservatives have sought to reduce the Labour impact upon a free market for land. The actual impact upon private housing of this long-running political battle – through the Town and Country Planning Act of 1947, the repeal of many of its features by the Conservatives in the 1950s, the 1967 Land Commission Act, the Community Land Act of 1975 and its repeal in 1980 – is unclear and cannot be considered here. This issue is mentioned, however, because it is important not to overlook the significance of land legislation for the housing market.

THE PRIVATE-RENTED SECTOR

The private-rented sector (excluding the housing association sector – see next section), which now houses only about 8 per cent of the population, is increasingly seen as the 'residual' sector. Since, however, its decline to this position is a relatively recent phenomenon (in 1951, over half the households in England and Wales were in this sector and in 1918 probably about 90 per cent were renting privately), it is important to consider the causes of this decline.

There has been a political, but now rather academic, argument about this. Was the decline of the private-rented sector inevitable, as better outlets for investment opened up, or was its decline produced by government-imposed controls? From 1916 onwards there were controls of varying kinds and varying degrees of stringency. Controversy raged over the protection of private tenants from both eviction and high rents. Between 1965 and 1988 the 'fair rent' principle was adopted for most forms of private tenure. This represented a political compromise based on a comparatively nonsensical formula in which rent officers were expected to assume that properties were let in a market in which there was no scarcity. The reality was that rents were determined by a system of comparisons at levels some way below what the market might be expected to bear. At the same time many landlords sought to evade the rent controls altogether by legal devices such as the granting of a 'licence to occupy' rather than a tenancy. The 1988 Housing Act effectively abandoned rent control, apart from various rather complex measures of protection to tenants with agreements dating from earlier rent control regimes.

In decontrolling this sector the government argued that returning it to the 'market place' would arrest its decline. Yet this depends upon the alternative opportunities available to renters. In particular, in the context of tax-system-subsidized house purchase (as described above), owning is likely to be a better prospect than renting for most people with the resources to pay market rents and proposing to stay in the same district for some time.

Excluding temporary residents of an area, amongst whom students figure as a significant group, this means that private tenants will tend to be low-income earners and recipients of social security benefits. To enable them to pay market rents the government has had to allow them access to the housing benefit scheme. However, the problem about this scheme is that receipt of benefit removes any incentive to the renter to behave like a free-market participant. The cost of the rent falls upon the state. To cope with this problem for the social security budget a complex procedure has been adopted, requiring rent officers to rule whether rents should be regarded as excessive for benefit purposes and requiring the hapless tenant (or sometimes the local authority) to find the balance, rather than central government. In other words, a special system of benefit control has replaced rent control.

The private-rented sector is unevenly distributed across the country. In some areas, and particularly in the North, there are still old, poor-quality houses occupied by elderly tenants who have been in them for very many years. With this property the main public concern has been about conditions. Local authorities have included many such houses in their slum clearance programmes. As they have removed the worst houses it has been increasingly questioned whether improvement is not preferable to demolition. A feature of the better estates of old houses has been the piecemeal extension of owner-occupation among the rented property. Owner-occupiers have been more ready than land-lords to make use of improvement grants. The consequence has been the patchy regeneration of such areas. To further this process, there-fore, local authorities have been able to designate 'general improve-ment areas' or 'housing action areas' where they can better the overall environment and pressurize or buy out private landlords in order to secure the improvement of the remaining houses. As time passes, the characteristic tenure in these areas is becoming owner-occupation rather than private renting.

Elsewhere the private sector may have rather different charac-teristics. In London in particular, but also in many other big cities, much of this accommodation is in the form of flats created out of large old houses. Local authorities may again tackle the problems of these areas through compulsory purchase or improvement, but they are often reluctant to go beyond the more limited powers they possess to curb the worst abuses of 'slum landlordism'. These areas tend to accommo-date people whom local authorities do not see as their responsibility (or at least place very low on their scales of priorities): in particular, newcomers to the area and the young single. The concentration of housing problems in areas of this kind, therefore, offers a challenge for the development of more-comprehensive local authority policies. As other housing problems have been solved, the gap between the good housing conditions of the majority and the often very poor conditions experienced in this part of the private sector has become increasingly evident.

HOUSING ASSOCIATIONS

It has already been noted that there is a housing association sector owning over half a million homes (around 3 per cent of the housing stock). Housing associations were important in the nineteenth century, as voluntary, charitable bodies, but declined with the growth of the public sector in the twentieth. But over the last 25 years housing association growth has been given government encouragement, being seen as an alternative form of 'social' housing to the large and bureaucratic local authority sector. Housing associations may receive grants and subsidies from government, through the Housing Corporation, and in the 1980s much new investment in rented housing was in this sector rather than the local government one. We have already noted how the 1988 Act encouraged some shifting of local authority tenants into housing association tenancies.

Housing associations vary widely in size, scope and character. Some differ little in their characteristics from private companies; these have grown in size recently, absorbing some associations along the way. Others have distinct charitable aims and objects, and many are specifically local in their coverage. A small number are co-operatives.

HOMELESSNESS

Homelessness has increased as a result of a combination of mobility in search of work in the overcrowded south and family breakdown with the decline in the supply of vacant accommodation, deriving from the lack of local authority building and the continuing shrinkage of the private-rented sector. It also has causes outside the direct control of housing policy, in the unwillingness of the social security system to pay adequate benefits to some groups (in particular the young). Finally, it must be noted that many amongst the homeless are in need of health and social care, to assist with problems of mental illness, alcoholism and drug abuse. Many provide evidence of undesirable consequences of the shift towards community care described in chapter 6.

In 1977 the Housing (Homeless Persons) Act imposed a duty upon local housing authorities to provide accommodation for homeless persons in certain 'priority' groups. These priority groups are, broadly, families containing children or elderly or sick persons, together with those made homeless by disasters such as flood or fire. However, authorities need not help families who are deemed to have become homeless 'intentionally'. This controversial provision was added to the Act by an amendment and may be used to justify refusal of help to someone who has been evicted for not paying rent.

This Act is interesting, since for many years there had been uncertainty about the relative responsibilities of the housing and the social services authorities for helping the homeless. In 1974 a government circular urged housing authorities to provide adequate help for the homeless. The resulting patchy response intensified the conflict between housing and social services in some areas, and created anomalies where neighbouring authorities treated the homeless very differently. The government decided, under strong pressure from some of the housing charities, to rectify this by legislation. However, they could not find time for this in the 1976–77 parliamentary session. But when a Liberal Member, Stephen Ross, promoted a private member's Bill they gave full governmental support. Hence the law was changed in an unusual way. The new legislation aimed to secure a more uniform response and, by making it mandatory for any authority to give temporary help and for more permanent help to be given where a homeless person has a (carefully defined) local connection, to end the buckpassing between authorities that caused great distress and hardship. The other important aspect of the clear shift of responsibility is that it is implicit within the Act that the homeless must be rehoused, except on a very temporary basis, in permanent homes, and not be herded into inadequate accommodation. In this sense they are in competition with those rehoused by the housing departments from their waiting lists. In practice many authorities, particularly in London, use poor-quality, temporary accommodation for housing homeless people for long periods of time.

It must, in conclusion, be emphasized that the policy response described above is principally for families. Local authorities' obligations to the single are simply to give advice! It is single homelessness which has grown visibly, particularly in London, during the 1980s. It has already been suggested that the roots of this problem lie in a complex of factors, only some of which concern housing policy. Certainly, however, the hard-pressed, under-resourced local authority housing departments are unable to pay much attention to the needs of this group, particularly if the individuals need some combination of housing and social care.

LOCAL AUTHORITY ALLOCATION PROCEDURES

Wherever there is competition for local authority housing the determination of rules to govern priorities is an emotive matter. As local authority housing became big business most authorities changed from systems that depended upon the judgements, or whims, of councillors or officials to waiting lists based upon some queuing principles. The main issues were, first, to what extent the simple queuing approach should be modified by the development of 'points systems' which enabled individual priorities to be weighted; secondly, what the balance should be in such systems between needs and waiting time; and thirdly, whether any preference should be extended to those who had resided in the area for some time.

Central government became critical of local schemes that did not give overwhelming importance to need. Local authorities were urged to abandon residence requirements, both because they may have an impact upon labour mobility and because they may facilitate a covert form of racial discrimination. An official advisory committee, the Cullingworth Committee (Central Housing Advisory Committee, 1969), strongly urged the adoption of need-based points schemes. There has been a distinct move towards the development of points schemes; this was particularly enhanced by the abolition of many smaller housing authorities when local government was reformed in 1974. However, local commitments to residence rules die hard.

However much a local authority endeavours to govern its allocation policies by fair and open points schemes, it has also to make allowance for housing priorities that do not fit those schemes. Homelessness has already been mentioned as one such example of this. Individual unfit houses may also require immediate responses. Demolition because of new roads or slum clearance schemes bring re-housing responsibilities that may cut across waiting-list allocation in a major way. With low levels of new house building such commitments may bring movement from waiting lists almost to a standstill. Finally, some authorities recognize special categories of need, which cannot readily be translated into housing 'points', that are determined by health or social work priorities, and allow other agencies to make special recommendations. These call for discretionary judgement by housing officials and by doctors or social workers, and there is also an inevitable tension between the maintenance of rules and special arguments for 'queue-jumping'.

HARD-TO-LET HOMES

Allocation of council houses involves achieving a balance between what people want, what they are deemed to need, and what is available. Under conditions of housing scarcity, individuals are, unless their co-operation is required with a redevelopment scheme, in a weak position to assert their wants. Housing authorities allocate on the basis of assessments of need, attempting to make the most efficient use of the housing stock. But in the past they often gave attention to capacity to pay, and many were also disposed to make judgements about potential tenants' suitability for 'good' houses. Elizabeth Burney portrayed this decision-making as follows:

> The principle is simple: a clean person gets a clean house and a dirty person gets a dirty house. In between are all kinds of subtle gradings which are the everyday material of housing management. Quiet, clean, steady-earning families with not more than three children are highly prized because they make life easy for management and their neighbours. They are usually repaid by being put near other 'good' families in better houses. The most unsatisfactory tenants may only get old terraced property awaiting demolition, or rehabilitated as part of the council's permanent stock; or simply one of the shabbier inter-war houses. (Burney, 1967, p. 71)

The Cullingworth Committee also attacked this aspect of housing management. Housing authorities have become increasingly sensitive to the problems entailed in, and following from, policies of this kind. However, as in some areas the numbers of families who are desperate for help decline, so the balance of power between housing officers who judge needs and potential tenants who express their demands inevitably shifts. Now, poorer houses are often only easily allocated to, for example, the homeless. However, a reshuffling of tenants proceeds all the while, and those allocated the 'bad' houses seek transfers to better ones. Often they secure such transfers only if they have been 'good' tenants, and in particular if they have been regular rent-payers. The only people who shift in the opposite direction are those who are punished for rent arrears or strikingly non-conforming behaviour by being evicted from 'good' houses into 'bad' ones.

Local authorities now have stocks of houses and flats of various kinds, in particular prewar semis, postwar semis built when standards were very low, modern houses built to very high standards, flats in blocks of various sizes, good old houses acquired from private owners, and patched houses with short lives pending demolition. Of course these dwellings vary in popularity, with perhaps high flats and short-life houses as the least popular. If through allocation and transfer policies there are various forms of segregation within an authority's housing stock, then the 'hierarchy of popularity' will have been influenced by social as well as architectural considerations. Indeed, these social factors may well complicate the hierarchy as certain estates, not necessarily characterized by severe design problems, also acquire reputations as 'rough' or 'respectable', perhaps as a result of some really rather complex accidents of history. This can obviously tend to involve differentiation by income, particularly if accessibility to employment opportunities influences tenant choices. Thus the unpopular areas may contain substantial proportions of households dependent on social security benefits. The sale of council houses (see next section) further enhances the social divisions, since houses on popular estates and on estates in which the more prosperous tenants live are more likely to be sold.

As a result of this mixture of factors local authorities now find that, where the demand for housing is falling, they have 'hard-to-let' houses. Families still in quite poor conditions in the private sector regard their existing situations as preferable to rehousing in, for example, a badly vandalized tower block. Authorities' problems may be compounded, moreover, by the fact that those families least able or likely to object to these undesirable dwellings may be the very families who, rightly or wrongly, are identified in the eyes of others as contributing to the stigma attached to them. Moreover, some aspects of this vicious circle have already been identified above. What do the authorities do about applications for transfers out of unpopular dwellings? And if an authority does not want to create homelessness, what weapon can it use against bad rent-payers but 'demotion' to less-desirable accommodation?

Authorities resort to a variety of devices in these situations. Some do halt transfers, and seek to allocate unwary 'good' tenants to unfavourable property, but this is unpopular and may have political repercussions. In some cases architectural and environmental improvements may help. In some areas a group whom hitherto local authorities have largely ignored, the young single, are accommodated in unpopular properties, particularly high flats. Some authorities have sold some blocks of flats cheaply to private owners. But in some cases demolition, even of relatively modern property, has been seen as the only answer. In many places local authorities are worried about the extent to which they are becoming new kinds of 'slum landlords'.

The Selling of Council Houses

The Conservative party has advocated the selling of council houses to their occupiers for some years. While Labour generally, and particularly Labour local authorities, resisted this policy, their line on this issue was modified in the 1970s.

The Conservatives came to power in 1979 determined to stimulate the sale of council houses. Their Housing Act of 1980 provided a statutory right of tenants to buy their own houses at market prices less a discount based on length of tenancy, ranging from 33 to 50 per cent. Subsequently the government put pressure on Labour-controlled authorities which dragged their feet in implementing this provision, going so far in one case, Norwich, as to secure legal intervention to enable them to put in a special commissioner to do the job.

The impact of this policy has been described as follows:

As a result of this legislation, almost 1.5 million local authority and new town tenants bought their homes during the 1980s. Annual sales peaked at 226 thousand in 1982, but fell to less than half this level in 1985 and 1986. Between 1986 and 1989 sales increased in each year before falling again in 1990 when only 140 thousand dwellings were sold ... (*Social Trends 22*, 1992, p. 147)

Since council tenants are, generally speaking, low-income people, sales will have been affected by unemployment, which was particularly high in the middle and end of this period. Moreover, the number with the resources to buy will ultimately be finite so some falling away in numbers is to be expected. In fact the recovery from the sales slump in 1985–6 was influenced by increased discounts and an increase in the range of properties which could be bought.

It is also the case that the success of the policy varies markedly from area to area, according to levels of prosperity (see Forrest and Murie, 1991, ch. 6).

The debate about the selling of council houses is partly a technical one about the actual effect of such a sale upon the housing effort as a whole, and partly an ideological one about council tenants' rights. Even if it believes that a council house sale diminishes its capacity to respond to unmet needs, Labour local authorities have been faced by a peculiar dilemma about putting the interests of potential future tenants above those of actual present ones.

This debate must also be seen in the light of what was said in the last section about hard-to-let houses. The houses that tenants are likely to buy will be in 'good' popular estates. The development within these of a mixture of owner-occupation and renting may be seen as desirable for the future of such estates, in the long run extending social mixing and social diversity to those estates. But such a development reinforces the growing gap between the 'good' estates and the 'bad'. In this way it reinforces a future for local authority housing, in a society in which owner-occupation is continuing to grow, in which public renting will be seen as a much inferior option to ownership. Britain is moving to a situation, like that in the United States, in which public-sector housing is not even 'housing for the working classes', as it was required to be in the original legislation, but housing for the poor. By 1986–7 almost two-thirds of local authority tenants were on means-tested benefits (figure from a Parliamentary answer quoted by Forrest and Murie, 1991, p. 69). This tendency is likely to be further enhanced by government policies (see pp. 183–5) which push rent levels up leaving subsidy to the benefit system. This increases the incentive of those required to pay full rents to seek to buy. The political problem is that owner-occupation is popular, and its growth seems therefore desirable, but this growth leaves a minority behind in possibly decreasingly satisfactory circumstances.

It is significant that in order to enhance the sale of council houses the government has been forced to provide large discounts. The fact is that for several years already the greater desirability for prosperous working-class people of owner-occupation as against council housing has been so clear that few who can readily afford mortgages for full-cost house purchase are left on council estates. Many who have incomes high enough to buy are already too old to take out a mortgage of normal length. The provision of discounts weakens the economic arguments for sales; older houses that are, perhaps quite reasonably, sold to long-term sitting tenants at low prices still have to be replaced, if there is outstanding housing need, by new, highly expensive houses. The issue draws our attention to a variation of the same anomaly as exists within the owner-occupied sector: there is a vast gap between the original 'historic' costs of housing and modern 'replacement' costs. In the owner-occupied sector someone who bought a house, say in the 1960s, for £2000 may today be repaying a minute (by modern standards) mortgage. If he or she dies, heirs will receive an asset worth many times the original price. In the local authority sector a similar house may, assuming rents have moved in line with prices, today be yielding the local authority a 'profit', which it returns to the rent pool to subsidize newer houses. What is a fair rent (in the true sense – not in the sense in which it is used in the Rent Acts) for such a house? And if the occupier wants to buy, what is a fair price? There are no right answers to these questions; the whole situation is riddled with anomalies. To treat such a tenant well is to give a privilege relative to those who are still seeking local authority accommodation. To treat him or her harshly is to emphasize his or her disadvantage relative to the long-term owner-occupier.

CONCLUSIONS

The latter part of this chapter has particularly emphasized the issues that arise from the interaction between Britain's various housing sectors as the growth of owner-occupation and the decline of renting continues. The interactions here are complex. Recent studies of housing have given attention to movement between the sectors, examining the filtering hypothesis which suggests that the benefits of new houses, even at the top of the owner-occupier market, filter down to contribute to the reduction of housing need. Superficially this seems plausible. However, the 'chains' that have been traced resulting from new houses at the 'top' end of the system are often short. Typically they extend down only to a young new entrant to owner-occupation, perhaps from that special part of the private sector where the needs of the young, mobile middle class are met, perhaps merely forming a new separate household for the first time (Murie, Niner and Watson, 1976; Forrest, Murie and Williams, 1990).

In this concluding section it is intended neither to overload the argument that can be developed from this sort of example nor to elaborate the findings of the research from which it is drawn at any length. What must be stressed is that at least three very different kinds of housing 'career' can be detected. Many involve movement into or entirely within the owner-occupied sector as described above. Some involve movement, either on separation from a parental home or via the private-rented sector, to council housing, but then stop there for the rest of life. And some, of diminishing significance, involve difficulty in moving from the private-rented sector to either of the other more privileged sectors. The argument in this chapter has involved acceptance that the last of these 'careers' is likely to die out. If this is correct, then some of the peculiar problems we have identified about the different expectations within the two major sectors become of increased importance. At the moment interchange between them takes the form of movement out of local authority housing (often by purchase of a council house).

What are the implications for social segregation in Britain if this remains the case? But equally, what are the implications of those interchanges that do occur since they may, as the examination of the issue of the sale of council houses implied, reinforce this new form of social segregation. It is a division in our society that does not precisely correspond with the social class division between manual and non-manual work which has received so much attention in the past. Yet it is a division that may have equally serious implications for the allocation of opportunities and for territorial justice in our society. Since, furthermore, owner occupation conveys benefits which pass on through inheritance, whilst the other sectors do not, these social divisions may be reinforced across time (this is an issue which is attracting increasing attention; see, for example, Hamnett, 1991).

Perhaps too little attention has been given so far to aspects of the interaction of housing policies and other policies – in particular employment and education policies. The progressive reshaping of our housing system over the past 20 to 30 years emphasizes the need for attention to this issue.

SUGGESTIONS FOR FURTHER READING

Balchin (1989) provides a good introduction to British housing policy, whilst Donnison and Ungerson's *Housing Policy* (1982) provides an overview of British housing policy which puts it in a European context. The many issues about housing finance are well discussed in Gibb and Munro's *Housing Finance in the UK* (1991) and in Malpass's *Reshaping Housing Policy* (1990). Merrett's *State Housing in Britain* (1979) provides an historical analysis of British housing policy rooted in a Marxist theoretical framework.

Two books which deal with contemporary developments are Malpass and Murie's *Housing Policy and Practice* (third edition, 1990) and Malpass's edited collection, *The Housing Crisis* (1986). A thorough account of the selling of council houses is contained in Forrest and Murie (1991).

CHAPTER 11

Social Policy and Society

INTRODUCTION

This book has given attention to the major policy areas that are conventionally labelled 'social policy'. It has shown that within these areas the state is responsible for a wide range of activities. In the chapters on individual policies a number of weaknesses were noted in the pattern of provision. Yet it is widely suggested today that the state takes on too much, and that the public service sector, of which the social policy areas account for a large proportion, is too large. We need therefore to look, in this final chapter, at some of the general issues about the role of social policy in society and at some of the attempts to make social policy, as a whole, more effective and more responsive to popular needs and attitudes.

SOCIAL EXPENDITURE IN THE CONTEXT OF NATIONAL PUBLIC EXPENDITURE

First, some figures must be considered to place social policy expenditure in the context of national expenditure. Table 11.1 provides figures setting out expenditure under the main functional headings with which this book has been concerned, together with some other functions, for the purposes of comparison. It compares expenditure just before the beginning of Conservative rule in 1979 with 1990–1, the last year for which 'out-turn' figures are available, using what are described as 'real terms' figures. These are figures adjusted to common price levels, in this case those prevailing in 1990–1, to try to eliminate the distorting impact of inflation.

TABLE 11.1 Public expenditure by function (£ billion in real terms, with proportion of total public expenditure in brackets)

	1978–9	1990–1	Rate of growth (%)	Average annual rate of growth (%)
Housing	11.6 (7.0)	4.9 (2.5)	−58	−4.8
Education and science	24.7 (14.9)	28.4 (14.5)	15	1.3
Health and personal social services	23.4 (14.1)	33.0 (16.9)	41	3.4
Social security	43.0 (26.0)	58.8 (30.1)	37	3.0
Industry, energy, trade and employment	10.5 (6.4)	7.4 (3.8)	−29.5	−2.5
Defence	19.0 (11.5)	21.8 (11.2)	14.7	1.2
Law, order and protective services	6.4 (3.9)	11.4 (5.8)	78.1	6.5
Total national public expenditure	190.1	216.1	13.7	1.1

Source: HMSO, 1992

The total amount of public expenditure in 1990–1 was about 40 per cent of the gross domestic product (GDP). The latter is defined as 'the value of goods and services produced by United Kingdom residents'. It had fallen to this level from about 44 per cent at the end of the seventies. Of course, the relationship of public expenditure to the GDP, depends upon *both* the level of public expenditure and the level of productive output. Politicians pay attention to the relationship between public expenditure and GDP, and some critiques of the welfare state suggest that it is dangerously high. However, much public expenditure involves no more in practice than transfers between citizens (as in social security payments). Hence the notion, sometimes expressed, that a large part of the output of the nation is absorbed into the 'unproductive' public sector is rather misleading.

Some points about the data in table 11.1 are worth underlining. If we treat the first four rows in the table as representing 'social expenditure', that is leaving out employment and including some items in the education budget which have not been considered (scientific research and library expenditure, particularly), we find that it represents 64 per cent of public expenditure. Between 1978–9 and 1990–1 social expenditure has grown slightly faster than public expenditure as a whole, largely because of the big increase in health and social security expenditure. The Conservative governments of this period were committed to public expenditure cuts but did not achieve them. We will come back to this, and discuss a little more the detailed changes to expenditure on the various services, but let us first digress a little to examine the ideological perspectives which may influence the way we assess the performance of the so-called 'welfare state'.

ALTERNATIVE PERSPECTIVES ON SOCIAL POLICY AND THE STATE

The financing of extensive public expenditure requires heavy taxation. It is argued that the size of the redistributive exercise via taxation into public expenditure undertaken by the British government has a disincentive impact upon private initiative and has contributed towards low productivity. It is also suggested that the scale and the scope of the state 'bureaucracy' is such that public resources are inevitably used inefficiently. The British people are alleged to be overtaxed and overgoverned. These are propositions about public expenditure found in the attack upon the welfare state which comes from the political Right (Harris and Seldon, 1979; Minford, 1984).

One way of examining propositions of this kind is to compare Britain with other countries. Newspaper articles regularly attempt to do this, skating cheerfully over the many problems about making such comparisons, in particular different definitions of public expenditure and the gross domestic product. Nevertheless such comparisons tend to show that, while in the United States public authorities proportionately tax less and spend less, Britain's position in league tables of comparable European countries is not particularly exceptional. Perhaps this merely proves that 'overgovernment' is a shared European problem.

Alternatively, it may be suggested that the important comparisons concern not overall taxation and expenditure but kinds of taxation, in particular, differences in the use made of direct and indirect taxation, and kinds of expenditure. There are some very clear differences in the extent to which different nations use insurance devices in relation to expenditure on social security and health; and widely differing uses are made of means tests to control spending on all the major services. In the last resort it is welfare outcomes which are important.

Hence, while attention to comparison between overall levels of public expenditure may not be very revealing, the more detailed examination of ways of providing social policies introduces us to some of the main standpoints in political debate. Government in modern industrialized societies is unlikely to be indifferent to the need to provide cash for those unable to earn, education for the young and health care for all, but it may choose various options for their provision. It may seek to encourage, regulate and strengthen broadly private provisions. It may devise very mixed forms of private and public services. Or it may lay its emphasis on public services, and in so doing endorse the possibility of extensive social engineering towards egalitarian goals.

Certainly, political theorists on the Right see the provision of health and social care, housing and education, together perhaps with social security (beyond some bare minimum), as the responsibility of the individual. It is asserted that instead of depending upon a paternalistic state people should be free to make choices about amounts and kinds of social benefits, just as they make choices about the purchase of ordinary consumer goods. This perspective is likely to embrace the view that a protective welfare state is undesirable, and that individual initiative and independence are desirable characteristics of society which are undermined by welfare measures. People of this persuasion generally regard the existing range of social policies as already too developed in this respect. They argue, therefore, in favour of the maintenance of private sectors in health and education, and of the rationing of services through charging policies.

The advocates of less government involvement, and of the extension of the role of the market, generally have a stance on social equality too. While it could be the case that bureaucratic rigidity and the lack of choice in the present social welfare system might be reduced by an extension of the free market system, changes to such a system might leave vulnerable low-income groups unprotected. In theory such problems might be countered by government interventions to enhance the incomes of the poor and decrease inequality. Hence, the poor would gain both more income and more choice. The difficulty with such compensating changes is that they would entail very extensive government interventions to equalize incomes. These would be anathema to those who expound the virtues of free enterprise. They require instead the distribution of incomes to be determined by the 'hidden hand' of the market. Modern British society is today an enormous distance away from such a free market. Clearly, political realists among the exponents of this view have a gradual programme of moves towards their ideal society. They look to means of enhancing private social policies using state policies to play underpinning roles.

The clearest alternative to this perspective sees social policies as potentially able to contribute to the redistribution of income in Britain. As Titmuss and his colleagues developed the study of social policy in Britain in the 1950s they were concerned to attack the complacent belief that the creation of a 'welfare state' has occurred, particularly through the social policy reforms of the 1940s, in which state-promoted policies had secured a very much more equal society. It was pointed out that the main beneficiaries of some of the key reforms were the relatively well-to-do. The free health service extended benefits to all, but was more used by the higher social classes. The middle classes could now send their children to grammar schools without having to pay fees. Even the main extensions of the social security system gave the better-off access to benefits from which they were previously excluded. At the same time, while it was true that the tax burden had considerably increased for higher earners, a wide range of concessions and untaxed fringe benefits offset this or provided compensating benefits (Titmuss, 1962; Atkinson, 1975; see also Le Grand, 1982, and George and Wilding, 1984, for more recent explorations of this issue).

Towards the end of the 1950s researchers, including notably Abel-Smith and Townsend (1965), showed that extensive poverty was still present in Britain. Not only were there large numbers of people dependent upon that subsistence level guaranteed by national assistance, but there were also many – a considerable proportion of whom were in families containing a full-time wage-earner – with incomes below or only a little above that level.

Hence it was argued that the 'welfare state' was neither markedly redistributive nor particularly effective at eradicating poverty. Studies of the overall distribution of income and wealth suggest that the degree of equalization that has occurred in the course of the twentieth century has been comparatively slight (HMSO, 1975).

But should social policy be redistributive? Is the prevailing degree of inequality acceptable? And is the extent and nature of poverty tolerable? Students of poverty (Townsend, 1979; Mack and Lansley, 1985) have tended to shift their attention away from consideration of an absolute definition, in terms of the minimum income necessary to sustain life, to one which is concerned with capacity to achieve a widely accepted standard of living and share in everyday social life. Probably most people in Britain today, no matter how tough their attitude to poverty, would accept some version of this thesis. Few would argue for a 'bowl of rice a day' level of nutrition or be content to see the children of the poor in our society without shoes. However, what is clearly more controversial is how such a poverty 'standard' is to be identified. Should the politically determined 'income support' level, which was described in chapter 5, be such a standard? Should the standard be related to average wages? Should the lowest quartile in the income distribution be deemed to be in poverty, whatever the nature of that distribution? In short, are the key political questions about poverty or about inequality?

Clearly, the way you answer these questions will determine your answers to the wider questions about the success of the government's interventions into social policy. They will determine whether you regard it as sufficient to ensure that all citizens secure access to free education, free primary health care and subsistence-level benefits when they are unable to work; or whether you believe that social policy should be a really powerful engine for social equality. It is quite likely that neither of these extreme statements fits your requirements for social policy, in which case you will be faced by rather more complicated questions about policy adequacy and the extent to which an element of redistribution should be built into social policy.

Here then are two rather different perspectives on the role of social policy in society. On the Right are those who see the provision of social services as the responsibility of the individual and who reject the idea that such services should be redistributive. The role of the state is merely to alleviate the most extreme forms of hardship, but otherwise to stand back from interfering in the market.

Alternatively, on the Left are those who evaluate social policy in relation to its commitment to equality. But there is also a 'Centrist' position of considerable importance for British politics. Not only does it have its adherents in both major parties, but there are also strong political forces which influence the adoption of this stance by governments regardless of their initial ideological inclinations. Labour governments have become inhibited from developing policies that expand the public sector, and particularly the social policy sector, for fear of its impact upon either inflation or taxation. It has been argued that public expenditure draws in so many resources that it inhibits investment in industry (Bacon and Eltis, 1976; see also the discussion in Hill and Bramley, 1986, ch. 5).

The Conservatives came to power in 1979 committed to cuts in public expenditure, other than defence and law and order, claiming that this would enable the economy to recover. They were, apparently, successful in curbing public expenditure on housing, but even that 'success' was not as great as it appears to be because (a) housing support for low-income people has increasingly been given through the housing benefit scheme (which is classified under social security expenditure), and (b) tax relief for mortgage interest payers has risen sharply. Expenditure on education has only risen slightly in real terms. Expenditure under the other two social policy headings has increased, markedly so in the case of social security. As far as health expenditure is concerned, the government has been inhibited from cutting by the continuing popularity of that service. Nevertheless, as was suggested in chapter 7, the actual growth level has been sufficiently low for it to be regarded in many quarters as involving a decline in the standard of service provided.

Hence, while the government has seen itself, and been seen, as engaged in an attack on social expenditure, what we actually find is some rather confusing changes. The government has gone to considerable lengths to cut social security benefits, but demographic trends (increased numbers of the elderly), economic trends (increased unemployment) and a tendency to shift other social expenses on to income maintenance (housing support, in particular, but also some of the costs of care of the elderly – see chapter 6) has sharply increased expenditure under this heading. Education and health expenditure have been attacked, but there has still been a considerable rise in real expenditure in the second case – albeit a rise insufficient to meet rising demands or expectations. The one big success has been in cutting *direct* expenditure on *public* housing (Hills (ed.), 1990).

Inevitably, in a situation in which social policy expenditure consumes a high proportion of national income and provides little room for political manoeuvre, yet leaves ample scope for dissatisfaction about what is provided, there is a search for better ways of delivering the social services. Political parties unable markedly to influence the overall pattern of public services will seek other ways of modifying their performance and enhancing the 'value for money' provided. The various forms this search has taken are the subject of the next section.

THE QUEST FOR EFFICIENT AND RESPONSIVE MODES OF SOCIAL POLICY DELIVERY

The view that social policy interventions have not achieved the success that might be expected from the effort put into them has been accepted by many politicians and public servants. It has been recognized that a complex bureaucracy has been developed to provide social services, and that efforts are therefore needed to overcome the resulting institutional and professional divisions within the system.

In the 1960s and 1970s governments devoted a considerable amount of attention to the organization of both central and local government. There was a search for the most rational form of organization. The search was always made difficult by a wide range of political considerations; reorganization may change the balance of power and alter individual opportunities and career prospects. Moreover, established patterns of organization develop supporting sentiments and loyalties. In any case, the rationalization of government is not an easy process. There are often competing criteria for rationalization which are hard to evaluate. For example, there is a conflict between the achievement of uniformity through centralization and the maximization of flexibility through decentralization. The close integration of particular services – for example health and the personal social services – may weaken links between those services and other related activities – for example the provision of housing and the achievement of high environmental standards. Rationalization seems to involve a search for the best arrangement, when perhaps in reality there are merely alternative arrangements, each carrying costs and benefits. These are hard to evaluate. Finally, there are 'informal' aspects to organizational arrangements which develop within formal structures. While in theory formal arrangements may be sought to maximize effective informal links, these are particularly hard to predict. Moreover, one of the effects of a formal reorganization is to distort and perhaps undermine informal links operating prior to reorganization.

At central government level there was, between the mid-1960s and the mid-1970s, a move towards super-departments embracing many different policy areas. The 1980s has seen some backing away from this approach. The largest of the social policy departments, the Department of Health and Social Security, has been broken into two. But probably more important than this has been the 'next steps' initiative under which small policy-making departments are gradually being achieved which delegate to executive agencies their day-to-day policy delivery tasks. The significance of this change for social security and for employment services has been discussed in chapter 4.

This new model enables the policy departments to set policy output goals and targets to which agencies can be held accountable. It is too early to judge whether this managerial approach to accountability is superior – in its outcomes and in its ultimate public accountability – to the older doctrines of ministerial responsibility.

A more 'radical' innovation in respect of accountability involves trying to get away from a situation in which there is one agency as a sole provider of a publicly required service. This is the model being

developed for the health and personal social services in which purchasers (health or local authorities) give contracts to providers. The
theory is that providers are placed in a market or quasi-market situation in which they may be in competition with each other and in which
failure to deliver contracted services can lead to non-renewal of a
contract. This model also allows of the possibility that the provider can
be a private body, even a profit-making body. Once again, it is too
early to evaluate this development. Its proponents see it as increasing efficiency with competition driving down costs, whilst accountability
is maintained because contracts can specify standards of work and
amounts of output. Its opponents argue that quantitative output criteria
will dominate at the expense of qualitative considerations, or that much
of the competition will be illusory. To many on the Left it is seen as the
thin edge of a wedge of privatization in which subsequent steps will be
to enable multinational companies to make profits out of British social
services or to compel consumers to become purchasers of what were
hitherto public services.

As pointed out above, the New Right advocates shifting, as far as
possible, to arrangements for individuals to purchase social services,
using vouchers if necessary towards that end. For them, real public
accountability must involve not purchasing agencies but rather
situations in which individuals buy services for themselves and their
families. Education has been seen as an area in which this market
approach can be readily advanced. So far the government has resisted
the voucher approach, which would be principally a subsidy to private
education, but has aimed to produce a system in which parents will be
supplied with information on schools' 'outputs' and will be free to
choose where their children will go. In practice, the costs of establishing and altering schools and the extent to which geographical considerations limit choices impose severe limits upon the realization of a
real market situation here. Furthermore, as was noted in the chapter on
education, this development occurs at the expense of the planned use
of educational resources and is enhancing various forms of social and
racial segregation and inequality.

The Conservative governments since 1979 have seen two, not necessarily compatible, approaches as important for the control of public
services. One of these has been a managerialist quest for ways of
controlling by creating accountable subdivisions within large organizations and by delegating services to accountable agencies. This process of delegation has involved strong budgetary controls and demands
for the achievement of specific quantitative outputs (see Pollitt, 1990,
for a further discussion of this). The other has involved the search for
devices which mimic markets and thus, as described above, use competition and choice as control devices. Since the fall of Mrs Thatcher, the

new Conservative regime led by John Major has put a strong emphasis on consumerism. Major's approach to consumerism lies in stressing the importance of information about service outputs to enable people to exercise choice and in exploring ways to provide financial compensation when services fail to deliver outputs or to deal with problems within a specific time-span.

It is important to contrast these approaches to public policy to an alternative which has been more popular on the Left. This is to see the key problem for public accountability as not public monopoly *per se* but rather the absence of devices for popular participation in decision-making (Donnison, 1991). The characteristic of this approach is to seek to establish ways of decentralizing decision-making. In the late 1970s and early 1980s the lead on this decentralization movement was provided by Labour- (and sometimes Liberal-) controlled local authorities (Gyford, 1985, 1991). Decentralization took the form of the breakdown of some authorities into sub-areas with local offices and local committees, the development of tenants' participation in housing management and so on.

Arguments for greater participation have developed against the backcloth of the elimination of the smaller organs of local government and the increased centralization of decision-making. Accordingly, in those areas where governments, or local authorities, have been willing to countenance the development of participatory devices, there have been grounds for regarding this as tokenism designed to disguise the retreat of the real locus of power. To put it a little more neutrally, there is a significant conflict between the desire for centralized uniformity and the suspicion of particularistic local interests on the one hand and real local accountability on the other.

Perhaps the most significant area in which participation rights have been extended is in strategic and local land-use planning, areas of policy outside the scope of this book. Within social policy two examples have been discussed in earlier chapters: community health councils (CHCs) in the health service, and school governors and managers in education. In the first of these cases actual power is very limited: CHCs are officially supported pressure groups. In the case of school management, significant steps have been taken to ensure parents' representatives an equal share with local authority nominees in a context of increasingly devolved powers over school arrangements but not over the curriculum.

The very considerable hostility of the Conservative government to local government has had the effect of increasing centralization, and perhaps making local delegations – like that in education – fairly meaningless (see Glennerster, Power and Travers, 1991). In chapter 3 the way in which the Conservatives have very firmly controlled local government finance was discussed. In health policy the Conservatives have removed the last vestiges of local authority participation in district decision-making. In community care policy local authorities are being forced to transfer services to private and voluntary providers. In education, as has been shown, local authority autonomy is now very limited. Local government aspirations to participate in employment policy have been almost totally suppressed and, such is the Conservative's distrust of them, in this policy field special Urban Development Corporations have been developed to operate in certain specific depressed areas.

An unfortunate feature of the political polarization of Britain in the 1980s was the conflict between the largely Labour-controlled governments of the major urban authorities and the central Conservative government, led by a woman who openly made a war against local government part of her strategy for eliminating socialism in Britain. Of course it did not help local government's cause that some Labour authorities matched Mrs Thatcher's extremism with a Leftist extremism of their own, but the damage done over this period to local government as a building block for genuine local democratic accountability was out of all proportion to the modest attempts to establish local socialist strongholds.

It is now necessary for Britain to look again at the whole structure of its local government, and at the relationship between central and local government. Both Labour and the Conservatives, now, recognize the case for simplifying the local government structure, delegating responsibilities to the lowest possible level. Interestingly, the purchaser/ provider principle allows of the possibility that purchasers may represent quite small areas, able to purchase services from specialist providers outside their own geographical patch. More difficult is the question whether there is a need to look at the structure of government for the United Kingdom as a whole, conceding social policy responsibilities to elected bodies within the constituent nations, and perhaps within the English regions as well.

Fortunately through all this conflict over local democracy, and despite the search for new methods of delivering services, mechanisms have survived for enabling citizens to take action over individual grievances. In principle, the two categories into which grievance procedures fall are nearly as old as the nation-state itself: appeals to courts and complaints to elected representatives. In practice, they take modern forms very different to these traditional grievance procedures. In centuries past in Britain litigation about dissatisfaction with an administrative agency depended upon an elaborate and costly legal procedure whereby the royal prerogative was invoked on behalf of the aggrieved citizen. These 'prerogative remedies' are still used from time to time, and today individuals may secure legal aid or the assistance of a powerful voluntary organization to enable them to take grievances against public authorities to the High Court. But for everyday purposes what is much more important is that a large number of lower 'courts', generally known as 'tribunals', have been set up to deal with appeals against decisions of public agencies. Furthermore, in many cases there may be direct appeals to the courts or a supervisory tribunal against the decisions of these bodies.

The area of social policy in which tribunals are most important is social security. Individuals may appeal against most decisions taken by social security officials. There is a two-tier appeal system for social security benefits, with commissioners who operate at the top level and whose decisions are regarded as precedents for lower tier decisions. Special systems, less detached from day-to-day decision makers, exist to deal with claimants dissatisfied with Social Fund and housing benefit decisions.

In the housing sector there are only tribunals to deal with a limited range of disputes over rent levels and security of tenure in the private sector. Disputes between tenants and local authorities are not covered. Family health service authorities in the national health service are required to set up what are, in effect, tribunals to hear complaints against doctors, dentists and pharmacists. There are also tribunals that review cases of compulsory detention under the Mental Health Acts. Parents may appeal against decisions on pupil allocations and exclusions, and a tribunal exists to hear appeals by private schools against ministerial decisions that they should be closed.

The case for tribunals is that they provide for the independent review of decisions, particularly where they involve official discretion. They are less important for the control of policy itself; it is comparatively rarely that tribunal decisions indicate a significant defect in policy. To aggrieved individuals they offer not so much a chance to change policy as an opportunity to check a controversial application of policy.

The system of tribunals in Britain has been improved considerably in recent years. As a result of the Franks Committee (HMSO, 1957), attempts have been made to make tribunal proceedings more consistent and impartial. A Council on Tribunals maintains an oversight of tribunal arrangement and reports (if necessary, publicly) its observations to the government. There is, nevertheless, still a suspicion that some tribunals are too closely identified with the government agencies whose decisions they are expected to examine. For example, the committees that adjudicate on complaints against doctors have been seen as rather too closely identified with the administration of the family practitioner services.

In the Scandinavian countries there are officials known as 'ombudsmen' who investigate complaints against the administration. When the appointment of such officials was first proposed for Britain one of the arguments used against it was that elected representatives perform this function. Eventually in 1967 the office of Parliamentary Commissioner was set up, but only to investigate individual public grievances passed on to him by members of Parliament. Later, when local government and the health service were reorganized, local government and health service commissioners were appointed. Complaints against local authorities were to be presented by councillors, but a provision was included to enable the local government commissioners to investigate direct complaints when they were satisfied that a member of the public might have had difficulty in securing a councillor's backing (presumably because of involvement in the decision at issue). However, in the absence of elected representatives within the health service, direct access was allowed to the health service, commissioners. Hence there is a curious mixture of direct and indirect access to these British 'ombudsmen'. Perhaps in due course direct access will become the rule for all.

The commissioners are solely concerned with maladministration. They do not deal with policy, so long as that policy has a clear statutory foundation. Nor do they deal with decisions that involve statutorily legitimate discretion or professional judgement. They provide, therefore, like the tribunals, only a limited protection for citizens against the worst abuses of administrative behaviour, and not an opportunity to participate in policy formulation or to comment upon its overall implementation.

The underlying issue throughout this section concerns the extent to which Britain has a political and administrative system in which it is generally difficult to conceive of meaningful participation, except through representative political institutions or through very specific devices to deal with individual grievances for consumers of social services. Concerns about participation, we have seen, tend to be channelled into two, often distinct, ideological streams. For some the key to control lies in the market place. Services should be privatized, and consumers put into a position in which they can make choices as the free purchasers of services. For others decentralization of public provision to the local level, breaking up big bureaucracies and offering local participation in service control, is the preferred approach to this problem.

CONCLUSIONS

This chapter has looked at the issue of social policy and society by considering, first, some of the political perspectives on the level and character of social service expenditure, and then some government- or local-authority-inspired attempts to improve social policy co-ordination, or to enable citizens to have some slight influence on the impact of policy upon themselves. It has thus concentrated primarily upon some of the more detailed questions about the relationship between policy and society. It could, however, have developed an entirely different level of analysis in which attention was focused upon the functions of social policy in our society and its relationship to our social structure.

Many of the propositions discussed in this chapter presuppose that social policy has developed out of a concern to protect, and to offer services for, weak and vulnerable groups in our society. For some writers on social policy such state activities have an integrative func- tion, serving to unite us in one mutually dependent community. Within such a community developments to enhance social equality may occur. A 'welfare state' advances us towards a 'welfare society'. But the devel- opment of social policy may also be seen very differently. Perhaps the clearest alternative view is provided by Marxists (as was suggested in chapter 1). Of course, they argue, various social benefits have been extended to the poor. These are designed to increase their productive efficiency, by educating them and keeping them in good health, and to stave off revolution by meeting their most salient grievances. But they are never likely to advance a capitalist society far along the road to social equality. In this sense democratic socialists are likely only to secure social policies that help to preserve the status quo, while the radical free-marketeers on the Right are likely to be restrained by the fact that a return to the open market-place would accelerate the drift towards the class warfare that Marx originally predicted. This modern Marxism rejects historical inevitability, arguing instead about capital- ism's capacity to retain its dominance in a changing society.

This argument secures credence from the fact that social policy has not so far been proved to be a powerful source of social change. It must be analysed in relation to political motives, and in terms of social struc- ture. At the level of the interpretation of political motives and political behaviour the Marxian position cannot be disregarded. Most political conflicts in a society like our own are battles between those who seek to gain from social change and those who benefit from the status quo. Those who seek change are always likely to be most successful when the defenders of the existing order see advantages in making concessions. Conservative politicians have at various times in the past spoken openly of the need to win popular support through specific measures. Countless government reports have drawn attention to the inefficiency of a society which is insufficiently fit to work hard, or fight wars, and insufficiently educated to provide the skills needed for industry. Social reformers with unquestionable humanitarian and altruistic motives have always fought alongside politicians who see new policies as expedient to protect the status quo and to win popular support.

The part of this argument most difficult to evaluate is that which deals with the role played by mass political movements. Marxist theorists have long been split between those who believe that the working class can force capitalism to change peacefully and gradually, and those who believe real change will be achieved only by revolution. Clearly, in twentieth-century Britain the organized working class has sought to secure gradual social change. How successful has it been? And how much more success is it likely to achieve?

These are questions to which readers will want to choose their own answers. Clearly, they raise issues that go far beyond the scope of the policies discussed in this book. However, there is one rather complicated answer to these questions which has a considerable bearing upon the interpretation of the making of social policy. This is that the organized working class has achieved quite considerable political success in Britain, forcing concessions from capitalism that nevertheless fall short of the transformation of Britain into a 'socialist society'. Moreover, those concessions are much more marked in some areas of social life than in others, and serve to benefit the better-organized segments of the working class more clearly than anyone else. These gains have thus been more likely to advantage males than females, and to favour the long established indigenous population as opposed to more recent migrants and their families. Hence, while it is true that the overall distribution of income and wealth has been affected but little, and particularly has changed little at the extremes, some groups of manual workers have advanced significantly in income relative to some groups of non-manual workers and small entrepreneurs. These new middle-income workers are also significant beneficiaries from the advancements in the health and education services, and from income maintenance reforms which provide good short-term benefits. However, their gains have done very little to benefit those who are less well organized, who remain low paid and highly vulnerable to unemployment. The more powerful groups of workers also have relatively little interest in some of the problems for social policy that have been described in this book (such as homelessness, mental handicap, racial disadvantage). Those most in need of help from the 'welfare state' are likely to be correspondingly ill-equipped to secure concessions from it.

That is a personal, and inevitably contentious, suggestion of the way in which an interpretation of the development of social policy that has its roots originally in the Marxian perspective may be of relevance. It is an argument about power in the social structure, seeing capitalist interests as still of considerable importance but being forced to compromise with some better-off, male and white sections of the organized working class. It is important to recognize that political action in our complex society is enormously complicated. In no way is it a simple confrontation between twin forces of capital and labour. Both of these forces tend to be segmented in various ways. In addition, the role of the state has grown to such an extent that it employs, at various levels and with various interests, a great army of people who are not necessarily readily aligned with any other forces in our society. In explaining social policy the impact of such groups of state employees as doctors, teachers, and central administrators need to be brought into the equation. In sum, readers are being asked to accept that social policies are not merely derived from humanitarian aspirations, but are also products of power conflicts in our society.

An understanding of social policy depends upon taking into account this balance between conflict and humanitarianism; it also depends upon relating to it a comprehension of the much more detailed factors that influence individual policies. This book certainly cannot claim to have made all the key connections in this complex field, but it is hoped that readers have been introduced to many of the more important ones.

SUGGESTIONS FOR FURTHER READING

The government's 'public expenditure White Papers' are the most thorough up-to-date sources on expenditure patterns. They are published early in each calendar year. *Social Trends* also provides a most valuable collection of official statistics, much used in this book. A collection edited by Hills (1990) provides a most authoritative examination of the impact of the Thatcher governments on public expenditure.

The two sides in the debate on social policy provision have been well put together in a collection edited by Loney (1987); other important contributions to this debate are Bosanquet's *After the New Right* (1983), Deakin's *The Politics of Welfare* (1987) and Donnison's *A Radical Agenda* (1991). A literature on the institutional changes and their implications is only just beginning to emerge; useful contributions to it come from Elcock (1991) and are contained in parts of Savage and Robins (1990) and Dunleavy, Gamble and Peele (1990).

References

Abel-Smith, B. 1976: *Value for Money in Health Services*. London: Heinemann.
Abel-Smith, B. and Townsend, P. 1965: *The Poor and the Poorest*. London: Bell.
Adler, M. and Asquith S. (eds) 1981: *Discretion and Welfare*. London: Heinemann.
Argyris, C. 1960: *Understanding Organisational Behaviour*. London: Tavistock.
Ashford, D. E. 1986: *The Emergence of the Welfare States*. Oxford: Blackwell.
Atkinson, A. B. 1975: Income distribution and social change revisited. *Journal of Social Policy*, 4(1), 57–68.
Audit Commission 1986: *Making a Reality of Community Care*. London: HMSO.
Bachrach, P. 1969: *The Theory of Democratic Elitism*. London: University of London Press.
Bacon, R. and Eltis, W. 1976: *Britain's Economic Problem: Too Few Producers*. London: Macmillan.
Balchin, N. 1989: *Housing Policy: An Introduction*. London: Routledge & Kegan Paul.
Baldwin, P. 1990: *The Politics of Social Solidarity*. Cambridge: Cambridge University Press.
Banting, K. C. 1979: *Poverty, Politics and Policy*. London: Macmillan.
Barclay, P. 1982: *Social Workers: Their Roles and Tasks*, Report of a Working Party. London: Bedford Square Press.
Bardach, E. 1977: *The Implementation Game*. Cambridge, Mass.: MIT Press.
Barnes, J. and Barr, N. A. 1988: *Strategies for Higher Education*. Aberdeen: Aberdeen University Press.
Barr, N. A. 1981: Empirical definitions of the poverty line. *Policy and Politics*, 9(1), 1–21.
Barrett, S. and Fudge, C. (eds) 1981: *Policy and Action*. London: Methuen.
Beer, S. H. 1969: *Modern British Politics*. London: Faber & Faber.
Bell, D. 1973: *The Coming of Post-Industrial Society*. New York: Basic Books.
Beveridge, W. 1942: *Social Insurance and Allied Services*, Cmd 6404. London: HMSO.
Blaug, M. 1970: *An Introduction to the Economics of Education*. Harmondsworth, Middx: Penguin Books.

Booth, C. 1889–1903: *Life and Labour of the People in London*, 17 vols.

Booth, T. (ed.) 1979: *Planning for Welfare: Social Policy and the Expenditure Process*. Oxford: Blackwell.

Bosanquet, N. 1983: *After the New Right*. London: Heinemann.

Bottomley, A. K. 1973: *Decisions in the Penal Process*. London: Martin Robertson.

Bottomore, T. B. 1966: *Elites and Society*. Harmondsworth, Middx: Penguin.

Braybrooke, D. and Lindblom, C. E. 1963: *A Strategy of Decision*. New York: Free Press.

British Association of Social Workers 1977: *The Social Work Task*. Birmingham: BASW.

Brittan, S. 1971: *Steering the Economy*. Harmondsworth, Middx: Penguin Books.

Burney, E. 1967: *Housing on Trial*. London: Oxford University Press.

Butrym, Z. T. 1976: *The Nature of Social Work*. London: Macmillan.

Byrne, T. 1990: *Local Government in Britain*, 5th edn. Harmondsworth, Middx: Penguin Books.

Carrier, J. and Kendall, I. 1977: Social Administration as social science. In H. Heisler (ed.), *Foundations of Social Administration*. London: Macmillan.

Central Advisory Council for Education 1954: *Early Leaving*. London: HMSO.

Central Advisory Council for Education 1959: *Fifteen to Eighteen* (Crowther Report). London: HMSO.

Central Advisory Council for Education 1963: *Half Our Future* (Newson Report). London: HMSO.

Central Advisory Council for Education 1967: *Children and Their Primary Schools* (Plowden Report). London: HMSO.

Central Housing Advisory Committee 1969: *Council Housing Purposes, Procedures and Priorities*, ninth report of the Housing Management Sub-Committee (Cullingworth Report). London: HMSO.

Central Statistical Office 1992: *Social Trends 22*. London: HMSO.

Clark, B. R. 1956: Organizational adaptation and precarious values. *American Sociological Review*, 21, 32–6.

Cole, D. and Utting, J. 1962: *The Economic Circumstances of Old People*. London: Codicote.

Corrigan, P. and Leonard, P. 1978: *Social Work Practice under Capitalism*. London: Macmillan.

Crossman, R. H. S. 1975–7: *Diaries of a Cabinet Minister*, 3 vols. London: Hamish Hamilton and Jonathan Cape.

Crozier, M. 1964: *The Bureaucratic Phenomenon*. Chicago, Ill.: University of Chicago Press.

Dahl, R. A. 1961: *Who Governs?* New Haven, Conn.: Yale University Press.

Dale, J. and Foster, P. 1986: *Feminists and State Welfare*. London: Routledge & Kegan Paul.

Davis, K. C. 1969: *Discretionary Justice*. Baton Rouge, La: Louisiana State University Press.

Deacon, A. 1976: *In Search of the Scrounger*. London: Bell.

Deacon, A. and Bradshaw, J. 1983: *Reserved for the Poor*. Oxford: Martin Robertson.

Deakin, N. 1987: *The Politics of Welfare*. London: Methuen.

Dearlove, J. and Saunders, P. 1991: *Introduction to British Politics*. Cambridge: Polity Press.

Department of Education and Science 1978: *Special Educational Needs* (Warnock Report). London: HMSO.

Department of Education and Science 1985: *Education for All* (a brief guide by Lord Swann to the Report of the Committee of Inquiry into the Education of Children from Ethnic Minority Groups). London: HMSO.

Department of Employment 1971: *People and Jobs*. London: HMSO.

Department of Employment, 1988a: *Training for Employment*, Cmnd 316. London: HMSO.

Department of Employment 1988b: *Employment for the 1990s*, Cmnd 540. London: HMSO.

Department of the Environment 1991: *Housing and Construction Statistics*. London: HMSO.

Department of Health 1991: *Health and Personal Social Services Statistics*. London: HMSO.

Department of Health and Social Security 1974: *Social Work Support for the Health Service*. London: HMSO.

Department of Health and Social Security 1976a: *Priorities for Health and Personal Social Services*. London: HMSO.

Department of Health and Social Security 1976b: *Sharing Resources for Health in England*. London: HMSO.

Department of Health and Social Security 1983: *NHS Management Inquiry* (Griffiths Report). London: HMSO.

Department of Social Security, 1991: *Social Security Statistics*. London: HMSO.

Dicey, A. V. 1905: *Lectures on the Relations between Law and Public Opinion*. London: Macmillan.

Dilnot, A. W., Kay, J. A. and Morris, C. N. 1984: *The Reform of Social Security*. Oxford: Clarendon Press.

Donnison, D. 1991: *A Radical Agenda*. London: Rivers Oram.

Donnison, D. V. and Ungerson, C. 1982: *Housing Policy*. Harmondsworth, Middx: Penguin Books.

Douglas, J. W. B. 1964: *The Home and the School*. London: Macgibbon & Kee.

Dunleavy, P. 1981: *The Politics of Mass Housing in Britain*. London: Oxford University Press.

Dunleavy, P., Gamble, A. and Peele, G. (eds) 1990: *Developments in British Politics 2*. London: Macmillan.

Eckstein, H. 1960: *Pressure Group Politics*. London: Allen & Unwin.

Edgell, S. and Duke, V. 1991: *A Measure of Thatcherism*. Glasgow: Harper Collins.

Elcock, H. 1991: *Change and Decay: Public Administration in the 1990s*. Harlow, Essex: Longman.

Enthoven, A. C. 1985: *Reflections on the Management of the NHS*. London: Nuffield Provincial Hospitals Trust.

Esping-Andersen, G. 1990: *The Three Worlds of Welfare Capitalism*. Cambridge: Polity Press.

Etzioni, A. 1961: *A Comparative Analysis of Complex Organisations*. New York: Free Press.

Finch, J. 1984: *Education and Social Policy*. London: Longman.

Finer, S. E. 1958: *Anonymous Empire*. London: Pall Mall.

Finn, D. 1987: *Training without Jobs*. London: Macmillan.

Floud, J., Halsey, A. H. and Martin, F. M. 1956: *Social Class and Education Opportunity*. London: Heinemann.

Ford, J. 1969: *Social Class and the Comprehensive School*. London: Routledge & Kegan Paul.

Forrest, R. and Murie A. 1991: *Selling the Welfare State*. London: Routledge.

Forrest, R., Murie, A. and Williams, P. 1990: *Home Ownership: Fragmentation and Differentiation*. London: Unwin Hyman.

Foster, P. 1983: *Access to Welfare*. London: Macmillan.

Fox, A. 1974: *Beyond Contract: Work, Power and Trust Relations*. London: Faber & Faber.

Fraser, D. 1973: *The Evolution of the British Welfare State*. London: Macmillan.

Friedman, M. 1962: *Capitalism and Freedom*. Chicago, Ill.: Chicago University Press.

Friedman, M. 1977: *Inflation and Unemployment: A New Dimension of Politics*. London: Institute of Economic Affairs.

Friedson, E. 1970: *Professional Dominance*. New York: Atherton.

Friend, J. K., Power, J. M. and Yewlett C. J. L. 1974: *Public Planning: The Inter-Corporate Dimension*. London: Tavistock.

Galligan, D. J. 1986: *Discretionary Powers*. Oxford: Oxford University Press.

George, V. and Wilding, P. 1984: *The Impact of Social Policy*. London: Routledge & Kegan Paul.

Gibb, K. and Munro, M. 1991: *Housing Finance in the UK*. London: Macmillan.

Gilbert, B. B. 1970: *British Social Policy, 1914–39*. London: Batsford.

Gilbert, R. 1989: *Employment in the 1990s*. London: Macmillan.

Glennerster, H. 1985: *Paying for Welfare*. Oxford: Blackwell.

Glennerster, H., Power, A. and Travers, T. 1991: A new era for social policy: a new Enlightenment or a new Leviathan? *Journal of Social Policy*, 20(3).

Goldberg, E. M. and Warburton, R. W. 1979: *Ends and Means in Social Work*. London: Allen & Unwin.

Gough, I. 1979: *The Political Economy of the Welfare State*. London: Macmillan.

Gowing, M. 1975: *Richard Morris Titmuss* (*Proceedings of the British Academy*, LXI). London: Oxford University Press.

Green, D. G. 1986: *The New Right*. Brighton: Wheatsheaf.

Gunningham, N. 1974: *Pollution, Social Interest and the Law*. London: Martin Robertson.

Gyford, J. 1985: *The Politics of Local Socialism*. London: Allen & Unwin.

Gyford, J. 1991: *Citizens, Consumers and Councils*. London: Macmillan.

Hadley, R. and McGrath, M. 1981: *Going Local: Neighbourhood Social Services*. London: Bedford Square Press.

Hall, P. 1976: *Reforming the Welfare*. London: Heinemann.

Hall, P., Land, H., Parker, R. and Webb, A. 1978: *Change, Choice and Conflict in Social Policy*. London: Heinemann.

Hallett, C. 1982: *The Personal Social Services in Local Government*. London: Allen & Unwin.

Hallett, C. and Stevenson, O. 1979: *Child Abuse: Aspects of Interprofessional Communication*. London: Allen & Unwin.

Halsey, A. H. (ed.) 1972: *Educational Priority*, vol. 1. London: HMSO.

Ham, C. and Hill, M. 1985: *The Policy Process in the Modern Capitalist State*. Brighton, Sussex: Wheatsheaf.

Ham, C. J. 1992: *Health Policy in Britain*, 3rd edn. London: Macmillan.

Hamnett, C. 1991: A nation of inheritors? Housing inheritance, wealth and inequality in Britain. *Journal of Social Policy*, 20(40), 509–36.

Handler, J. 1973: *The Coercive Social Worker*. Chicago, Ill.: Rand McNally.

Hanson, A. H. and Walles, M. 1970: *Governing Britain*. Glasgow: Fontana.

Harris, J. 1972: *Unemployment and Politics*. London: Oxford University Press.

Harris, J. 1977: *William Beveridge: A Biography*. Oxford: University Press.

Harris, R. and Seldon, A. 1976: *Pricing or Taxing*. London: Institute of Economic Affairs.

Harris, R. and Seldon, A. 1979: *Overruled on Welfare*. London: Institute of Economic Affairs.

Harrison, S., Hunter D. J. and Pollitt, C. 1990: *The Dynamics of British Health Policy*. London: Unwin Hyman.

Hartley, T. C. and Griffith, J. A. G. 1975: *Government and Law*. London: Weidenfeld & Nicolson.

Heclo, H. H. 1974: *Modern Social Politics in Britain and Sweden*. New Haven, Conn.: Yale University Press.

Heclo, H. [H.] and Wildavsky, A. 1981: *The Private Government of Public Money*. London: Macmillan.

Hickson, D. J. 1966: A convergence in organisation theory. *Administrative Science Quarterly*, 11, 224–37.

Higgins, J. 1978: *The Poverty Business*. Oxford: Blackwell.

Higgins, J. 1988: *The Business of Medicine: Private Health Care in Britain*. London: Macmillan.

Hill, M. 1969: The exercise of discretion in the National Assistance Board. *Public Administration*, 47.

Hill, M. 1972: *The Sociology of Public Administration*. London: Weidenfeld & Nicolson.

Hill, M. 1990: *Social Security Policy in Britain*. Aldershot: Edward Elgar.

Hill, M. and Bramley, G. 1986: *Analysing Social Policy*. Oxford: Blackwell.

Hill, M. and Laing, P. 1979: *Social Work and Money*. London: Allen & Unwin.

Hills, J. (ed.) 1990: *The State of Welfare*. Oxford: Clarendon Press.

HMSO 1957: *Report of the Committee on Administrative Tribunals and Enquiries* (Franks Report) Cmnd 218. London: HMSO.

HMSO 1963: *Higher Education* (Robins Report) Cmnd 2154. London: HMSO.

HMSO 1967: *The Future Structure of the National Health Service*. London: HMSO.

HMSO 1968a: *Report of the Committee on Local Authority and Allied Personal Social Services* (Seebohm Report) Cmnd 3703. London: HMSO.

HMSO 1968b: *The Administrative Structure of Medical and Related Services in England and Wales*. London: HMSO.

HMSO 1969: *Report of the Royal Commission on Local Government in England* (Redcliffe Maud Report) Cmnd 4040. London: HMSO.

HMSO 1972: *Proposals for a Tax-Credits System*, Cmnd 5116. London: HMSO.

HMSO 1975: *Royal Commission on the Distribution of Income and Wealth, Initial Report on the Standing Reference*, Cmnd 6171. London: HMSO.

HMSO 1977: *Housing Policy: A Consultative Document*, Cmnd 6851. London: HMSO.

HMSO 1978: *Royal Commission on the Distribution of Income and Wealth. Report no. 6: Low Incomes*. London: HMSO.

HMSO, 1979: *Report of the Royal Commission on the National Health Service* (Merrison Report) Cmnd 7615. London: HMSO.

HMSO 1985: *Reform of Social Security: Programme for Action*, Cmnd 9691. London: HMSO.

HMSO 1989: *Caring for the People: Community Care in the Next Decade and Beyond*, Cm 849. London: HMSO.

HMSO 1992: *The Government's Expenditure Plans 1992–3 to 1994–5*, Cm 1913. London: HMSO.

Holman, R. 1978: *Poverty*. London: Martin Robertson.

Holme, A. and Maizels, J. 1978: *Volunteers in Social Work*. London: Allen & Unwin.

Hood, C. C. 1976: *The Limits of Administration*. Chichester, Sussex: John Wiley.

House of Commons 1977: *Seventh Report from the Expenditure Committee, Session 1976–7*, London: HMSO.

Inland Revenue 1991: *Inland Revenue Statistics*. London: HMSO.

Jackson, B. and Marsden, D. 1962: *Education and the Working Class*. London: Routledge & Kegan Paul.

Jacques, E. 1967: *Equitable Payment*. Harmondsworth, Middx: Penguin.

Jenkins, W. I. 1978: *Policy Analysis*. London: Martin Robertson.

Jordan, A. G. and Richardson, J. J. 1987: *British Politics and the Policy Process*. London: Unwin Hyman.

Jordan, B. 1974: *Poor Parents*. London: Routledge & Kegan Paul.

Jowell, J. 1973: The legal control of administrative discretion. *Public Law*, 178.

Jowell, J. and Oliver, D. (eds) 1985: *The Changing Constitution*. Oxford: Clarendon Press.

Judge, K. 1982: The public purchase of social care. *Policy and Politics*, 10(4).

Judge, K. 1987: *Rationing Social Services*. London: Heinemann.

Keynes, J. M. 1936: *The General Theory of Employment, Interest and Money*. London: Macmillan.

Kincaid, J. 1973: *Poverty and Equality in Britain*. Harmondsworth, Middx: Penguin Books.

Klein, R. 1989: *The Politics of the NHS*. London: Longman.

Kogan, M. 1978: *The Politics of Educational Change*. Glasgow: Fontana.

Land, H. and Rose, H. 1985: Compulsory altruism for some or an altruistic society for all. In P. Bean, J. Ferris and D. Whynes (eds), *In Defence of Welfare*, London: Tavistock.

Le Grand, J. 1982: *The Strategy of Equality*. London: Allen & Unwin.

Le Grand J. and Robinson, R. (eds) 1984: *Privatisation and the Welfare State*. London: Allen & Unwin.

Lee, J. M. 1963: *Social Leaders and Public Persons*. London: Oxford University Press.

Lindsey, A. 1962: *Socialised Medicine in England and Wales*. Chapel Hill, N.C.: University of North Carolina Press.

Lipsky, M. 1980: *Street-level Bureaucracy*. New York: Russell Sage.

Loney, M. (ed.) 1987: *The State or the Market*. London: Sage.

Loughlin, M. 1986: *Local Government in the Modern State*. London: Sweet & Maxwell.

Lynes, T. 1962: *National Assistance and National Prosperity*. London: Codicote.

Mack, J. and Lansley, S. 1985: *Poor Britain*. London: Allen & Unwin.

Malpass, P. 1990: *Reshaping Housing Policy*. London: Routledge.

Malpass, P. (ed.) 1986: *The Housing Crisis*. London: Croom Helm.

Malpass, P. and Murie, A. 1990: *Housing Policy and Practice*, 3rd edn. London: Macmillan.

Marsden, D. 1973: *Mothers Alone*. Harmondsworth, Middx: Penguin Books.

Marshall, T. H. 1970: *Social Policy*. London: Hutchinson.

McCarthy, M. 1986: *Campaigning for the Poor*. London: Croom Helm.

McCarthy, M. (ed.) 1989: *The New Politics of Welfare*. London: Macmillan.

McKeown, T. 1980: *The Role of Medicine*. Oxford: Blackwell.

Merrett, S. 1979: *State Housing in Britain*. London: Routledge & Kegan Paul.

Minford, P. 1984: *State Expenditure: A Study in Waste*. Economic Affairs, Supplement, 4(3).

Mishra, R. 1977: *Society and Social Policy*. London: Macmillan.

Mishra, R. 1984: *The Welfare State in Crisis*. Brighton, Sussex: Wheatsheaf.

Moon, J. and Richardson, J. J. 1985: *Unemployment in the U.K.* Aldershot: Gower.

Morgan, K. O. 1984: *Labour in Power, 1945–51*. Oxford: Oxford University Press.

Morgan, K. O. 1990: *The People's Peace: British History, 1945–89*. Oxford: Oxford University Press.

Moynihan, D. P. 1969: *Maximum Feasible Misunderstanding*. New York: Free Press.

Mukherjee, S. 1972: *Making Labour Markets Work*. London: PEP.

Murie, A., Niner, P. and Watson, C. 1976: *Housing Policy and the Housing System*. London: Allen & Unwin.

Murray, C. 1984: *Losing Ground*. New York: Basic Books.

O'Connor, J. 1973: *The Fiscal Crisis of the State*. New York: St Martin's Press.

Packman, J. 1975: *The Child's Generation*. Oxford: Blackwell.

Parker, H. 1989: *Instead of the Dole*. London: Routledge.

Pater, J. E. 1981: *The Making of the National Health Service*. London: King's Fund Publishing.

Piven, F. F. and Cloward, R. A. 1972: *Regulating the Poor*. London: Tavistock.

Pollitt, C. 1990: *Managerialism and the Public Services*. Oxford: Blackwell.

Pressman, G. and Wildavsky, A. 1973: *Implementation*. Berkeley, Cal.: University of California Press.

Ralphs, Sir F. Lincoln 1973: *The Role and Training of Education Welfare Officers*. Luton, Beds.: Local Government Training Board.

Regan, D. E. 1977: *Local Government and Education*. London: Allen & Unwin.

Rex, J. and Tomlinson, S. 1979: *Colonial Immigrants in a British City*. London: Routledge & Kegan Paul.

Roberts, D. 1960: *Victorian Origins of the British Welfare State*. New Haven, Conn.: Yale University Press.

Roberts, G. K. 1970: *Political Parties and Pressure Groups in Britain*. London: Weidenfeld & Nicolson.

Robinson, R. and Judge, K. 1987: *Public Expenditure and the NHS: Trends and Prospects*. London: King's Fund Institute.

Rose, H. 1981: Rereading Titmuss: the social division of welfare. *Journal of Social Policy*, 10(4), 477–502.

Rowtree, B. S. and Lavers, G. R. 1951: *Poverty and the Welfare State*. London: Longman.

Rowntree, S. 1901: *Poverty: A Study of Town Life*. London: Macmillan.

Sabatier, P. 1986: Top-down and bottom-up approaches to implementation research: a critical analysis and suggested synthesis. *Journal of Public Policy*, 6(1).

Sanderson, M. 1991: Social equality and industrial need: a dilemma of English education since 1945. In T. Gourvish and A. O'Day (eds), *Britain since 1945*. London: Macmillan.

Savage, S. P. and Robins, L. (eds) 1990: *Public Policy under Thatcher*. London: Macmillan.

Schattschneider, E. E. 1960: *The Semi-sovereign People*. New York: Holt, Rinehart & Winston.

Schon, D. 1971: *Beyond the Stable State*. London: Maurice Temple Smith.

Schumpeter, J. 1950: *Capitalism, Socialism and Democracy*. New York: Harper & Row.

Selznick, P. 1949: *TVA and the Grass Roots*. Berkeley, Cal.: University of California Press.

Semmel, B. 1961: *Imperialism and Social Reform*. London: Oxford University Press.

Simon, B. 1988: *Bending the Rules*. London: Lawrence & Wishart.

Sinfield, A. 1978: Analysis in the social division of welfare. *Journal of Social Policy*, 7(2), 129–56.

Sinfield, A. 1981: *What Unemployment Means*. Oxford: Martin Robertson.

Sinfield, R. A. 1969: *Which Way for Social Work?* London: Fabian Society.

Smith, B. 1976: *Policy Making in British Government*. London: Martin Robertson.

Social Security Consortium 1986: *Of Little Benefit*. London: Social Security Consortium.

Specht, H. and Vickery, A. 1977: *Integrating Social Work Methods*. London: Allen & Unwin.

Stanworth, P. and Giddens, A. 1974: *Elites and Power in British Society*. Cambridge: Cambridge University Press.

Stoker, G. 1988: *The Politics of Local Government*. London: Macmillan.

Stone, M. 1981: *The Education of the Black Child in Britain*. Glasgow: Fontana.

Taylor-Gooby, P. 1985: *Public Opinion, Ideology and State Welfare*. London: Routledge & Kegan Paul.

Thane, P. 1982: *The Foundations of the Welfare State*. London: Longman.

Therborn, G. 1986: *Why Some Peoples are More Unemployed than Others*. London: Verso.

Titmuss, R. M. 1958: *Essays on the Welfare State*. London: Allen & Unwin.

Titmuss, R. M. 1962: *Income Distribution and Social Change*. London: Allen & Unwin.

Titmuss, R. M. 1968: *Commitment to Welfare*. London: Allen & Unwin.

Titmuss, R. M. 1974: *Social Policy: An Introduction*. London: Allen & Unwin.

Titmuss, R. M. 1987: *The Philosophy of Welfare*. London: Allen & Unwin.

Townsend, P. 1954: Measuring poverty. *British Journal of Sociology*, 5(2), 130–7.

Townsend, P. 1979: *Poverty in the United Kingdom*. Harmondsworth, Middx: Penguin Books.

Townsend, P. (ed.) 1970: *The Concept of Poverty*. London: Heinemann.

Townsend, P., Davidson, N. and Whitehead, M. (eds) 1988: *Inequalities in Health*. Harmondsworth, Middx: Penguin Books.

Travers, T. 1986: *The Politics of Local Government Finance*. London: Allen & Unwin.

Tuckett, D. (ed.) 1976: *An Introduction to Medical Sociology*. London: Tavistock.

Unemployment Unit 1992: *Working Brief* (issued monthly). London: Unemployment Unit.

Urry, J. and Wakeford, J. (eds) 1973: *Power in Britain*. London: Heinemann.

Van Meter, D. and Van Horn, C. E. 1975: The policy implementation process: a conceptual framework. *Administration and Society*, 6(4).

Walter, J. A. 1988: *Basic Income: Escape from the Poverty Trap*. London: Marion Boyars.

Webb, A. 1985: 'Alternative futures for social policy and state welfare'. In R. Berthoud (ed.), *Challenges to Social Policy*. Aldershot: Gower.

Webb, A. and Wistow, G. 1986: *Planning, Need and Scarcity*. London: Allen & Unwin.

Webb, A. and Wistow, G. 1987: *Social Work, Social Care and Social Planning: The Personal Social Services since Seebohm*. London: Longman.

Weber, M. 1947: *The Theory of Social and Economic Organization*, trans. A. M. Henderson and T. Parsons. Glencoe, Ill.: Free Press.

Wilensky, H. and Lebeaux, C. 1965: *Industrialism and Social Welfare*. New York: Free Press.

Williams, F. 1989: *Social Policy: A Critical Introduction*. Cambridge: Polity Press.

Willis, P. 1977: *Learning to Labour*. Farnborough, Hants.: Saxon House.

Wootton, B. 1959: *Social Science and Social Pathology*. London: Allen & Unwin.

Wootton, G. 1970: *Interest Groups*. Englewood Cliffs, N.J.: Prentice-Hall.

Index